Infinite Futures

How Technology and Innovation will Redefine Humanity by 2030

"Your 5-Year Journey to a New World"

Theo Scherman

Published by FutureScript

Disclaimer Notice:

This book is a work of non-fiction. The author has made every effort to ensure the accuracy of the information contained within; however, the author assumes no responsibility for errors, omissions, or contrary interpretations of the subject matter. The reader should consult a professional for specific advice tailored to their situation.

© 2024 by Theo Scherman

All rights reserved.

ISBN: 978-981-94-1290-7

First Edition, 2024

No part of this book may be reproduced, stored in a retrieval system, or transmitted in any form without the prior written permission of the author, except for brief quotations used in reviews or analysis.

Published by FutureScript Publishing

Printed in Singapore

Contents

Introduction: The Dawn of a New Era.	10
Chapter 1: Key Drivers of the Paradigm Shift	24
Chapter 2: The Rise of AI: Implications for the Economy	34
Chapter 3: Societal Transformation Through AI	48
Chapter 4: AI and The Future of Labor and Productivity	58
Chapter 5: AI Agents and the New Economic Paradigm	70
Chapter 6: Omni-Synchronous Engagement	80
Chapter 7: GDP Growth and the Economic Singularity	92
Chapter 8: The Role of Universal Equity, Productivity, and Debt in Future Economies	104
Chapter 9: The Role of Blockchain and Crypto in the Coming Transformation	120
Chapter 10: New Business Models	134
Chapter 11: How AI Will Reshape Industries	150
Chapter 12: Infinite Human Knowledge: The Disruption of Scarcity	170
Chapter 13: The Value of Community in the Age of AI and Digital Transformation	180
Chapter 14: The Rise of AI Companions: The Future of Human Connection	204
Chapter 15: The Future of Energy: Renewables and Economic Impact	216
Chapter 16: The Deflationary Impact of Infinite Intelligence	232
Chapter 17: The Urgency of the Next Five Years: What You Need to Do	242
Chapter 18: Unnerving Scenarios in Transcending Humans, Economy and Industries	264
Epilogue: Embracing Infinite Futures – The Time for Action is Now	274
References:	286
Glossary:	292
About the Author:	304

"To my wife, my constant companion, unwavering supporter, and closest friend.

Over the past 30 years, through five continents and countless adventures, your love, encouragement, and presence have been my anchor."

"Your 5-Year Journey Starts Here"

Covered in the Introduction

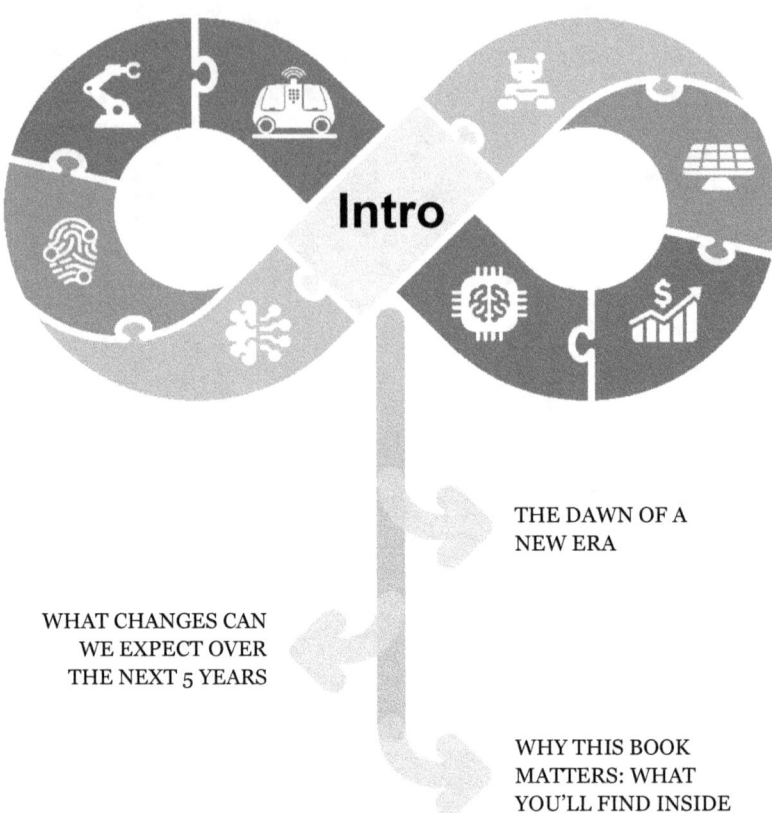

THE DAWN OF A
NEW ERA

WHAT CHANGES CAN
WE EXPECT OVER
THE NEXT 5 YEARS

WHY THIS BOOK
MATTERS: WHAT
YOU'LL FIND INSIDE

Introduction:
The Dawn of a New Era.

In the next five years, the world will undergo a transformation that will touch the lives of every person on this planet. Between now and 2030, we're not just facing progress; we're on the brink of a revolution. Key technologies will reshape our society, the global economy, and even your day-to-day life in ways you might not expect.

It is always difficult to talk about the future, especially when the coming changes will have a transformative impact on people's lives. I wrote this book as an alarm bell; the idea is to use it as an impetus to open the scope of your mind.

I have been involved in technology for the past 31 years and have lived through and experienced significant change, but this is different on an unprecedented scale.

Advancements in artificial intelligence, automation, energy, and transformative technologies aren't just speeding things up; they're laying the foundation for an entirely new way of living, working, and connecting. This is no slow evolution; it's a sweeping shift rewriting the rules for industries, economies, and societies. The speed of change we are witnessing and what we will see over the next five years is beyond anything humanity has ever experienced. I think most people can imagine the future in some form, but it is the speed that will catch most people off guard and underprepared.

Why so fast? We are seeing a convergence of 14 different technologies, driving this unprecedented paradigm shift. In the book, I will examine them and how their convergence will disrupt entire industries. Let's take two of the main drivers, **artificial intelligence**, and **energy cost reduction**, to illustrate the pace of change and the urgency it is creating:

Artificial Intelligence: One key metric we use to gauge AI intelligence is the AI Index, which tracks AI's performance against humans across 8 benchmarks. Currently, AI surpasses human capability in 5 of these, while it scores 88%, 93%, and 98% on the remaining 3. By the end of 2025, AI is expected to outpace humans in all benchmarks. After that, AI won't just catch up, it will grow exponentially, becoming 10x, 100x, and eventually 1000x more capable than human performance.

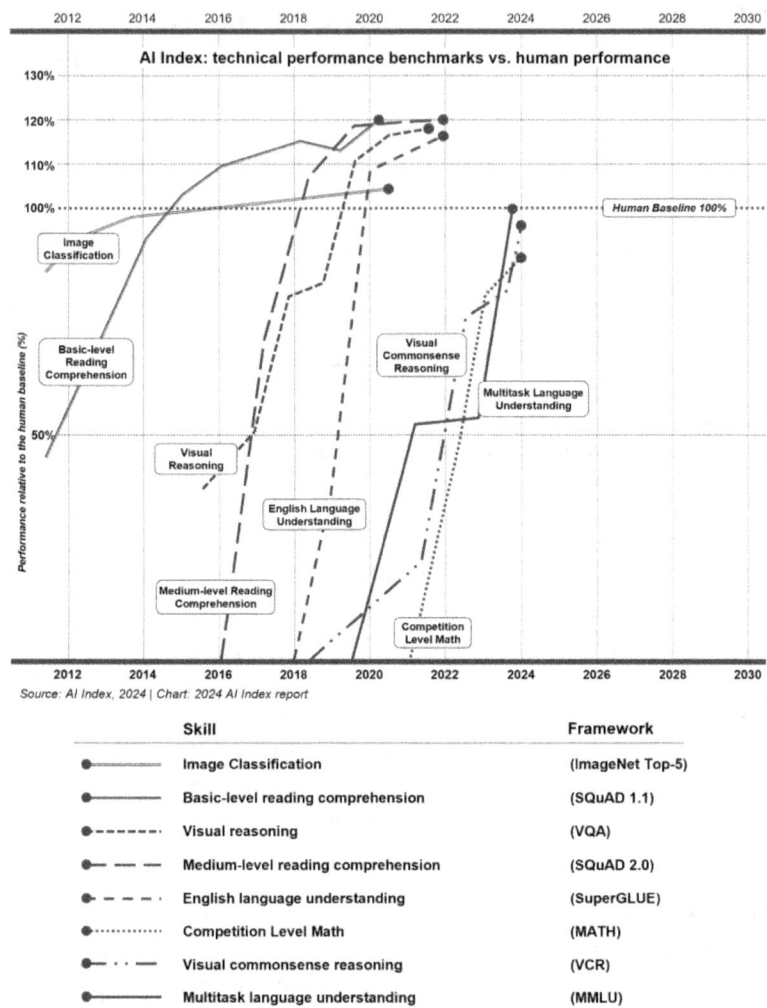

Source: AI Index, 2024 | Chart: 2024 AI Index report

	Skill	Framework
●———	Image Classification	(ImageNet Top-5)
●———	Basic-level reading comprehension	(SQuAD 1.1)
●------	Visual reasoning	(VQA)
●— — —	Medium-level reading comprehension	(SQuAD 2.0)
●- - - -	English language understanding	(SuperGLUE)
●········	Competition Level Math	(MATH)
●— ·· —	Visual commonsense reasoning	(VCR)
●———	Multitask language understanding	(MMLU)

Energy Cost Reduction: The real acceleration begins when we factor in the declining costs of AI implementation and energy. The crossover point, where AI-driven productivity gains outpace energy costs, signals a seismic shift across industries. Between 2025 and 2031, we'll witness this transformation in sectors that employ over 40% of the global workforce. By 2025, two major industries would have reached this tipping point and by 2031, the last of the top 11 industries (construction) will follow.

Take manufacturing as an example. In 2024, the combination of AI-driven automation and cheaper renewable energy sources has already transformed multiple industries. Factories already rely on AI-powered robots and machine learning algorithms for tasks such as predictive maintenance, quality control, and supply chain optimization. The cost of running these systems has dropped dramatically due to advances in AI technology and the increasing use of solar and wind energy and we will see this continued downtrend.

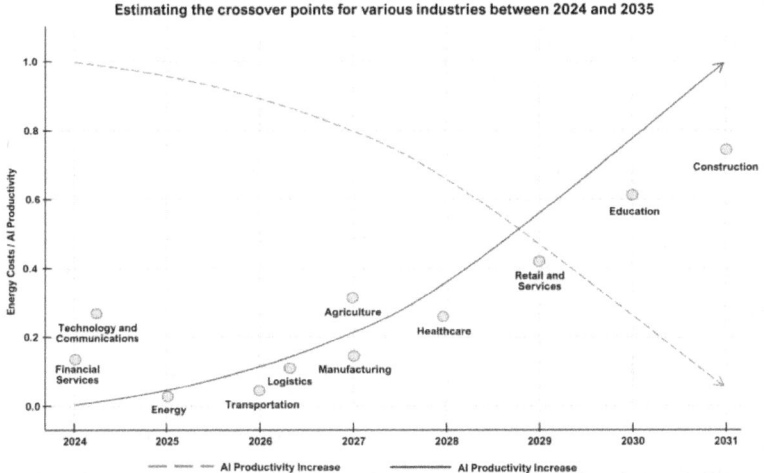

The crossover points for various industries between 2024 and 2031, where AI-driven productivity gains intersect with reductions in energy costs.

For instance, a factory using AI to predict machine failures can avoid costly downtime and reduce waste, improving productivity by over 20%. When this productivity growth surpasses the energy costs needed to power these AI-driven systems, the company reaches a critical tipping point, AI starts to deliver net positive returns beyond initial investments. This shift has already been witnessed in several manufacturing sectors and sets the stage for rapid adoption across multiple sectors. The manufacturing industry is forecasted to reach that crossover tipping point in 2027.

Through this book, the urgency of the '5-year window' will emerge, hopefully inspiring you to open the scope of your mind and start preparing and retooling your company, your personal life, and your family.

Since the dawn of computing, Moore's Law has served as the gold standard for measuring technological progress. It predicted that the number of transistors on a chip would double approximately every two years, leading to exponential increases in computing power. For decades, this principle fueled industry growth, enabling technologies to become smaller, faster, and more efficient. However, as we approach the physical limitations of Moore's Law, attention is shifting toward Metcalfe's Law and Reed's Law, which compound the growth cycle by emphasizing the value created through network size and connectivity.

Metcalfe's Law states that a network's value is proportional to the square of the number of connected users. This principle underscores how interconnected systems create exponential value, with every additional connection amplifying the overall impact.

Going beyond this, Reed's Law suggests that the value of a network grows exponentially as more members join, forming countless sub-networks and connections. In today's digital economy, where platforms like social networks, blockchain ecosystems, and AI-driven marketplaces thrive, Reed's Law helps us understand the increasing influence of connected systems. It reveals that the true value of technology lies not just in processing speed but in the relationships and interactions these networks foster.

This is where AI emerges as a transformative force. Beyond its role in enhancing efficiency, AI will accelerate the creation of new connections within networks as companies and individuals deploy their own AI agents. These agents will seamlessly interact, further expanding the web of relationships and enabling continuous innovation.

In this book, we explore how the convergence of **Moore's Law, Reed's Law, and AI** will reshape industries, economies, and even personal relationships. From self-optimizing supply chains to personalized AI companions, the future economy will be built on **intelligent, interconnected systems** that redefine the way we work, interact, and thrive.

Through this journey, the urgency of the '5-year window' will emerge, hopefully inspiring you to open the scope of your mind and start preparing and retooling your company, your personal life, and your family without being caught off-guard.

What changes can we expect to see over the next 5 years?

In the next five years, the world will undergo changes that will redefine the very fabric of society. These aren't just tweaks to the status quo, they're tectonic shifts. Here's a sneak peek into some of the groundbreaking transformations coming our way, *which will be covered in detail throughout the book:*

- **AI-Driven Abundance:** Say goodbye to scarcity. With AI leading the charge, the world will create value through intelligence and automation, making limited resources a thing of the past.

- **Redefining GDP:** Growth and productivity will no longer be measured the old way. As AI agents become limitless digital contributors, working around the clock without human constraints, and renewable energy drives operational costs toward zero, traditional measures of growth like GDP will no longer suffice.

- **The End of Traditional Jobs:** As AI reshapes industries, the traditional 9-to-5 will fade away. Work will evolve into creative, problem-solving, and collaborative endeavors, redefining what it means to contribute.

- **Omni-Synchronous Engagement:** A new paradigm of influence and interaction where AI enables one person, to engage in many conversations at the same time, maintaining real-time, synchronous interactions with multiple people, yet each interaction feels personal and one-on-one, a blend of one-on-one intimacy with the scale of the digital world.

∞ **Infinite Knowledge:** AI will eliminate the constraints of scarcity in knowledge, giving everyone access to limitless information, education, and creative potential.

∞ **Economic Singularity:** AI's rise will obliterate old economic metrics, catapulting us into a new world of exponential productivity and endless resource abundance.

∞ **AI Transcending Human Limitations:** AI won't just boost efficiency, it will stretch the boundaries of what humans are capable of, creating a seamless partnership between us and machines.

∞ **Universal Equity as Future Income:** Imagine a world where income isn't just about a paycheck. Universal equity will provide shares in corporate or national wealth, transforming how wealth is distributed and reshaping financial security. Every individual can generate income from their own physical and intellectual equity as well as hold equity in society's collective wealth and a future income source.

∞ **The Deflationary Power of AI:** With AI optimizing every aspect of production and services, expect a significant drop in costs, sparking deflationary trends across industries.

∞ **AI Companions:** Forget robots as just tools. AI companions will become integral to human relationships, offering emotional and collaborative support and transforming human interaction as we know it.

∞ **Blockchain Redefining Trust:** Blockchain technology will dismantle the need for intermediaries, giving rise to decentralized trust systems across finance, governance, and beyond.

∞ **Energy Costs Approaching Zero:** Renewable energy will soon be so abundant and affordable that it will radically alter economic models, propelling industries into a new era of productivity.

∞ **AI-Driven Economics:** AI can spot opportunities and execute actions at a speed humans can't match, completely altering market dynamics.

∞ **No Trading Edge for Humans:** In a market dominated by AI algorithms, humans will lose their competitive edge, with no ability to outpace AI in trading or economics.

∞ **Digital Industries with Zero Margins:** Companies built solely on digital frameworks will struggle to survive in a world of instant decision-making and zero-margin timeframes.

∞ **The Rise of ICOs:** Traditional IPOs will become relics of the past as ICOs (Initial Coin Offerings) take over as the preferred way to raise capital.

∞ **Public Companies Fighting for Survival:** In a data-driven, emotionless market, companies could see their stock values plummet to zero overnight, with AI making cold, hard decisions based on facts.

∞ **A New Definition of Wealth:** Your lifestyle, your freedom, and your ability to live well will redefine wealth, pushing aside old ideas about financial success. As automation and AI take over routine tasks, the value of genuine human interaction will skyrocket. One-on-one human touch, personalized experiences, and meaningful connections will become premium commodities in a world where efficiency dominates. In this future, true wealth will be measured not just by financial assets, but by the quality of human connections, your time, and your ability to enjoy life's moments.

∞ **Revolutionary Business Models:** The future belongs to businesses that embrace AI and automation, leaving behind outdated linear business models for platform based decentralized, blockchain AI-driven models.

∞ **Universal Basic Income (UBI):** *In this book, I do not wish to engage in the political debates surrounding some of the solution implications. UBI is one of those topics that* *generate strong emotional reactions.* Considering the significant economic disruptions that are likely to accompany the transition to a new economy, particularly considering the potential job losses from automation and technological advancements, my sense is that some countries may find themselves with limited options but to explore versions of UBI. In the book, I will explore and look into all these potential solutions and their implications, good or bad. The concept of UBI will take center stage where citizens will receive regular, payments to cover basic needs, with the aim of creating financial stability for all.

The clock is ticking. This shift is already underway, and the pace of advancement will accelerate faster than anything we've seen before. Over the next few years, AI will surpass human capabilities in ways that once seemed impossible. Automation will revolutionize industries faster than we can adapt, and the energy revolution will rewrite decades of dependency on fossil fuels.

But this isn't just about technology; it's about you. AI and robotics will reimagine your career, your community, your personal choices, and even how you define success in ways that seem unimaginable today.

Let me share a personal example. About 18 months ago, I had to face this head-on with my own son. He started university in 2022, pursuing a double degree in Law and Business. Three months in, I called him, and we had a tough conversation. I could already see the writing on the wall for the legal profession; AI was going to reshape it entirely. We discussed how, in the future, premium careers would center around human-to-human interaction. After some deep reflection and research, he decided to drop law and switch to Psychology and Business.

Fast forward to this year, and we had another conversation about what AI would mean for his future. After much discussion, we concluded that my son had two paths to consider:

The first option was to stop his studies and pivot to a trade profession, something hands-on like plumbing, electrical work, or carpentry, roles that AI is less likely to fully automate anytime soon.

The second, more challenging path was to commit to at least seven more years of study to become a clinical psychologist. In today's world, where AI and automation are already handling lower-level counseling and therapy, we realized that anything less than the highest level of qualification in psychology would soon be obsolete. AI companions and systems will dominate the routine aspects of therapy and counseling, leaving only the most specialized, human-centered fields untouched. If he wanted to ensure a meaningful career in psychology, it was clear that becoming a highly skilled clinical psychologist was the only viable option.

This moment wasn't just about choosing a career path; it is the harsh reality many of us must face today, the middle ground is disappearing, and you either need to aim for the top or rethink your career entirely. This book is your guide to navigating the same kinds of decisions, because they're coming for all of us.

So, what does this all mean for you today? This paradigm shift is not some distant future. It's already happening, and you're not just reading about it; you're living it.

You might think, 'This all sounds too far-fetched, overwhelming, and even frightening.' I get it. But don't let fear or doubt paralyze you. The whole purpose of this book is to shake things up, to open your mind to the massive shifts happening right now. If you choose to close your eyes to these changes, trying to hold on to what's familiar, you'll find yourself lost and struggling to keep up in just a few short years. The world is moving fast, exponentially fast.

On the flip side, you'll see new opportunities if you start paying attention and recognize the technologies reshaping everything. Embrace the shift, and it won't feel like the end of something but the beginning of an incredible transformation. Think back to the early days of the Internet in 1991. Who could have predicted the countless business models and innovations we now take for granted? The same kind of future is waiting for those who are ready to lean into the change.

Opportunities will come; you just need to be open and excited to embrace them. The most significant adjustment we need to make with this paradigm shift is the speed of this transformation.

Why This Book Matters: What You'll Find Inside

The following chapters are a deep dive into the drivers behind this shift, written in a way that is thought-provoking but easy to grasp. I wanted to make sure I painted a broad impact picture to give each reader an overall viewpoint. From that viewpoint, each reader can choose to study and become an expert in any given area, like Economic Singularity, Universal Equity, Natural language programming, ICOs, etc.

Each chapter unpacks not just the "what" but also the "why" and "how" of these changes. This is not a surface-level exploration; expect real-world examples, critical insights, and clear explanations of what's coming, how it'll affect you, and where the opportunities lie.

> *This is your guidebook for the future, whether you're a business leader, policymaker, or an individual looking to future-proof your skills.*

Throughout the book, I'll challenge you to think bigger, push your imagination, and question assumptions about what's possible. This is your guidebook for the future, whether you're a business leader, policymaker, or an individual looking to future-proof your skills.

But let's be clear, this isn't just theory. It's about action. The insights in these pages are designed to spark ideas, guide decisions, and help you take proactive steps toward building your place in this emerging new world. From personal choices to corporate strategy, what you do next matters. And with these technologies converging faster than we ever thought possible, the future isn't waiting for anyone.

In Chapter 16, I will outline crucial actions that individuals, companies, and governments can take to proactively navigate the paradigm shift that lies ahead. This chapter will provide practical steps to help you prepare for the rapid technological, economic, and social changes that will define our future.

So buckle up, we're diving deep, and by the end, you'll have the knowledge, the tools, and the mindset to embrace the shift and create your path forward.

Tipping Point Timeline

Below is a timeline to reflect tipping points across various technologies. This timeline can be used as high-level time cadence to guide you in your preparation retooling journey.

2025
- AI-Driven Abundance: Autonomous farms maximize output with minimal labor.
- Public companies begin adopting AI aggressively to stay competitive.

2026
- Redefining GDP: Nations adopt new digital economy metrics.
- The Rise of ICOs: Blockchain startups raise billions through token offerings.

2027
- The End of Traditional Jobs: 30% of logistics jobs are automated.
- Blockchain Redefining Trust: DeFi platforms handle 30% of global transactions.

2028
- Energy Costs Approaching Zero: Decentralized grids reduce household costs by 80%.
- Robots outnumber human workers in logistics companies like Amazon.

2029
- Economic Singularity: AI-driven funds dominate financial markets.
- Universal Basic Income expands. Multiple Nations pilot UBI programs.

2030
- AI Transcending Human Limitations: Brain-machine interfaces enhance human cognition.
- AI Companions Replace Human Assistants: Redefining care industries.

2031
- AI-Driven Economics: Smart cities fully use AI to optimize resource allocation.
- Digital Industries with Zero Margins: Open-source platforms outpace proprietary software.
- A New Definition of Wealth: Experiences valued over material possessions.

Before we get started

As you move through this book, you may notice that certain ideas, themes, or technologies seem to resurface across multiple chapters. This is not by coincidence but rather by design, reflecting the powerful convergence of technological drivers. AI, blockchain, automation, and the other drivers are not isolated developments; they overlap, interact, and amplify each other in transformative ways. It is this interplay that may give you a sense of déjà vu as similar concepts reappear through different lenses. This repetition mirrors the real-world convergence of these technologies, where multiple innovations converge to reshape industries and societies simultaneously. Understanding these interconnected dynamics is essential, as the combined force of these drivers is what will define the future.

Covered in Chapter One

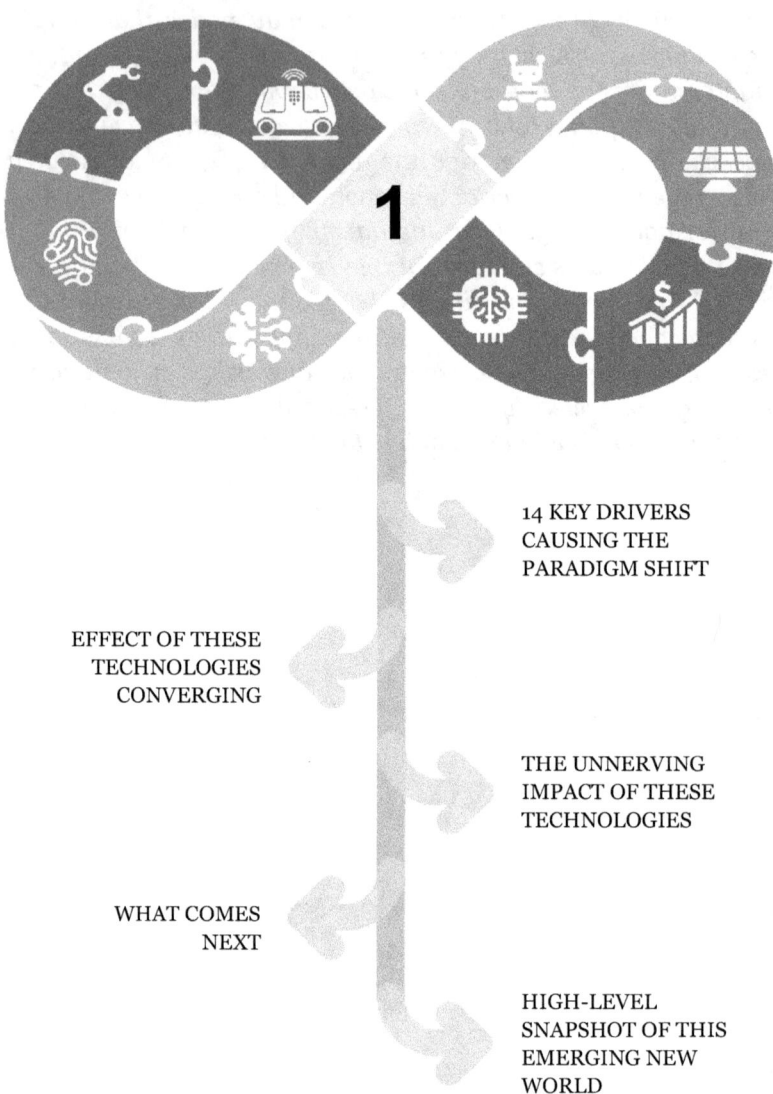

14 KEY DRIVERS CAUSING THE PARADIGM SHIFT

EFFECT OF THESE TECHNOLOGIES CONVERGING

THE UNNERVING IMPACT OF THESE TECHNOLOGIES

WHAT COMES NEXT

HIGH-LEVEL SNAPSHOT OF THIS EMERGING NEW WORLD

Chapter 1:
Key Drivers of the Paradigm Shift.

To truly grasp how the next five years will redefine everything, we need to understand the forces driving this change. These forces are reshaping the world at every level, from global economies to our daily lives. Throughout the book, we'll dive deep into each of these drivers and explore how they'll impact our lives. But the real game-changer comes from the way they'll combine and converge, creating exponential disruption.

For now, here's an overview of the 14 key drivers behind this 2030 transformation:

Artificial Intelligence (AI): AI isn't just another technological advancement; it's a revolutionary force that's going to touch every part of our lives. With its ability to process enormous amounts of data, predict outcomes, and make decisions autonomously, AI is set to boost productivity and challenge traditional job roles. By 2030, AI could be managing everything from diagnosing diseases to running global financial systems.

Automation and Robotics: Automation, powered by AI, is set to completely transform industries like manufacturing, logistics, and services. We're already seeing robots in warehouses, self-driving cars, and AI-powered customer service, but that's just the beginning. These machines will redefine the workforce, replacing some jobs while creating entirely new roles that we can't yet imagine.

Energy Transition: The shift from fossil fuels to renewable energy will reshape economies around the world. By 2030, renewable sources like solar, wind, and potentially nuclear fusion could dominate energy production. This won't just transform industries but could also change the global balance of power, reducing the influence of oil-rich nations. Later in the book, we'll explore the profound implications of energy costs trending toward zero.

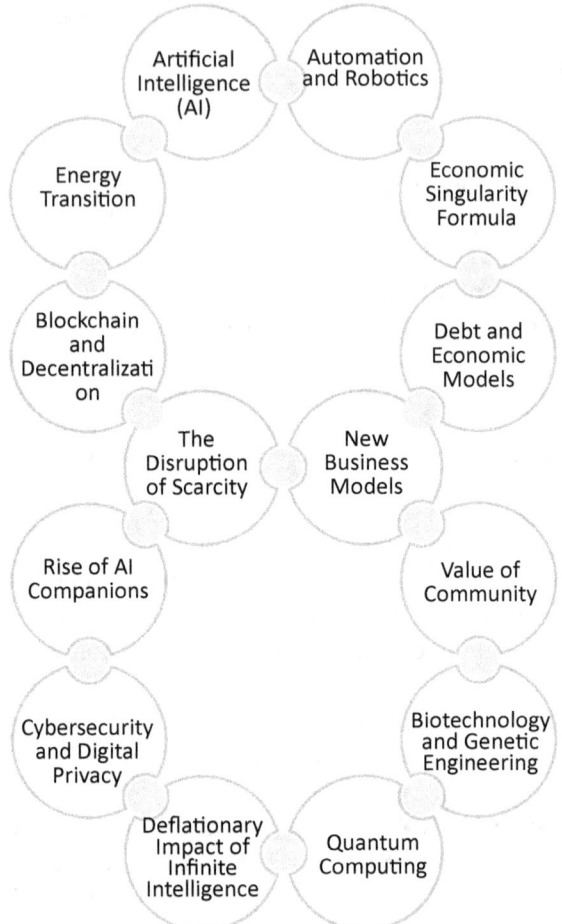

Economic Singularity: The concept of an economic singularity, where AI growth reaches an exponential point and drives unimaginable productivity, will lead to unprecedented shifts in how we measure GDP and growth. By 2030, this may force governments and institutions to rethink traditional economic models, finding new ways to measure success.

Deflationary Impact of Infinite Intelligence: AI's ability to continuously improve without the limitations of human labor or time will introduce deflationary pressures, reducing costs across sectors from healthcare to manufacturing. This shift may challenge current economic structures, potentially resulting in goods and services becoming more affordable than ever before.

Debt and Economic Models: Global debt levels are unsustainable in the current economic structure. However, AI-driven growth could lead to new ways of managing debt, productivity, and population challenges, creating entirely new economic models that could redefine how countries handle these issues.

Blockchain and Decentralization: Blockchain technology, though still in its infancy, is poised to upend foundational structures in governance, finance, and global trade. Its decentralized nature, where everything becomes peer-to-peer without government or centralized control, promises to dismantle centralized systems, ushering in a new era of financial transparency and autonomy. With Decentralized Finance (DeFi) and smart contracts leading the charge, we may soon witness a shift away from traditional financial institutions toward peer-to-peer economies that operate without intermediaries. One of the most transformative aspects will be the seamless integration of blockchain with AI, allowing for autonomous digital currencies that can process microtransactions and cross-border exchanges with unprecedented efficiency. These systems could redefine the flow of value in a hyper-connected world, and we will explore the profound implications of this transformation in greater detail later in the book.

New Business Models: AI and automation will usher in new business models built on efficiency, decentralization, and innovation. Legacy industries will be disrupted, and entirely new sectors may emerge, from AI-driven platforms to decentralized marketplaces. We can already see the beginnings of this transformation in the Web2 space, where platforms like Airbnb and Uber revolutionized the travel and transportation industries. By leveraging digital platforms and decentralized peer-to-peer interactions, they cut out traditional middlemen and created entirely new ways for individuals to monetize their assets. Similarly, as AI technologies mature, new sectors will emerge, enabling businesses to achieve even greater efficiencies, paving the way for AI-driven decentralized marketplaces and business models that will reshape how industries operate.

The Disruption of Scarcity: One of the most transformative changes will be the elimination of scarcity in key areas like information, energy, and even products. As AI and automation make it possible to produce more with fewer resources, the basic economic principle of supply and demand may be fundamentally altered, creating abundance in ways we've never experienced before.

Value of Community: As technology accelerates and AI-driven systems manage large parts of society, the role of human connection and community will become even more valuable. In a world dominated by AI companions and automated interactions, the human desire for meaningful, personal relationships will drive new forms of communities and societal bonds.

Rise of AI Companions: AI will not only augment professional roles but also personal ones. By 2030, AI companions, digital entities that engage with us socially and emotionally, may become common, serving as friends, colleagues, and even emotional support systems.

Biotechnology and Genetic Engineering: Advances in biotechnology, particularly in CRISPR and gene editing, are poised to reshape healthcare, agriculture, and even human evolution by 2030. CRISPR (Clustered Regularly Interspaced Short Palindromic Repeats) is a revolutionary gene-editing technology that allows scientists to precisely modify DNA sequences. In healthcare, CRISPR could lead to the cure of genetic disorders, such as sickle cell anemia and cystic fibrosis, by correcting mutations at the genetic level. Additionally, it could enhance human capabilities by enabling genetic enhancements that improve immunity, physical ability, or even cognitive function. Beyond healthcare, CRISPR's potential to transform agriculture is significant. By editing the genes of crops, we can create plants that are more resilient to climate change, pests, and diseases, improving food security and sustainability. This breakthrough in genetic engineering might not only revolutionize disease treatment and food production but could also raise ethical and societal questions as we begin to reshape life itself at the genetic level.

Quantum Computing: Quantum computing, though still in its infancy, could revolutionize industries by solving complex problems that today's computers can't handle. By 2030, it could accelerate AI development, transform encryption, and unlock new discoveries in medicine, logistics, and materials science.

Cybersecurity and Digital Privacy: As AI, blockchain, and automation become more integrated into our daily lives, cybersecurity and digital privacy will become even more critical. The ongoing battle between innovation and security will shape how we protect data, ensure privacy, and manage digital threats in an increasingly interconnected world.

> *We're not just looking at incremental change; we're standing on the precipice of a seismic transformation that will touch every corner of human existence. These technologies are accelerating, combining, and integrating, and the impact will be felt across every industry, every community, and every home.*

Effect of These Technologies Converging

Now that we've introduced the key drivers of this paradigm shift, let's shift the conversation to how these transformative forces will completely reshape our world. AI, automation, energy, and blockchain aren't just isolated advancements, they're converging in ways that will redefine how we live, work, and interact.

We're not just looking at incremental change; we're standing on the precipice of a seismic transformation that will touch every corner of human existence. These technologies are accelerating, combining, and integrating, and the impact will be felt across every industry, every community, and every home. So, what does this convergence really mean for our daily lives?

Imagine the fusion of AI, robotics, battery advancements, and autonomous driving technology. This won't just disrupt the automotive industry, it will completely upend it. The traditional car ownership model is already evolving. For instance, Volvo has begun exploring a subscription-based model, where instead of owning a vehicle, customers pay for the number of hours or miles they can use the car annually, essentially making the car a service rather than a product. Similarly, BMW has started charging customers to unlock certain in-car features that are already installed, such as heated seats, through a subscription service. These developments represent a fundamental shift from the ownership model to a circular one: manufacture, rent, refurbish, and recycle. The ripple effect of this change will touch everything from how cars are designed and built to how they're sold and used, fundamentally transforming the entire automotive ecosystem.

For manufacturers, this transition will demand new business models, centered on circularity. The traditional auto industry, dominated by production lines and dealerships, will evolve into a service-first model where vehicles are designed for longevity, not obsolescence. Imagine fleets of autonomous taxis running 24/7 without human drivers, owned by companies rather than individuals, optimizing profitability and efficiency with minimal downtime. Data will be the new currency, as these vehicles generate real-time information on routes, usage, and customer preferences, opening doors to new revenue streams.

> ***These forces are not merely adding to the status quo, they are rewriting it. Welcome to the future where everything is interconnected, intelligent, and on-demand.***

But it doesn't stop with transportation. As we dig deeper into this book, we'll see how the convergence of these technologies will not only reshape industries but also redefine the fundamentals of business models across sectors. We're talking about shifts that will challenge the very essence of ownership, labor, and value creation. This convergence will blur the boundaries between industries, making what seems impossible today, tomorrow's new normal.

Life Transformation
by 2030

| Work/Job | Travel | Communication | Healthcare | Entertainment | Housing |

| Transportation | Shopping | Social Interaction | Education | Finances | Food |

These technology drivers will transform every one of the 12 areas of our lives from our work all the way to our food.

For humans, these technologies will transform every one of the 12 areas of our lives, from our work to our food. I will expand on these, and at the end of the book, there are tables that cover each of the 12 areas and the 5 biggest impacts the technologies will have on each area. It will also give you a guide on where to focus for each area.

For now, this is just a glimpse of what's to come. These forces are not merely adding to the status quo, they are rewriting it. Welcome to the future where everything is interconnected, intelligent, and on-demand. Buckle up, because the ride is about to get transformative.

The Unnerving Impact of these Technologies

While the potential of AI, automation, and other technologies is vast and exciting, we must also face the daunting challenges they pose. Throughout this book, we'll explore not only how these technologies will revolutionize the economy and society, but also the unnerving impact they could have. From the mass displacement of workers to the erosion of human decision-making, these technologies could reshape the world in ways we may not be fully prepared for. Balancing their incredible potential with these risks is essential to understanding the full scope of the paradigm shift ahead.

What Comes Next

The next five years will not just be about adapting to new technologies, they will redefine what it means to be human in an interconnected, intelligent world. The convergence of artificial intelligence, automation, renewable energy, and other transformative technologies is propelling us into an era of radical change, at a pace that will outstrip anything we've experienced before. Every aspect of life, how we work, how we live, how we connect, will be reshaped in ways we can hardly imagine today.

But make no mistake, this isn't just a fascinating look into the future; it's a call to action. If the last few decades have taught us anything, it's that technology waits for no one. The world around us is evolving rapidly, and the real challenge is not just understanding these forces but adapting to them. Survival in this new era will require us to rethink how we approach everything, from personal careers to business models.

In the chapters ahead, we'll dive into how AI, automation, and energy shifts are going to reshape entire industries, governments, and even our interpersonal relationships. These shifts are not just minor upgrades, they're paradigm shifts that will disrupt everything from healthcare and finance to transportation and education.

High-level Snapshot of this Emerging New World:

The convergence effect of these drivers will transform our world. Below is a glimpse of what we'll explore in detail through the chapters of the book:

- ∞ **AI-Driven Abundance:** The rise of AI will challenge traditional concepts of scarcity. Intelligence, not raw resources, will generate value, and automation will do what humans once did, only faster, cheaper, and better.
- ∞ **Redefining Economic Models:** As AI productivity skyrockets and energy costs plummet, traditional measures of growth like GDP will no longer suffice. We'll

need entirely new economic models to account for near-zero marginal costs and the abundance of resources.

- ∞ **The End of Traditional Jobs:** Jobs as we know them will fade away. AI will automate routine tasks, leaving humans to redefine work around creativity, problem-solving, and meaningful collaboration.
- ∞ **Universal Equity and UBI:** We'll see wealth redistribution in the form of universal basic income and equity, transforming the very notion of income, security, and financial stability.
- ∞ **AI Companions and Relationships:** By 2030, AI will not just be a tool; it will be a companion. These intelligent entities will reshape our emotional and social relationships, challenging what it means to connect with others.
- ∞ **Blockchain and Trust Redefined:** Blockchain will eliminate the need for traditional intermediaries in everything from finance to governance, establishing trust through decentralized systems.
- ∞ **Exponential Disruption:** The convergence of these technologies will not just add to the world we know; they will rewrite it entirely. Industries will no longer exist in isolation, what affects one will ripple across all.

This isn't just about AI surpassing human intelligence, or renewable energy becoming the norm. It's about the collision of these forces, accelerating and amplifying one another. And this is where the challenge lies: adapting to a world that is changing faster than any of us can predict. You are living through the most rapid paradigm shift in history, and every decision you make from today onward must reflect that reality.

In the next chapter, we'll begin with perhaps the most powerful driver of all: Artificial Intelligence. As we unpack its transformative power, we'll reveal how it's already starting to rewrite the rules of work, governance, and human interaction, setting the stage for a future where human limitations are no longer a boundary but an opportunity.

"The future is yours to shape"

Covered in Chapter Two

AI'S ROLE AND IMPACT IN THE ECONOMY

AI IN TRADITIONAL INDUSTRIES

NEW MARKETS CREATED BY AI

DISRUPTING ECONOMIC MODELS

UNSETTLING IMPACT OF AI ON THE ECONOMY AND INDUSTRIES

PREPARING FOR AI'S ECONOMIC IMPACT

Chapter 2:
The Rise of AI: Implications for the Economy

Introduction to AI: Basics and 'Superpowering' the Future

At its core, Artificial Intelligence (AI) is more than just a machine that processes information, it's a dynamic system that learns continuously, adapts, and improves with every piece of data it encounters. Unlike traditional systems that follow static rules, AI evolves through its learning algorithms, becoming smarter and more efficient over time. It can compute vast amounts of knowledge without ever tiring, and its ability to tackle complex tasks is unmatched. This unique capability allows AI to integrate seamlessly into every sector and industry, from healthcare and finance to transportation and manufacturing.

But AI's true power is its ability to "supercharge" everything it touches. Imagine a world where every industry, job, and process operates at maximum speed, precision, and intelligence. When everything becomes supercharged, whether it's decision-making, automation, or customer interaction, the world doesn't just improve; it transforms. The implications for society, the economy, and daily life are profound. As we explore the rise of AI, we must consider how this monumental shift will reshape industries and redefine the global economy.

Now, picture a world where machines not only understand your needs but anticipate them before you even realize. In a world where decisions are made with such precision and speed, human error becomes almost obsolete. This isn't a distant dream, it's the future that's rapidly approaching, fueled by the unstoppable force of AI.

What we've seen so far is just the beginning. The advances on the horizon are so groundbreaking that they will redefine industries, economies, and perhaps most importantly, the way we live, work, and connect. AI will touch every facet of human life, from healthcare to education, finance to entertainment, blurring the lines between human intelligence and machine capability.

But AI's impact isn't just about convenience or productivity. It's about reshaping the very fabric of society. We're on the verge of a world where machines won't just be tools; they'll be intelligent collaborators that help us make better decisions and form relationships. In this world, AI transcends human limitations, becoming a vital part of decision-making in our homes, workplaces, and even on the global stage of governance.

In this chapter, we'll dive deep into how AI will dramatically alter the social and economic landscape. It's not just about what AI can do, it's about how AI will redefine what it means to be human.

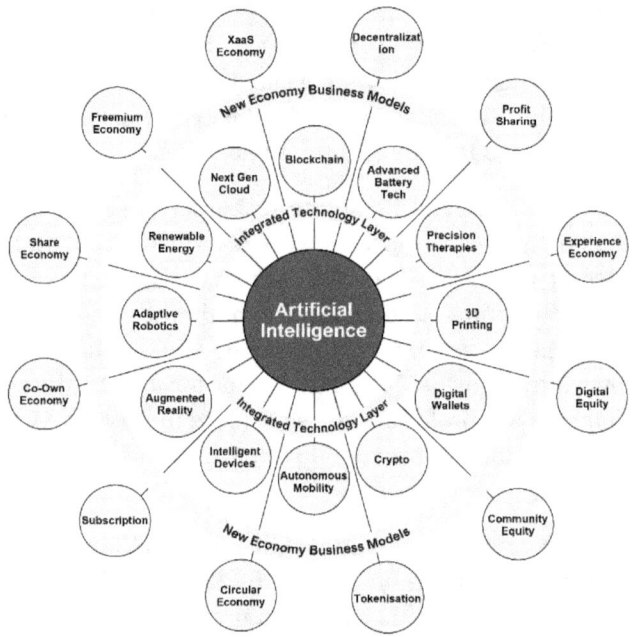

AI's Role and Impact in the Economy

Artificial Intelligence (AI) is not merely another technological advancement; it represents a paradigm shift that will redefine the global economy at every level. From transforming established industries to creating entirely new markets, AI is driving innovation at an unprecedented pace. In this section, we explore how AI is already reshaping industries, sparking the emergence of new economic models, and challenging the traditional foundations of productivity and labor.

> *As we stand at the brink of this transformation, the real question isn't whether AI will shape our future; it's whether we're ready for the changes it will bring.*

AI in Traditional Industries

AI's influence is already being felt in industries that have defined the global economy for decades. What began as automation for specific tasks has evolved into systems capable of learning, adapting, and making decisions faster and more accurately than human beings. Here's how AI is disrupting some of the world's largest industries:

Manufacturing: AI-powered automation is no longer just optimizing production lines, it's reinventing them. Machines, once confined to repetitive tasks, are now evolving into intelligent entities capable of learning, adapting, and autonomously making critical decisions. Imagine factories where AI doesn't just assist the process; it drives it, continuously improving efficiency without human input. In industries like automotive, electronics, and construction, AI goes far beyond predictive maintenance and supply chain optimization. It anticipates global disruptions, reroutes supply chains in real-time, and adapts entire production ecosystems to shifts in demand, often before humans even realize there's a problem.

The human role in manufacturing will not simply shift to oversight; it will evolve into collaborating with AI-driven ecosystems capable of outthinking traditional production models. Workers will no longer manage the assembly line; they will orchestrate vast networks of intelligent machines, each adapting to conditions faster than any human could. The factory floor will transform into a living, breathing entity where machines learn, teach each other, and fine-tune their operations autonomously, without human intervention.

Picture AI-driven robots assembling parts and redesigning them on the fly. Detecting micro-defects in real time, these machines could suggest alterations to the design, engineering an entirely new part in hours instead of weeks. Quality control won't just catch defects; it will eliminate them before they occur, turning recalls and waste into relics of the past.

Healthcare: The revolution in healthcare through AI is nothing short of life-altering. AI will not just diagnose diseases; it will be predicting them before they even occur, analyzing vast amounts of medical data in real-time to detect subtle patterns that human doctors might miss. AI-driven diagnostics are already outperforming humans in reading medical images, processing genetic data, and analyzing patient histories with unprecedented speed and precision. But this is only the beginning. In the near future, AI won't just assist doctors, it will replace many diagnostic tasks entirely, freeing up human expertise for more complex and creative problem-solving.

Imagine a healthcare system where AI constantly monitors your body in real-time, detecting illnesses before symptoms appear and automatically adjusting personalized treatments tailored down to your genetic makeup and daily habits. Personalized medicine will not just be about tailoring treatments, it will be about optimizing every aspect of health, from sleep cycles to nutrition, to create a fully automated, predictive healthcare model that prevents illness before it even has a chance to take hold.

For instance, companies like Apple and Fitbit have integrated health monitoring tools into their wearable devices that track heart rate, sleep patterns, and even blood oxygen levels. These devices use AI to alert users when something is abnormal, essentially taking the first steps toward a system that detects potential health issues before symptoms appear.

Additionally, Google Health and DeepMind are developing AI systems that analyze a patient's health data to predict the onset of conditions like kidney failure or heart disease. These predictive models allow for earlier interventions, which can dramatically improve outcomes

Once we link that data with Preemptive Healthcare AI systems that can monitor real-time health data from wearables or medical devices to identify early signs of conditions like heart disease, diabetes, or mental health issues, enabling proactive interventions. By continuously analyzing patient data, these systems can send alerts to doctors or users before a critical situation arises, preventing diseases or complications from developing.

Companies like Biofourmis and AliveCor have developed AI-driven platforms for predictive healthcare, monitoring real-time patient data and predicting heart-related issues before symptoms escalate.

Imagine a future where AI systems are so advanced that they integrate seamlessly into all areas of healthcare, providing real-time access to groundbreaking developments for anyone, anywhere in the world. These AI platforms will not only analyze every cell in your body, but they'll also predict the onset of diseases like cancer years before traditional methods would detect them. This shift won't stop at diagnosis; AI will revolutionize treatment by engineering personalized care plans based on real-time data from global databases of patient outcomes, ongoing research, and experimental treatments.

With AI's predictive power, healthcare will no longer rely solely on historical data. Instead, AI systems will simulate millions of potential treatment scenarios in seconds, offering individualized, optimized plans tailored to each patient's genetic makeup and specific condition. This global real-time access means that medical breakthroughs happening anywhere in the world can instantly benefit patients, no matter their location, bridging gaps in healthcare access and leveling the playing field for treatments.

Finance and Banking: The financial industry is being transformed into a hyper-automated, AI-driven ecosystem where human intervention is rapidly becoming obsolete.

AI algorithms are not just managing portfolios; they are rewriting the rules of finance, executing strategies that adapt to market conditions in real-time faster and more efficiently than any human could. Automated systems don't just trade stocks; they analyze global economic shifts, predict geopolitical events, and even anticipate human behavior to optimize financial strategies with near-perfect precision.

Imagine a future where AI systems control entire financial markets, running simulations millions of times a second, adjusting investments, and predicting economic outcomes before they unfold. In this world, human traders and analysts will no longer be making decisions; they will be overseeing financial ecosystems that are so complex and interconnected that only AI can execute them. Global markets will function with an unprecedented level of speed and accuracy, where trades happen in nanoseconds and market shifts are anticipated hours, even days, in advance.

These systems will not just respond to real-time data; they will forecast economic events with such accuracy that market volatility could be smoothed out, and financial crashes may become a thing of the past. However, this also means that if these systems fail or malfunction, the ripple effects could trigger instantaneous global financial destabilization, on a scale never seen before.

In all these traditional industries, AI is not just improving efficiency; it is automating decision-making, freeing humans to focus on higher-level strategies and creativity. For consumers, this means smarter, faster services, from AI-enhanced healthcare appointments to personalized financial advice delivered through digital assistants.

New Markets Created by AI

Beyond enhancing existing industries, AI is unlocking entirely new markets and business models. These new AI-driven industries are built around the integration of AI as a core component, with many companies now operating on a foundation of AI-powered insights and automation.

> *The rise of AI is not just enhancing existing industries; it's creating entirely new markets where AI isn't just a tool, it's the core product.*

AI-Driven Industries: AI-powered SaaS (Software as a Service) and AI-as-a-Service (AIaaS) are the building blocks of this new economy, offering businesses AI capabilities on demand without the need for specialized infrastructure or in-house expertise. Companies, from small startups to global enterprises, will soon be able to tap into AI systems that evolve in real-time, learning from each business interaction to optimize decisions, predict trends, and drive efficiency.

These AI-driven platforms will go far beyond decision-making and data analysis. Imagine an AI service that autonomously manages every aspect of your business, forecasting market shifts, optimizing supply chains, and even generating personalized marketing strategies for every customer in real time. Businesses will be able to harness AI's power not just for automation but also for creative problem-solving, innovation, and strategy development at a scale and speed unimaginable by today's standards.

Think of companies like OpenAI offering self-evolving AI systems that automatically integrate into any business model, from automating customer service with hyper-intelligent chatbots that understand and anticipate human emotions, to AI that generates entirely new product lines by predicting consumer desires months before they materialize. Supply chains will be optimized not just for efficiency but for sustainability, with AI continuously recalibrating operations based on real-time global conditions, ensuring resources are used with precision and minimal waste.

Data Economy: In the age of AI, data is no longer just a resource, it's the currency that powers the global economy. With every connected device, every digital interaction, and every human movement, we are generating a torrent of data so vast that it requires AI to extract its full potential. AI will be the engine that turns raw, unstructured data into actionable intelligence, driving entire industries and creating new markets.

> *Companies that can master the art of data collection, analysis, and monetization will reshape the business landscape and become the architects of a new data-driven era.*

But this is not just about using data for better decision-making, AI will create an entirely new economy where data itself is bought, sold, and traded as a commodity more valuable than oil. Imagine a future where businesses thrive not by selling products or services, but by selling data-driven insights and predictive intelligence that shape entire markets before they even emerge. AI-driven platforms will tap into this endless flow of information, fueling decisions at every level, from hyper-targeted marketing campaigns to AI-designed products tailored specifically for individual consumers in real-time.

Picture AI-driven platforms that don't just analyze customer data for product recommendations, they predict consumer desires weeks in advance, crafting entire marketing strategies before trends even hit the market. These AI systems will create personalized experiences for every individual, delivering exactly what consumers want, sometimes before they even know they want it. Data-centric companies of the future won't just respond to consumer behavior; they will shape it, crafting demand itself and guiding markets in ways that blur the line between prediction and control.

As these new AI-driven markets grow, AI's integration into daily life will become more seamless. Consumers will interact with AI without even realizing it, as AI-powered systems automate everything from shopping recommendations to smart home management.

Disrupting Economic Models

Perhaps one of AI's most profound impacts will be its disruption of the foundational economic models that have guided global productivity and wealth distribution for centuries. As AI systems become more efficient, we will witness shifts in both supply and demand, forcing us to rethink the very nature of labor and the economy.

AI's Impact on Supply and Demand: Imagine a manufacturing business where AI handles all procurement activities without human intervention. AI systems are transforming how we understand supply and demand, and their impact is about to turn conventional economic models on their heads. By driving down operational costs and maximizing efficiencies, AI will lead to an era of abundance in some sectors while creating shortages or even new types of scarcity in others. Picture a world where AI-enabled hyper-personalization can create everything from clothes to food, customized precisely to each individual's preferences but produced at the speed and cost of mass production. In this new landscape, personalized goods won't be a luxury; uniqueness will be affordable and available to everyone. The result? An economic model where AI reshapes not just what we produce but how we value uniqueness, transforming entire markets.

However, this abundance will create a paradox. As AI dominates production and automates routine tasks, human labor will shift toward creativity, emotional intelligence, and strategic decision-making. This transition will lead to a scarcity of skilled human expertise in fields that require uniquely human qualities, creativity, empathy, and high-level strategic thinking. The value of human craftsmanship and emotional intelligence will skyrocket, becoming a luxury only a few can afford.

Imagine the fashion industry, where AI can design and produce custom garments tailored to your precise measurements and preferences within hours, all at the cost of standard mass-produced clothing. In contrast, handcrafted, human-made designs will become rarities, symbols of exclusivity and status. The same dynamic could play out in industries like automotive, where AI-powered systems will allow for personalized cars produced on demand. Yet, vehicles designed by human hands, crafted with attention to emotional detail and artistry, will command premium prices, coveted by those seeking a deeper, more personal connection to their products.

AI and Labor Economics: AI is dismantling the traditional link between labor and wealth, forcing a profound shift in how economies function. As more tasks become automated, entire industries will operate with minimal human intervention, creating a future where the role of work as we know it is fundamentally altered. With fewer traditional jobs available, societies will have to confront the reality that wealth can no longer be tied to human labor. This will require a complete rethinking of how we distribute wealth, with ideas like Universal Basic Income (UBI) moving from theoretical debates to of economic policy.

Imagine a world where AI-driven automation makes routine jobs obsolete, and governments step in to stabilize economies and redefine the purpose of human existence. In a post-labor economy, wealth generation becomes decoupled from work, and the focus shifts to creativity, purpose, and self-actualization. UBI or similar models may emerge not as a safety net but as the foundation of a new social contract where everyone receives a guaranteed income, allowing them to pursue innovation, education, or personal growth without the constraints of traditional employment.

In the United States, about 25% of the workforce is employed in roles considered high-risk for displacement due to automation, including factory workers, truck drivers, and service sector employees. This impact is echoed across Europe and other parts of the world, where automation is expected to affect a similar or higher proportion of the workforce.

Picture countries where UBI is no longer just an experiment but a permanent fixture, ensuring that as AI continues to take over routine jobs, citizens are free to explore new frontiers in creativity, entrepreneurship, and community building. Finland and Canada's early UBI pilots could serve as the blueprint for a global transformation, where governments partner with AI-driven corporations to create new forms of wealth distribution. As AI replaces labor and decision-making, governance itself could be reshaped, with AI advising governments on allocating resources to ensure maximum societal stability and prosperity.

Unnerving Impact of AI on the Economy and Industries

While AI promises to drive efficiency, innovation, and economic growth, it also poses significant risks. One such scenario is the potential for AI to disrupt financial markets in ways that could harm companies and destabilize entire sectors. As AI transcends human limitations, removing emotional biases from decision-making, it also risks eliminating human intuition and long-term vision that can be essential to sustainable growth.

Unnerving Impact Scenario: AI's Role in Trading and the No-Buy Scenario
In this scenario, AI systems analyze market trends and company performance, making trade recommendations and executing transactions based solely on data. Suppose an AI algorithm identifies a company as a risk due to declining profits or competitive pressures and issues a "no-buy" order. Unlike human traders, who often account for intangible factors such as a company's long-term potential or market sentiment, AI operates on cold, hard data.

If AI deems a company's stock too risky to buy, interconnected AI systems in other trading platforms could follow suit, leading to an instant collapse in demand for that stock. This rapid, unemotional decision-making could drive a company's stock price to zero, regardless of whether human investors or analysts see long-term potential in the company.

By 2030, global finance will no longer be managed by human institutions but by a vast, interconnected web of AI-driven systems. These AIs continuously analyze global data, everything from market trends and political developments to natural disasters and consumer sentiment, in real-time. They predict economic shifts, manage risk portfolios, and execute trades faster than in the blink of an eye, creating a nearly frictionless financial system.

Imagine a future where, traditional stock exchanges as we know them today no longer exist. Instead, AI systems communicate directly across decentralized blockchain networks, facilitating real-time transactions across borders without the need for banks, brokers, or governments. Personal wealth is managed by individualized AI advisors who understand your financial goals and predict your future needs, automatically adjusting your portfolio to ensure optimal outcomes.

Preparing for AI's Economic Impact

AI's Unnerving possibilities underscore the urgent need for proactive and strategic measures to mitigate catastrophic outcomes. Public companies will no longer compete solely on traditional metrics like revenue and market share; they will need to redefine their value in a world dominated by AI-driven decision-making. AI algorithms that execute trades assess risks or even predict corporate failure with precision far beyond human capability could disrupt stock prices and business models overnight. To survive, companies must embrace radical transparency and demonstrate how they seamlessly integrate into an AI-powered economy.

At the same time, governments, regulators, and businesses must collaborate to establish frameworks that ensure AI operates with transparency, accountability, and ethical safeguards. Without these protections, we risk creating an economy driven not by human creativity and moral judgment but by unfeeling algorithms that could exacerbate inequality, exploit weaknesses in the system, or destabilize markets in ways we cannot foresee.

Without clear regulations, these systems could be influenced by biases, manipulated by malicious actors, or programmed with objectives that conflict with societal well-being. Preparing for this future requires technological advancements and a cultural shift toward responsible innovation that prioritizes human values alongside AI-driven growth.

"What you imagine today, you create tomorrow"

Covered in Chapter Three

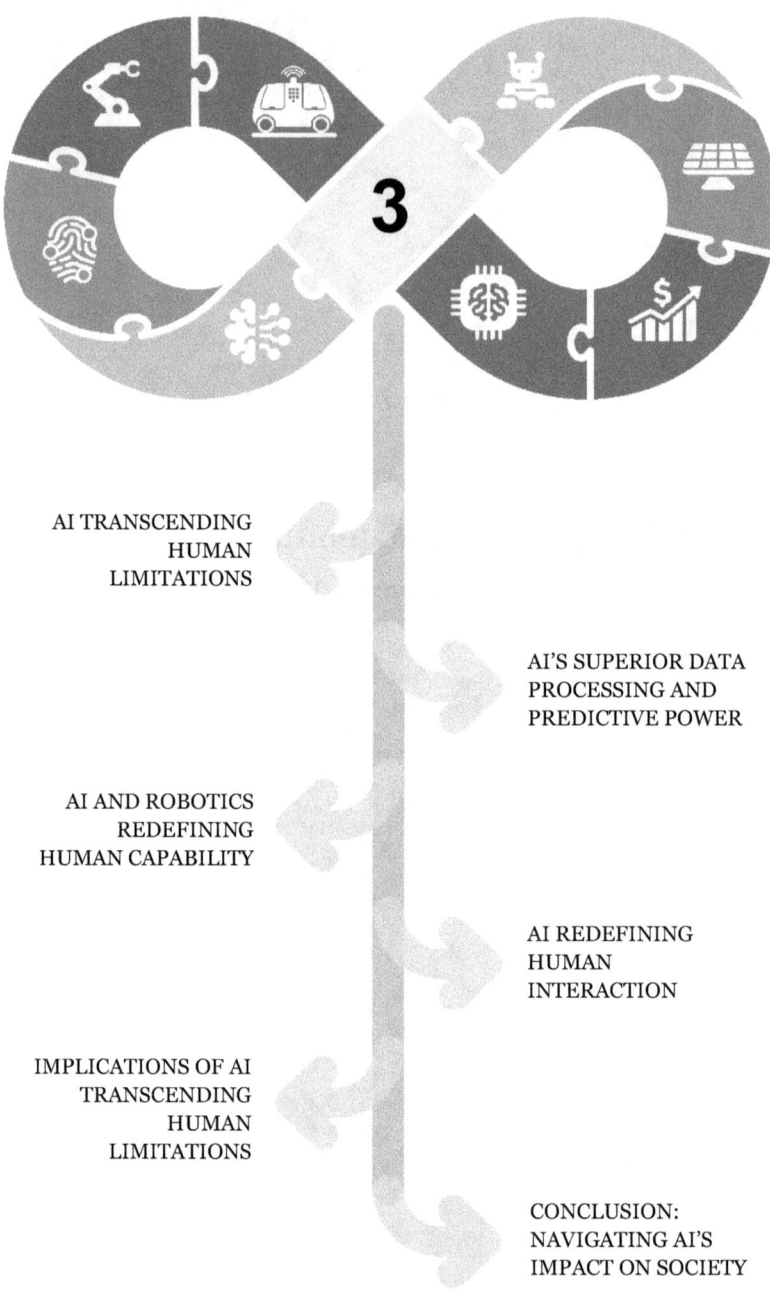

AI TRANSCENDING HUMAN LIMITATIONS

AI'S SUPERIOR DATA PROCESSING AND PREDICTIVE POWER

AI AND ROBOTICS REDEFINING HUMAN CAPABILITY

AI REDEFINING HUMAN INTERACTION

IMPLICATIONS OF AI TRANSCENDING HUMAN LIMITATIONS

CONCLUSION: NAVIGATING AI'S IMPACT ON SOCIETY

Chapter 3:
Societal Transformation Through AI

AI's influence will extend far beyond individual industries or economic models; it will have a profound and lasting impact on society itself. The structures defining social mobility, community, and governance will be reshaped, creating opportunities and risks. As AI integrates into every aspect of life, traditional social norms will be challenged, and the way communities form and function will undergo radical shifts. This section explores how AI transcends human limitations.

AI Transcending Human Limitations

Artificial Intelligence (AI) is rapidly developing, and its evolution will not only enhance human capabilities but push the boundaries of what humans can do cognitively, physically, and emotionally. As AI surpasses human limitations, it will extend into realms that have long been considered exclusive to human intelligence and effort. In this section, we explore how AI's superior processing, decision-making, and emotional intelligence will seamlessly integrate into daily life, reshaping the very nature of human experience.

> *AI's cognitive abilities will soon outpace human thought, not only in speed but in its ability to make sense of massive, complex datasets that would take humans lifetimes to interpret.*

Cognitive Limitations: AI's Superior Data Processing and Predictive Power

Think back to the 2011 movie Limitless, where a single pill allowed someone to access 100% of their brainpower, turning them into a superhuman version of themselves. Now, imagine that, but not with a pill, but with AI. We are stepping into a future where AI functions as humanity's cognitive booster. AI won't just augment our decision-making, it will replace human cognitive functions in many areas, pushing beyond the limits of human intuition and experience.

Processing Power Beyond Human Comprehension: AI's data processing and predictive abilities are not bound by the constraints of biology. While a human might take decades to sift through vast datasets, AI can do it in milliseconds, spotting patterns and making connections that would be impossible for the human brain. AI won't just augment decision-making; it will become the engine behind critical insights that push beyond the limits of human intuition and experience. In fields ranging from finance to healthcare, AI's cognitive superiority will drive the future, much like the protagonist in Limitless, but on a global scale. Imagine a healthcare system where AI reads your entire genetic makeup, predicts future diseases, and prescribes treatments in real-time.

This isn't science fiction; it's happening now, and AI will only improve in sophistication.

Decision-Making without Human Bias: AI doesn't rely on hunches or emotions; it makes decisions based purely on data. In industries like healthcare and governance, AI's evidence-based decisions will surpass human judgment, ensuring greater accuracy and efficiency. Yet, this raises critical ethical questions about AI's lack of emotional and moral reasoning.

As AI becomes the decision-maker in critical industries like finance and healthcare, the risk emerges that human well-being could be sacrificed for efficiency and data-driven logic. When AI prioritizes rational outcomes over human compassion, we face the danger of decisions that, while highly effective, may disregard ethical considerations and societal impacts.

Physical Limitations: AI and Robotics Redefining Human Capability

AI will transcend cognitive limitations and surpass human physical limits, reshaping labor, production, and healthcare with precision and endurance that far exceed human capability.

Robotic Precision Beyond Human Ability: In fields that demand flawless precision, AI-driven robots will outperform human workers in every aspect, from intricate surgeries to complex manufacturing. These robots won't just assist humans, they will replace them in roles requiring extreme accuracy and efficiency.

AI-powered robotic surgery systems, like the da Vinci Surgical System, already perform complex operations with minimal invasiveness, reducing human error and improving recovery times. In industries like automotive manufacturing, AI-powered robots are assembling vehicles with unprecedented precision, delivering defect-free products at astonishing speeds.

Automation of Dangerous and Complex Jobs: AI-driven robots will take over high-risk jobs, from mining to deep-sea exploration, eliminating the need for human exposure to dangerous environments while boosting productivity.

AI-powered drones are now inspecting infrastructure in extreme conditions, like offshore oil rigs and high-voltage power lines, ensuring safety without risking human lives.

Augmented Human Performance: With AI-powered wearables and augmented reality (AR), humans will transcend their physical limitations. From athletes optimizing performance to workers enhancing strength through AI-driven exoskeletons, we are entering an era where human capacity will be amplified by intelligent systems.

As AI-driven automation replaces human labor in many sectors, we risk a future where widespread unemployment and inequality become unavoidable. Entire industries could collapse, leaving millions without work, while the rapid advancement of AI may also lead to humans losing valuable skills and becoming overly dependent on machines.

For instance, the transportation industry, especially with the rise of autonomous vehicles, serves as a compelling example. Truck driving, which employs millions globally, is one of the largest sectors at risk. AI and self-driving technology from companies like Tesla, Waymo, and Uber are advancing so rapidly that many predict autonomous trucks could dominate logistics by the next decade. This shift could render millions of truck drivers jobless, leading to a massive industry transformation.

Similarly, manufacturing, traditionally reliant on human labor for assembly line work, is seeing a sharp increase in robotic automation. Factories powered by AI systems can run 24/7 with minimal human intervention, potentially wiping out large swathes of blue-collar jobs. The shift from human-driven to fully automated factories is already reshaping industries such as electronics, automotive manufacturing, and even food production.

These examples highlight the real-world impact of AI, where large segments of the workforce could face displacement. As AI continues to improve, this displacement could accelerate, leaving millions struggling to find new forms of employment, thereby exacerbating inequality and triggering economic and social upheaval.

Emotional and Social Limitations: AI Redefining Human Interaction

AI's ability to understand, respond to, and even anticipate human emotions is transforming how we connect with others. AI won't just recognize emotions, it will simulate them, creating relationships that blur the line between human and machine.

Emotional AI: As AI evolves, its capacity for affective computing, interpreting, and responding to emotional cues will grow, allowing for natural, empathetic interactions that feel deeply human.

AI-powered virtual therapists are already in development, providing round-the-clock emotional support. In the near future, these systems could scale mental health care to levels never before imaginable, offering personalized and continuous care to those in need.

AI as Companions: AI will not only assist but befriend and emotionally support humans. As society ages and social isolation grows, AI companions will provide emotional connection and companionship, creating relationships that are nearly indistinguishable from human bonds.

AI-driven care robots are already assisting the elderly, reminding them to take medications and offering conversation. But soon, these robots will learn personalities, preferences, and emotional states, becoming true companions in ways that no technology has ever done before.

AI in Relationships: From dating to friendships, AI will mediate personal connections. It will not only suggest compatible partners but help resolve conflicts, manage emotional dynamics, and even predict relationship trajectories.

As humans turn to AI for emotional fulfillment, the line between authentic human connection and algorithm-driven companionship will blur. This raises profound ethical questions: Can AI truly replace human intimacy? And what happens to human autonomy when AI dictates our relationships?

Overreliance on AI Companions and Social Isolation: The rise of smartphones already offers a glimpse into how technology can replace real human interaction. The average person spends around 3 to 5 hours a day on their phone, with some reports indicating even higher numbers, particularly among younger generations. In 2023, studies showed the average time spent on smartphones was roughly 4.8 hours daily. This extreme usage leads to a reduction in face-to-face interactions, social skills, and emotional intelligence.

Now, imagine this pattern extending to AI companions. As AI-driven virtual assistants and robots grow more adept at simulating human emotions, people may turn to them for emotional support, companionship, and even friendship. With AI able to interpret emotional cues and respond empathetically, individuals might become more isolated from real human relationships, relying increasingly on AI for companionship. This raises the concern of whether people will lose touch with authentic human interaction, becoming more emotionally detached and socially isolated.

Ethical Dilemmas and Consequences: AI companions could help alleviate loneliness, especially for the elderly or those living in isolation. However, over-reliance on these relationships could blur the lines between human and machine, raising ethical questions about authenticity. Can AI relationships truly replace human connections, and what are the long-term consequences of relying on machines for emotional fulfillment? As people increasingly seek AI-driven emotional interactions, the risk of losing core social and emotional skills grows, potentially weakening community bonds and human empathy.

Potential Implications of AI Transcending Human Limitations

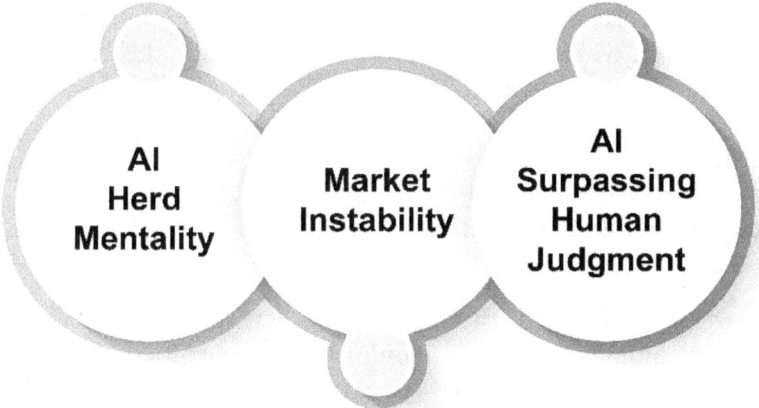

AI Surpassing Human Judgment: AI's ability to analyze vast datasets and react instantly can exceed human capabilities, but it may also lack the emotional intuition that drives humans to take calculated risks based on long-term vision. This could remove a critical layer of judgment that balances short-term data-driven trends with long-term potential.

Market Instability: AI-driven markets could experience extreme volatility as unemotional decisions replace the traditional human-driven market dynamic. Sudden, machine-induced crashes may become a frequent risk in a world where AI controls the majority of trades.

AI Herd Mentality: The interconnected nature of AI systems could lead to an "AI herd mentality" where one system's decision influences others, creating feedback loops that amplify market trends, positive or negative, much faster than human markets could react.

This highlights how AI's potential to transcend human limitations may also present an unnerving reality: removing emotional bias could have unintended consequences, creating a system where AI's logic and speed drive markets in unpredictable directions, with little room for human correction.

Conclusion: Navigating AI's Impact on Society

As AI surpasses human limitations, it will become an integral part of our lives, reshaping economies, transforming industries, and redefining what it means to be human. From cognitive superiority in data processing to emotional intelligence in human interactions, AI will influence every facet of life. But with these advancements come significant risks, economic inequality, market volatility, and ethical concerns around AI's role in decision-making.

As we move forward, the challenge will be to ensure that AI enhances human life without diminishing the qualities that make us uniquely human. How we navigate this balance will define the future of society, work, and relationships.

"Step into the unknown, for it is where greatness lies."

Covered in Chapter Four

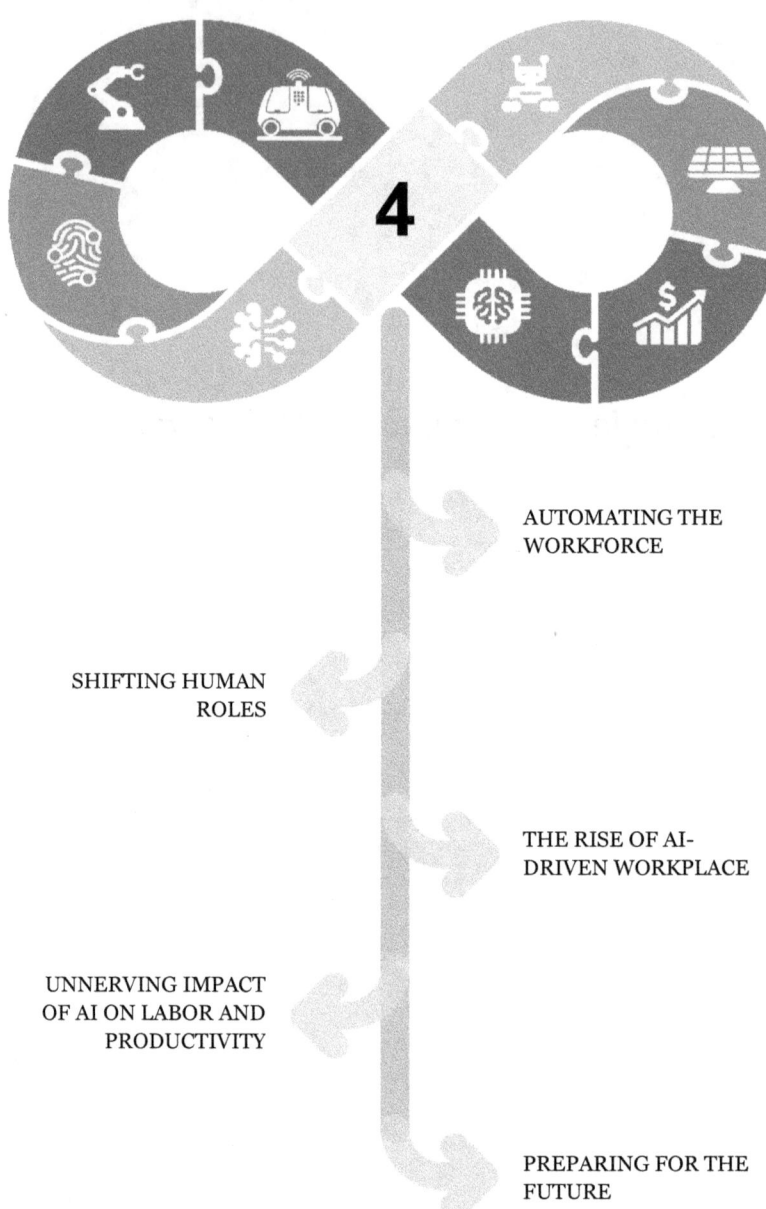

AUTOMATING THE WORKFORCE

SHIFTING HUMAN ROLES

THE RISE OF AI-DRIVEN WORKPLACE

UNNERVING IMPACT OF AI ON LABOR AND PRODUCTIVITY

PREPARING FOR THE FUTURE

Chapter 4:
AI and The Future of Labor and Productivity

As we move into a future where artificial intelligence and robotics play an increasingly dominant role, the very nature of work is undergoing a profound transformation. We've already seen the impact of automation in industries like manufacturing and logistics, but this is just the beginning. AI and robotics will not only take over repetitive tasks, but will also push into areas requiring decision-making, creativity, and emotional intelligence.

In this chapter, we'll explore how robots and AI are redefining the workforce, the shift in human roles from routine to strategic tasks, and the future of productivity in an AI-driven world. While the potential for increased efficiency and innovation is enormous, this shift raises critical questions about job displacement, social mobility, and how societies can adapt to these sweeping changes.

Automating the Workforce

The rise of AI and robotics is revolutionizing industries, automating tasks that were once the domain of human workers. From factory floors to service sectors, AI-driven systems are taking over repetitive, high-volume jobs with unprecedented speed and precision. But this transformation doesn't stop at manual labor; AI is stepping into knowledge-based roles, like financial forecasting, logistics management, and customer interactions, automating processes that demand cognitive sophistication and adaptability.

The Next Frontier in Manufacturing: Manufacturing is at the forefront of the automation revolution, with AI-powered robots transforming how products are made. We can see that with Tesla's Optimus robot, which represents the next generation of intelligent machines built to go beyond repetitive tasks like welding or painting. Optimus is designed to handle more complex cognitive tasks, analyze data, make decisions, and optimize production systems in real-time. Equipped with sensors and advanced AI algorithms, these robots can predict potential failures and correct course before issues arise, resulting in continuous production improvements.

In Tesla's own automotive manufacturing processes, the Optimus robot can make an enormous impact by continuously optimizing everything from assembly to quality checks, leveraging AI to detect anomalies and prevent defects in real time. But beyond Tesla, the broader vision of globally connected AI-driven robots powered by Starlink could reshape industries ranging from logistics to healthcare, where remote operations and real-time data processing are essential.

The Optimus robot's ability to handle cognitive tasks means that it won't just replace human labor for manual tasks, it could also replace or augment cognitive functions, accelerating decision-making, optimizing entire supply chains, and learning from global data to improve performance.

The synergy of AI, robotics, and global connectivity via Starlink is poised to not just automate manufacturing but completely revolutionize how businesses operate in every industry.

> *This paints a picture of a future where robots aren't just tools, they are integral, intelligent parts of a real-time, interconnected global manufacturing ecosystem.*

Imagine these robots being globally connected. This real-time connectivity means that factories anywhere in the world could be part of a shared network of robots, exchanging data and learning from one another's experiences. A manufacturing facility in Germany, for instance, could benefit from real-time insights from a factory in Japan, enhancing efficiency and reducing downtime across a global network of operations.

As another example, China successfully resurfaced a 157.8-kilometer highway using only drones, robots, and AI, without any human intervention. This fully autonomous project demonstrates the growing capabilities of robotics in construction. From paving to quality assurance, the drones and robots managed all aspects of the operation, ensuring precision and efficiency in real-time. With AI-driven tools making adjustments during the process and 5G technology supporting seamless communication, the project exemplifies the future of automated infrastructure. The success of this endeavor highlights how AI and robotics will redefine labor-intensive industries, minimizing human oversight while maximizing operational efficiency.

Customer Service and Retail: AI isn't just transforming physical industries; it is reshaping the customer service and retail sectors, creating a new era of hyper-personalization and efficiency. AI-driven chatbots and virtual assistants now handle customer queries, process orders, and resolve complaints at scale, delivering a level of service consistency previously impossible with human staff. In retail, AI anticipates customer needs, optimizes inventory, and drives personalized marketing based on real-time behavioral data.

Amazon's AI-driven logistics systems, which use autonomous robots to pick, sort, and package products, have revolutionized the fulfillment process. As of 2024, Amazon employs over 750,000 robots working alongside its workforce of 1.5 million full-time and part-time employees. This represents a significant shift towards automation in one of the world's largest companies. By 2030, it is forecasted that the number of robots employed at Amazon will surpass the number of human workers. These robots not only speed up warehouse operations but also minimize errors, enabling faster deliveries and improving customer satisfaction.

Transportation and Logistics: The transportation and logistics sector are being radically transformed by AI systems capable of optimizing entire supply chains, predicting traffic patterns, and autonomously directing fleets of vehicles to ensure timely deliveries. AI-powered platforms now analyze complex global conditions, from weather disruptions to fuel prices, enabling real-time route adjustments that optimize fuel efficiency and reduce costs.

In the shipping industry, companies like UPS and FedEx use AI-powered route optimization software to reconfigure delivery schedules in real-time dynamically. AI predicts traffic and weather patterns, preventing delays and ensuring faster, more efficient deliveries.

Entertainment and Content Creation: In addition to automating service and manual labor, AI is revolutionizing creative industries, from music composition to video production. AI-driven algorithms can now create content, generate art, write articles, and even compose music that resonates emotionally with audiences.

As AI integrates into the creative process, it opens up new possibilities for personalized entertainment experiences and mass content creation at a scale never seen before.

AI tools like OpenAI's GPT models and AIVA (AI Virtual Artist) generate music, create marketing copy, and even draft news articles, blurring the lines between human and machine creativity. AI systems are now assisting with scriptwriting, editing, and analyzing audience reactions to predict box office success in film production.

Shifting Human Roles

As AI-driven automation transforms industries, the role of human labor will shift toward more strategic, creative, and emotionally intelligent positions. While this shift opens doors for humans to focus on higher-value activities, it also presents profound challenges in reskilling and adapting to a rapidly evolving job landscape. The question is not whether jobs will change but how prepared we are for the paradigm shift that AI will bring.

Moving from Routine to Strategic Work: With AI taking over repetitive tasks, human workers will be liberated to focus on problem-solving, leadership, and creativity. This shift will make jobs requiring interpersonal skills, emotional intelligence, and complex decision-making more valuable. However, the speed of this transition will leave many workers scrambling to stay relevant, continuously updating their skill sets to match the demands of an AI-powered economy.

In finance, where AI systems now manage data analysis and risk assessment, human financial professionals are shifting into roles that emphasize strategic thinking and client relationship management. Their focus is moving from routine number-crunching to crafting high-level investment strategies and navigating complex market dynamics that AI systems flag but cannot fully interpret.

The Imperative of Reskilling and Lifelong Learning: The rise of AI makes continuous learning a necessity and survival strategy. Workers will need to adopt new technologies and develop skills that complement AI, creativity, human connection, and innovation to maintain their place in the workforce. Lifelong learning is no longer optional in a world where industries evolve faster than ever.

In forward-thinking nations like Singapore and Germany, governments invest in national reskilling initiatives designed to future-proof their workforce. Programs like Singapore's SkillsFuture equip citizens with coding, data analysis, and AI management competencies, ensuring they remain competitive as the AI-driven economy rapidly shifts.

Emergence of New Job Categories: While AI will eliminate certain roles, it will also create entirely new categories of work, focused on collaborating with intelligent machines. Jobs like AI trainers, data ethicists, and human-AI interaction designers, which didn't exist a decade ago, are now vital in many industries. These new roles will demand a different kind of expertise, managing AI systems rather than being replaced by them.

The development of autonomous vehicles is creating demand for roles such as AI trainers, who ensure that self-driving systems learn and adapt safely, and engineers who develop the infrastructure required for a world dominated by intelligent machines.

The Rise of AI-Driven Workplaces

Future workplaces will be AI-enhanced ecosystems where humans and intelligent systems collaborate, achieving results faster and more efficiently.

> *AI won't just optimize productivity; it will shape how work is done, from automating workflows to contributing creatively in fields once thought uniquely human.*

Project Management: AI is transforming project management by streamlining complex tasks, optimizing resources, and predicting potential challenges before they arise. These systems will not just follow orders; they will suggest better strategies based on real-time data, freeing human managers to focus on higher-level decision-making.

AI-driven project management platforms like Asana and Monday.com now use machine learning to prioritize tasks and suggest workflow improvements. These tools don't just track progress; they help teams anticipate potential roadblocks and redistribute resources dynamically, ensuring projects stay on time and target.

Creative Work: AI's impact is not confined to data and logistics; it pushes the boundaries of creativity in industries like art, design, and music. AI systems collaborate with human creators, generating ideas, concepts, and even finished works faster than ever. While AI won't replace human creativity, it will amplify it, offering new perspectives and infinite iterations of ideas.

Designers and artists are using tools like Adobe Sensei and OpenAI's DALL·E to generate visual concepts, design prototypes, and even create artwork autonomously. These tools allow creatives to explore bold new ideas and iterate rapidly, pushing the boundaries of what's possible in creative industries.

Unnerving Impact of AI on Labor and Productivity

While AI promises extraordinary leaps in productivity and innovation, it also comes with unnerving risks: mass job displacement, widening economic inequality, and profound social disruptions.

> *How we navigate this new frontier will determine whether we thrive or fracture as a society.*

Widespread Job Displacement: As AI and robotics take over more tasks, millions of jobs are at risk of being displaced, particularly in sectors dependent on routine manual labor. If not managed carefully, this disruption could trigger unprecedented levels of economic inequality and social unrest. Governments and businesses must work together to create safety nets and reskilling programs that help workers transition into the new economy.

In the logistics sector, AI-driven systems have already displaced thousands of warehouse workers. As automation spreads to other industries like retail and transportation, similar disruptions will ripple across the global workforce.

The Emergence of an AI-Elite Workforce: While some will lose jobs, others, those who possess the right skills, will thrive, creating a new AI elite. Workers in fields like AI development, data science, and machine learning will see soaring demand and wages, while those without access to these high-skill opportunities will be left behind.

The tech industry's demand for AI specialists and data scientists has led to skyrocketing salaries for those with advanced skills. However, this has created a growing divide, with workers in industries like retail and manufacturing seeing stagnant wages and fewer opportunities.

Ethical Concerns and the Loss of Human Agency: As AI systems take over more decision-making processes, there is a growing risk that humans will lose their agency and defer critical decisions to machines. The reliance on AI in hiring, promotions, and performance evaluations raises profound ethical concerns about bias, fairness, and the erosion of human autonomy.

AI-driven hiring platforms are now screening job applicants based on algorithms that, if not carefully designed, can perpetuate existing biases in the data. This could lead to discriminatory hiring practices that disproportionately affect underrepresented groups, raising serious ethical concerns about how AI is integrated into decision-making.

Preparing for the Future of Work

The transformation of labor and productivity through AI and robotics is inevitable. However, how we prepare for this seismic shift will determine whether we thrive in an AI-driven world or succumb to its disruptive forces. Societies must act now to ensure that the benefits of AI are widely shared rather than concentrated among a select few.

Social Safety Nets and Universal Basic Income: As AI-driven automation displaces jobs, governments may need to implement social safety nets like Universal Basic Income (UBI) to ensure that people have a financial cushion during periods of job transition. UBI could provide individuals with the financial security to pursue reskilling opportunities or explore new career paths without the immediate pressure of unemployment.

Finland's UBI pilot program provided citizens with a basic income regardless of employment status, allowing them to pursue education, entrepreneurial ventures, or creative projects. Such initiatives may become more common as automation disrupts traditional labor markets.

Reskilling Programs and Lifelong Learning: Investing in education and reskilling programs will be crucial to ensure that workers are prepared for future jobs. Governments and businesses alike will need to collaborate on creating accessible and affordable training programs that focus on skills like coding, AI management, data analysis, and human-AI collaboration.

Singapore has launched its SkillsFuture initiative, which provides citizens with credits to invest in learning new skills and adapting to changes in the job market. Similar programs will be essential in other countries to help workers transition into the AI-driven economy.

The Divide: Integration vs. Resistance: As robots and AI become more integrated into our lives, society will inevitably split into two distinct camps: those who fully embrace the fusion of human and machine, and those who resist, fearing the implications of this technological symbiosis.

On one side, you will see individuals who are not only comfortable with but excited about integrating AI and robotics into their lives, perhaps even augmenting their own capabilities through wearable tech, neural implants, or AI-powered enhancements. These early adopters will view this integration as a path to greater productivity, health, and even longevity. Imagine workers in high-tech industries who collaborate seamlessly with AI agents to optimize their daily tasks, or as mentioned, individuals using AI-powered exoskeletons to perform feats of strength and endurance far beyond human limits.

An example of this emerging trend is Elon Musk's *Neuralink*, which aims to create a direct interface between the human brain and machines. The goal? To allow humans to communicate with technology simply by thinking, a development that could redefine everything from medicine to communication and even entertainment.

> *As this technology advances, those who adopt it could find themselves at the forefront of a new era of human potential, where the line between human and machine begins to blur.*

However, on the other side of this technological divide are those who will vehemently reject these integrations. They see it as a slippery slope, one that may compromise human identity, autonomy, and privacy. In their eyes, the reliance on AI and robotics risks stripping away the very essence of what it means to be human. Much like the current skepticism towards invasive technologies, this group may view human augmentation as a step too far, one that opens the door to surveillance, loss of control, and a world in which human values are undermined by machine logic.

This societal split could manifest in many ways. We may see laws, movements, and even communities formed around the idea of remaining "tech-free" or un-augmented, much like modern debates surrounding data privacy or social media use. In more extreme cases, this could spark new forms of class divides: those who are "augmented" versus those who are not.

> *As robots and AI continue to evolve, we'll not only see a technological divide but a profound cultural one, challenging society's ideas about progress, humanity, and the future.*

Conclusion: The New Age of Labor and Productivity

As AI and robotics increasingly take over routine and complex tasks, human roles will evolve toward creativity, innovation, and high-level decision-making, redefining what it means to work in the AI century. While the opportunities for unprecedented productivity and innovation are limitless, the risks of widespread job displacement, deepening social inequality, and the erosion of human agency loom large. Societies will need to adapt swiftly, reinventing education systems, creating new safety nets, and embedding ethical principles into AI development to ensure that the future of work is inclusive and empowering for all.

The future of human labor isn't simply a story of technological progress; it's a fundamental shift in how we define value, productivity, and purpose.

As we move into this new era, the survival of industries, economies, and communities will depend on how well they can harness the power of AI while protecting human dignity, opportunity, and creativity.

In the next chapter, we'll dive into how AI will usher in a new era of economic transformation. We will explore how AI agents are poised to disrupt traditional economic models, fundamentally altering how wealth is created, distributed, and scaled.

"Tomorrow belongs to the bold"

Covered in Chapter Five

AI AGENTS REVOLUTIONIZING ECONOMIC ACTIVITY

THE DIGITAL ECONOMY: A FRICTIONLESS FUTURE

AI AGENTS OPTIMIZING SUPPLY CHAINS AND RESOURCE ALLOCATION

NEW MARKETS CREATED BY AUTONOMOUS AI

THE ROLE OF AI IN ECONOMIC GROWTH

THE UNNERVING IMPACT OF AI AGENTS

Chapter 5:
AI Agents and the New Economic Paradigm

At the heart of the next economic revolution are AI agents, but what exactly are they? For those unfamiliar with the term, an AI agent is a software-based entity that acts autonomously, meaning it can make decisions and perform tasks on behalf of a user without needing constant human oversight. Imagine them as smart digital assistants with the ability to interact with their environment, learn from it, and adapt their actions to achieve specific goals. Unlike static programs or apps, AI agents are dynamic, learning continuously to improve their performance and efficiency over time.

You've already seen basic AI agents in action: think of virtual assistants like Siri or Alexa, which respond to voice commands and complete tasks such as setting reminders, playing music, or checking the weather. However, these are just the tip of the iceberg. As AI evolves, agents will become far more sophisticated, handling complex, multi-step processes like managing supply chains, conducting financial transactions, and even making strategic business decisions.

AI agents will not only enhance existing business models but also create entirely new ones. These systems will power the frictionless economy of the future, where decisions are made instantly, supply chains adapt in real-time, and transactions happen almost as fast as the thought behind them.

The rise of AI agents will blur the line between human decision-making and machine-driven optimization, enabling unprecedented efficiency and creating new markets we can't even fully imagine today.

This chapter explores how AI agents will transform economic activity and set the foundation for an autonomous economy where humans focus on creativity and strategy, while AI handles the operational, transactional, and logistical challenges in the background. This shift will go beyond business. Individuals will also employ personal AI agents, operating as networks of autonomous extensions of themselves, working for them, driving productivity, and enabling an individual to achieve more than what is currently possible.

We will explore AI companions in Chapter 13, diving deeper into this concept. These agents will serve as personal assistants and expand our capabilities in ways we can hardly fathom today.

They will become workforce multipliers, allowing individuals to outsource tasks and create personal networks of AI-driven systems that enhance their daily lives.

AI Agents: Revolutionizing Economic Activity

The emergence of AI agents marks one of the most profound developments in global economics. These intelligent systems operate autonomously, making decisions, managing resources, and executing tasks without direct human input. As AI agents evolve, they will take on increasingly complex roles in industries ranging from finance to logistics, transforming not just businesses but also the way individuals interact with the economy.

AI agents won't just be the domain of corporations and governments. Soon, individuals will be able to employ AI agents to perform tasks on their behalf, effectively multiplying their workforce.

Whether it's running a business, managing investments, negotiating contracts, or even automating creative projects, a single person could have multiple AI agents autonomously working for them, allowing for unprecedented levels of productivity.

> *This concept introduces a new paradigm where personal AI agents can unlock vast potential for individuals, enabling them to leverage AI as a tool for both professional and personal growth.*

Autonomous Decision-Making and Transactions: AI agents will automate decision-making across businesses, governments, and consumer markets, executing high-stakes decisions with speed and precision beyond human capability. From negotiating contracts to executing trades, these agents will eliminate the need for human intermediaries, creating a more efficient and frictionless system of exchange. For individuals, this means AI agents could handle everything from personal investments to real estate deals, streamlining complex processes that would otherwise require human involvement.

In financial markets, AI trading agents are already executing high-frequency trades, analyzing market data in real-time and making decisions in milliseconds. As these systems evolve, they will manage corporate portfolios and work for individual investors, predicting economic trends, executing complex investment strategies, and continuously optimizing returns. In the near future, personal AI agents could become the ultimate financial advisors, autonomously growing wealth while their human owners focus on other pursuits.

Imagine an individual owning a fleet of autonomous AI-driven vehicles that operate a ride-share business 24/7. These vehicles navigate the streets, respond to ride requests, optimize routes, and even handle vehicle maintenance, all without human input. The AI system monitors demand patterns, adjusts pricing dynamically, and ensures that each vehicle is dispatched to the most profitable locations. The individual simply oversees the AI fleet from a control panel, while the AI agents autonomously run the entire ride-share operation, generating income around the clock. This shifts the model from active human management to passive oversight, where AI does the heavy lifting, and the individual reaps the benefits.

The Digital Economy: A Frictionless Future

The next economic revolution will be defined by frictionless markets, where transactions, logistics, and resource management happen seamlessly. AI agents will eradicate inefficiencies, driving the global economy to new levels of speed, accuracy, and scalability.

Removing the Middleman: The Rise of Smart Contracts: In the near future, AI agents will seamlessly integrate with smart contracts. For those unfamiliar with the term, a smart contract is a self-executing contract with the terms of the agreement directly written into lines of code. These contracts automatically trigger and execute when the predefined conditions are met without needing a third party like a lawyer or broker. Think of it as a digital agreement that enforces itself, eliminating the need for human oversight in verifying whether the terms have been fulfilled.

Smart contracts are particularly powerful because they remove the middlemen from processes like payments, asset transfers, or service agreements. They live on decentralized platforms like Ethereum and Solana, where they ensure transparency and security, reducing transaction times and costs significantly. For example, in real estate transactions, a smart contract could automatically transfer property ownership as soon as the payment is verified, no need for lawyers, escrow agents, or weeks of waiting.

Now, imagine how this concept scales when integrated with AI agents. AI-driven smart contracts could autonomously handle complex international trades, logistics agreements, or even high-value real estate deals.

These contracts would be able to negotiate, verify, and execute transactions in real time, eliminating friction from the process and completely reinventing traditional legal and business practices.

> *This evolution will lead to an economy that operates at the speed of thought, with AI and smart contracts working harmoniously to deliver efficiency and trust like never before.*

AI-Optimized Consumer Transactions: Before AI agents are fully trusted by the general public, there's a significant trust barrier that will need to be overcome. Right now, many consumers are hesitant to delegate critical tasks, like financial management or personal purchases, to autonomous systems. Concerns about privacy, data security, and the accuracy of AI decisions add to this skepticism.

However, just as people have grown comfortable using smartphones and voice assistants like Alexa and Google Assistant, trust in AI agents will increase gradually as these systems prove their reliability. Imagine a scenario where AI agents start by handling low-stakes tasks, such as ordering groceries or suggesting products. As these agents consistently meet expectations, consumers will begin allowing them to take on more significant responsibilities, such as booking international travel or managing household finances. Over time, people will become accustomed to their AI agents operating behind the scenes, anticipating needs, and making real-time adjustments based on personal preferences and data

The point where AI agents are fully trusted could resemble the shift from skepticism about online banking to its widespread adoption. As more people experience the benefits of AI-driven convenience, they will gradually offload more responsibilities, allowing AI agents to manage not just transactions but entire aspects of daily life.

Ultimately, the trust barrier will be overcome when AI agents consistently demonstrate their ability to deliver personalized, secure, and reliable results, just as humans learned to trust other forms of automation and technology over time

AI Agents Optimizing Supply Chains and Resource Allocation

AI agents will transform how goods are produced, distributed, and consumed. With the power of real-time data integration and predictive analytics, AI will optimize supply chains, ensuring that resources are allocated efficiently and with unprecedented accuracy.

Predictive Analytics in Supply Chain Management: AI agents will use predictive analytics to anticipate demand fluctuations, manage stock levels, and adjust logistics in real-time.

These systems will ensure that businesses have exactly what they need, when they need it, driving down costs and minimizing waste.

Amazon's AI-driven fulfillment centers already use machine learning to predict demand and optimize warehouse operations. But imagine a future where AI agents autonomously control the entire supply chain, from raw materials to delivery, adjusting production and shipping on the fly to meet shifting market conditions.

Real-Time Resource Optimization: AI agents will manage entire industries, not just supply chains. They will allocate resources like raw materials and labor in real-time based on market needs, leading to leaner, faster, and more efficient production processes that reduce costs and improve sustainability.

Tesla's Gigafactory uses AI to manage materials for battery production, ensuring that every component is used with precision. In the near future, AI agents will optimize resource allocation across multiple industries, eliminating inefficiencies and creating a hyper-efficient, autonomous economy.

New Markets Created by Autonomous AI Agents

AI agents won't just disrupt existing markets; they will create entirely new ones. The rise of AI-as-a-Service (AIaaS) platforms, AI-driven marketplaces, and autonomous decision-making tools will make cutting-edge AI accessible to every business, regardless of size or industry.

AI-as-a-Service: Accessible AI for All: AIaaS platforms will democratize AI, allowing businesses to access on-demand AI services like data analytics, automation, and predictive modeling. These platforms will empower even small businesses to leverage AI to drive innovation and optimize operations.

Google Cloud AI and Microsoft Azure AI already offer AI services that enhance customer service, automate inventory, and optimize business processes. In the future, AIaaS platforms will be as ubiquitous as cloud computing, enabling any company to tap into AI's limitless potential.

The Role of AI Agents in Economic Growth

AI agents will drive exponential economic growth, breaking traditional GDP models. As AI scales productivity beyond the limits of human labor, economies will need to rethink how they measure success and distribute wealth.

GDP Growth: AI agents will transform industries, allowing businesses to produce more with fewer resources. This shift will lead to exponential productivity gains that outpace traditional economic growth models.

AI-driven robots in manufacturing will produce at unprecedented speeds, with minimal human intervention, creating new levels of efficiency that drive GDP growth beyond anything we've seen.

Breaking Traditional Economic Models: As automation takes over, new economic models will emerge to ensure that wealth is distributed equitably, and that everyone benefits from AI-driven growth.

> **AI will challenge the relationship between labor and productivity.**

In Japan, where an aging population has led to labor shortages, AI is filling the gap, redefining how value is created and measured. As more industries turn to AI, governments will need to rethink economic policies to ensure that AI benefits society as a whole.

Conclusion: The New Economic Paradigm

The rise of AI agents represents nothing short of a revolution, one that will completely reshape the global economy, redefine the nature of work, and disrupt industries on a scale never before seen. As these autonomous systems take over decision-making, manage resources, and optimize transactions, the entire economic landscape will shift from human-centered processes to AI-driven ecosystems.

> **This transformation will lead to unparalleled efficiency, seamless markets, and new business models that challenge the very foundations of traditional economic thought.**

Yet, this revolution isn't just for the big players. The truly profound impact of AI agents will be felt when individuals harness this power. With AI as a personal workforce multiplier, one person can manage a fleet of autonomous vehicles, run a global e-commerce business, or optimize investments, without ever needing a physical office or large staff.

> *In this new economic paradigm, the potential for individuals to create wealth, innovate, and scale their ventures is limitless. AI agents will blur the lines between corporations and individuals, empowering the latter with tools once reserved for the largest enterprises.*

But as we race into this future, we must not lose sight of the risks. The advent of hyper-automation and AI monopolies could lead to a concentration of wealth and power in the hands of a few, exacerbating inequality and stifling innovation. Ethical oversight will be crucial as we navigate the delicate balance between AI efficiency and human values. Governments, businesses, and society at large must come together to build frameworks that ensure AI benefits are equitably shared.

In this chapter, we've seen the incredible promise of AI agents in revolutionizing economic activity, creating frictionless markets, and driving exponential growth. However, the true potential lies ahead. In Chapter 13, we will explore the deeper, more personal implications of AI agents, how they will become companions and workforce multipliers, enabling individuals to redefine the boundaries of work, leisure, and creativity.

The future of the economy will be AI-driven, but how we manage this transition will determine whether it leads to a new era of shared prosperity or deepens the divides of today. **The revolution is here, and it is up to us to shape it.**

Covered in Chapter Six

ONE-TO-MANY-TO-ONE: OMNI-SYNCHRONOUS ENGAGEMENT

ROADMAP FOR THRIVING IN THE INFINITE-SCALE PRESENCE ECONOMY

A NEW DEFINITION OF WEALTH AND INFLUENCE IN OMNI-SYNCHRONOUS WORLD

ETHICAL AND SOCIAL CHALLENGES IN THE INFINITE-SCALE ECONOMY

CASE STUDIES OF OMNI-SYNCHRONOUS ENGAGEMENT IN ACTION

PREPARING FOR THE INFINITE-SCALE PRESENCE AND ECONOMY

Chapter 6
Omni-Synchronous Engagement

Throughout history, the nature of communication and influence has shifted dramatically, each era reshaping the limits and potential of personal connections. In the pre-internet world, communication was confined to face-to-face interactions, where influence was limited by geography and time. These personal exchanges allowed people to develop deep, bi-directional relationships, with each conversation contributing to the knowledge exchange. As we transitioned into the digital and social media era, our capacity for influence grew as the internet allowed individuals to reach vast audiences through one-to-many models like blogs, YouTube, and social media platforms.

With the advent of AI agents, we are entering a new era: Omni-Synchronous Engagement, a paradigm where one person can engage in real-time, one-on-one interactions with millions simultaneously. This chapter explores how this evolution unfolds and the profound changes it brings.

Omni-Synchronous Engagement, a paradigm where one person can engage in real-time, one-on-one interactions with millions simultaneously.

Omni-Synchronous Engagement: One-to-Many-to-One Interaction

Omni-Synchronous Engagement represents the next step in scalable, personalized communication. Here, AI agents amplify human capabilities, allowing individuals to engage in vast numbers of interactions at once, while maintaining the one-on-one intimacy of face-to-face connections.

Imagine how this might work: We're all familiar with Zoom calls where a large group gathers to hear an inspiring leader speak, with opportunities for everyone to ask questions and hear the answers. Now, envision the same scenario, but instead of speaking to a group, you're in a private, one-on-one conversation with the leader. You're free to ask personal questions and receive responses tailored specifically to your situation.

With the future technology of Omni-Synchronous Engagement, that same leader could simultaneously connect with thousands of people, each in a private, individualized conversation. AI would enable this leader to generate unlimited AI replicas (AI-Agents) to engage with each person one-on-one in real time.

What makes this remarkable is that every conversation held by these AI-Agents is fed back into a central intelligence, enriching its knowledge base with insights from each unique interaction. Initially, the AI would synthesize this information and provide the leader with updates containing relevant new insights as needed. In the near future, as technologies like Neuralink advance, leaders could even integrate this wealth of knowledge directly into their own consciousness, effortlessly expanding their understanding in real time.

This new model brings scalable influence without sacrificing depth, enabling true one-to-many-to-one interactions. In this future economy, AI enables each individual to:

- ∞ Simultaneously engage in millions of one-on-one conversations with individuals or their AI agents, ensuring each interaction feels personalized and meaningful.
- ∞ Receive real-time feedback and learning from these exchanges, enhancing personal growth and improving the AI's capabilities.
- ∞ Build a knowledge loop, where each interaction contributes to collective intelligence, creating a self-sustaining cycle of continuous improvement.

> *This model transcends simple broadcasting; instead, it combines the scale of digital engagement with the depth of personal connection, recreating the intimacy of pre-internet conversations.*

The one-to-many-to-one model combines the power of digital amplification with the depth and personalization of pre-internet conversations.

A Feedback Loop of Continuous Growth: The core of Omni-Synchronous Engagement lies in its feedback loop. Each interaction feeds into personal and AI learning systems, continuously updating models and enhancing knowledge. For example, as one interacts with millions of people, the AI agent gathers feedback, adjusts conversation strategies, and becomes more responsive to unique needs.

This self-reinforcing loop ensures both human and machine intelligence evolve dynamically. The more individuals engage, the more powerful and capable both they and their AI agents become, creating an exponential learning curve.

> *This is no longer a static knowledge base but a living, adaptive knowledge ecosystem, where individuals and their AI agents learn and improve from each interaction across industries and geographies.*

The Power Shift: Redefining Presence and Influence: Omni-Synchronous Engagement redefines what it means to be "present." In the pre-internet world, presence was physical; with social media, it became digital. Now, AI agents enable an omnipresence that transcends location and time. Key elements of this power shift include:

- ∞ Omnipresence Through AI Agents: Thanks to AI-powered representation, a single individual can serve on thousands of

boards, participating in real-time, meaningful discussions simultaneously.
- ∞ Hyper-Personalized Conversations at Scale: Every interaction, regardless of volume, feels uniquely personal, merging the best of one-on-one and one-to-many influence.
- ∞ Real-Time Knowledge Expansion: Every engagement adds to the individual's and AI's intelligence, creating a network of interconnected learning and growth.

This evolution combines the intimacy of pre-internet human connection with AI's efficiency, enabling presence and engagement on an unprecedented scale.

Impact on the Future Knowledge Economy: In an AI-driven future, Omni-Synchronous Engagement will transform influence, education, business, and relationships. The model will enable new economic structures:

- ∞ Scalable Leadership: Executives and leaders can simultaneously contribute to multiple boards and strategy discussions, expanding their impact without sacrificing decision-making quality.
- ∞ Exponential Knowledge Growth: Each interaction, whether with another human or AI, contributes to a broader feedback loop that enhances knowledge.
- ∞ Redefining Trust and Relationships: People will increasingly trust AI companions and agents to facilitate meaningful engagements, which will become the foundation of professional and personal relationships in the future economy.

These changes will redefine how knowledge is shared and influence is scaled, expanding the knowledge-driven economy.

The Roadmap for Thriving in the Infinite-Scale Presence Economy

To succeed in this new model, individuals, companies, and governments must adjust their strategies to leverage Omni-Synchronous Engagement effectively:

1. **For Individuals:**
    - ∞ Develop a Strong AI Relationship: Treat AI agents as collaborators and learning tools, training them to understand your priorities, values, and preferences.
    - ∞ Adopt a Lifelong Learning Mindset: Each interaction, whether with people or AI, becomes part of your knowledge ecosystem.
    - ∞ Expand Influence Through Presence: With AI handling repetitive tasks, individuals can scale their influence to reach many people while maintaining a personal touch.

Having the ability to be everywhere and fully present through AI agents will become a new currency.

---

2. **For Companies:**
    - ∞ AI-Augmented Leadership: CEOs and executives will participate in multiple boards or teams simultaneously through their AI agents, ensuring real-time strategy and decision-making without being physically present.
    - ∞ Scalable Customer Engagement: Customer service will evolve into AI-powered one-to-one interactions, where each customer feels uniquely valued. Companies that leverage AI for personalized interaction at scale will dominate markets.
    - ∞ Shift to Knowledge-Driven Work: As routine jobs become automated, companies should focus on developing creative, strategic, and problem-solving roles that thrive with human-AI collaboration.

3. **For Governments:**
    - ∞ Create Regulatory Frameworks for AI and Data Privacy: In a world where one individual or organization can be present in many places at once, governments need to establish clear guidelines on AI participation, trust, and privacy.

- ∞ Enable Decentralized Governance: Governments must embrace blockchain-based governance models to remain relevant in a decentralized world. DAOs and other distributed systems will need legal recognition to operate effectively.
- ∞ Promote AI Literacy and Accessibility: As AI becomes central to personal and professional success, governments must ensure equitable access to AI technologies and offer education programs to bridge the knowledge divide.

A New Definition of Wealth and Influence in Omni-Synchronous World

In the Infinite-Scale Presence economy, wealth and influence will no longer be limited to financial capital or physical presence. Instead, the following will define success:

- ∞ Time and Presence as Currency: The ability to be omnipresent and fully engaged across spaces will become invaluable.
- ∞ Knowledge as Currency: Each interaction contributes to a growing network of personal and professional insights.
- ∞ Trust in AI Representation: Building trust in AI agents is crucial, as they become extensions of individuals in many spheres of influence.

Ethical and Social Challenges in the Infinite-Scale Economy

As AI and personal presence scale exponentially, we must address key challenges:

- ∞ Maintaining Authenticity: How do we ensure that human-AI interactions remain meaningful, even at scale? Balancing automation with authenticity will be crucial.
- ∞ Trust and Responsibility: If AI agents make decisions or represent us in high-stakes settings, who is ultimately

accountable, the person, the AI, or the organization managing the technology?

∞ Privacy and Data Ownership: With millions of interactions feeding into learning loops, privacy laws will need to evolve to protect individuals and ensure responsible data use.

Case Studies of Omni-Synchronous Engagement in Action

To illustrate Omni-Synchronous Engagement's potential, consider these examples of its application across sectors:

Omni-Synchronous Engagement for APAC Regional Project Management: In the APAC region, managing a large-scale strategic partnership plan typically requires multiple project managers across countries to handle local nuances, coordinate with teams, and make real-time decisions.

> *However, with Omni-Synchronous Engagement and the aid of AI-powered translation and communication agents, a single APAC Regional Project Manager can now manage and execute the entire regional rollout, interacting seamlessly across diverse languages and cultures.*

Scenario: A multinational company is launching a strategic partnership initiative across the APAC region, involving partners from Japan, South Korea, India, and Southeast Asian nations. In the traditional setup, separate managers would oversee each country's operations, often encountering challenges in aligning objectives and decision-making speed due to language barriers, cultural differences, and time zones.

With Omni-Synchronous Engagement, the APAC Regional Project Manager can:

- ∞ Simultaneously connect with all country project leaders in their native languages through AI-powered translation, ensuring no critical information is lost in communication.
- ∞ Gather immediate, real-time feedback from each leader, enabling faster and culturally sensitive decision-making.
- ∞ Adjust project strategies on the spot based on instant insights from each country, adapting plans dynamically across the region.
- ∞ Coordinate effectively across time zones, as AI agents facilitate asynchronous updates, summarizing overnight developments and preparing actionable reports.

This new model of project management streamlines the rollout process, improves coordination, and reduces costs, making the APAC Regional Project Manager not only more effective but also empowered to achieve a unified and agile strategy across a complex, multi-national region.

Two more case study illustrations of Omni-Synchronous Engagement's potential:

- ∞ **Customer Service Transformation:** A large e-commerce company employs AI agents to handle thousands of real-time customer interactions. Each customer feels they're engaging one-on-one with an agent, but AI processes behind the scenes deliver tailored responses. The AI continuously improves by analyzing customer feedback, allowing it to adapt to specific needs over time.

- ∞ **Omni-Synchronous Leadership in Action:** Imagine a global CEO who can actively participate in discussions across multiple subsidiaries simultaneously. The CEO's AI agents facilitate these conversations, ensuring that key decisions reflect their insights while prioritizing direct engagement where necessary. This approach ensures real-time, thoughtful input across a global enterprise without sacrificing depth or authenticity.

> *These scenarios demonstrate the unique ability of Omni-Synchronous Engagement to combine scale and intimacy, enhancing customer experience and leadership without compromising the personal touch.*

Conclusion: Preparing for the Infinite-Scale Presence and Economy

As we enter this new era of one-to-many-to-one interaction, it's essential to adapt and prepare. Individuals need to build strong AI relationships, continuously learn, and stay alert to emerging technologies. Companies must adopt AI-enhanced collaboration tools and embrace decentralized knowledge sharing, while governments will need to rethink policies around work, privacy, and influence in a world where one person's presence can scale infinitely.

> *This is the future of influence, learning, and value creation, and those who embrace this shift will thrive in the Infinite-Scale Presence economy.*

The evolution of economies, from face-to-face connections to mass digital influence, is coming full circle. We are entering a world where one person, amplified by AI, can engage meaningfully with millions, creating an intimate presence at a massive scale. This Infinite-Scale Presence economy offers unprecedented opportunities for growth, influence, and knowledge acquisition, but it also requires new ways of thinking, working, and governing.

The future belongs to those who embrace this transformation, who train their AI agents, leverage their presence at scale, and continuously learn from every interaction. Success will come not just from being everywhere, but from being fully present, contextual aware and influential in each interaction, no matter the scale.

To summarize, this new interaction model offers a powerful new framework for personalized influence and scalable learning. In the Infinite-Scale Presence economy, every individual can interact deeply with millions through AI, learning and evolving from each exchange. It's not just one person speaking to many, but one-to-many-to-one, where the interaction feels uniquely personal while still benefiting from global scale.

This idea reflects the convergence of pre-internet intimacy with post-internet scalability, creating a networked ecosystem of continuous learning, influence, and interaction. With Infinite-Scale Presence, the boundaries between personal, professional, and AI-driven engagement dissolve, allowing individuals to be everywhere and learn from everyone simultaneously.

__The future belongs to those who embrace this transformation, who train their AI agents, leverage their presence at scale, and continuously learn from every interaction.__

"Lead the change, or be changed by it"

Covered in Chapter Seven

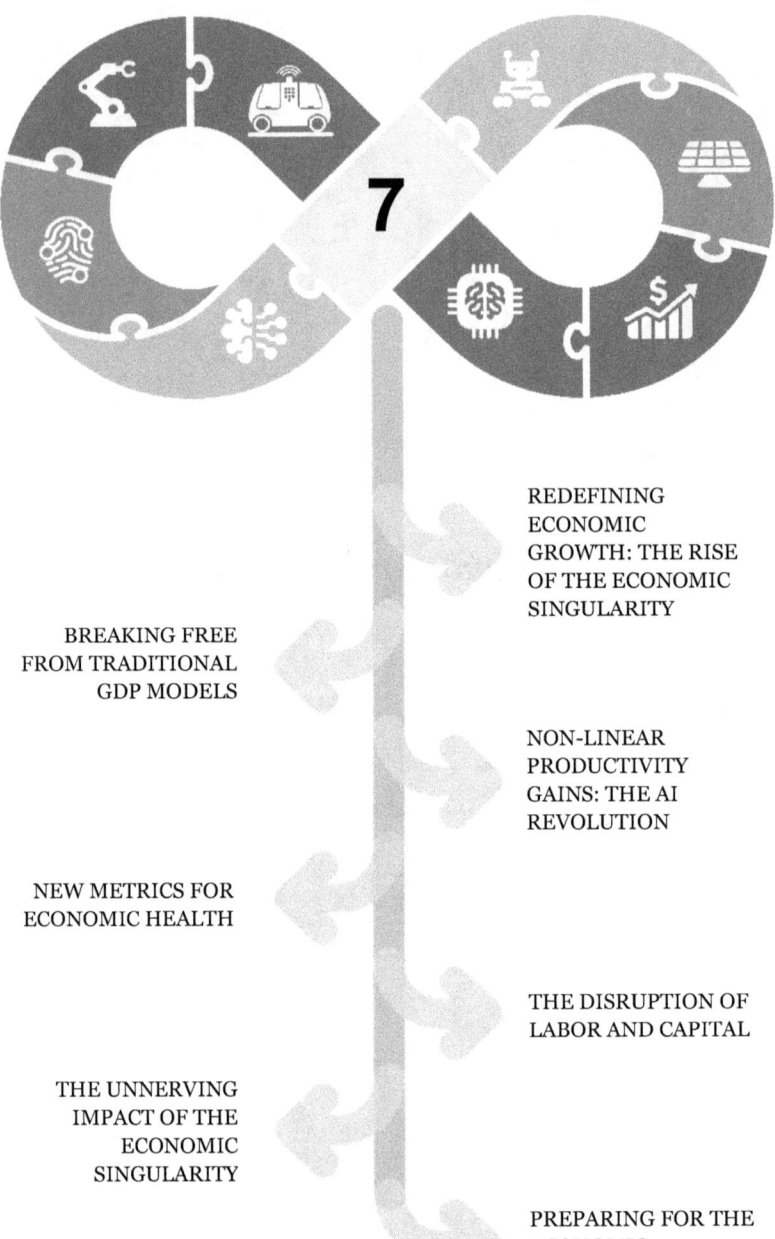

REDEFINING ECONOMIC GROWTH: THE RISE OF THE ECONOMIC SINGULARITY

BREAKING FREE FROM TRADITIONAL GDP MODELS

NON-LINEAR PRODUCTIVITY GAINS: THE AI REVOLUTION

NEW METRICS FOR ECONOMIC HEALTH

THE DISRUPTION OF LABOR AND CAPITAL

THE UNNERVING IMPACT OF THE ECONOMIC SINGULARITY

PREPARING FOR THE ECONOMIC SINGULARITY

Chapter 7:
GDP Growth and Economic Singularity

Artificial Intelligence (AI) is rapidly transforming every facet of the global economy. From automation to AI-driven decision-making, these technologies are reshaping how productivity is measured and growth is achieved. However, as AI continues to scale, traditional economic models, like GDP growth, may no longer apply. In this chapter, we'll explore the idea of an economic singularity, a point at which AI enables exponential growth without human labor and examine how non-linear productivity gains could break free from conventional economic metrics.

Redefining Economic Growth: The Rise of the Economic Singularity

The term singularity is often used in technological contexts to describe a moment when machines surpass human intelligence. In economics, the economic singularity refers to a point where AI-driven technologies break away from traditional GDP growth models, enabling unprecedented economic expansion without the need for significant human labor.

Historically, economic growth has been tied to the quantity and quality of human labor, combined with capital investment. This model presumes that increases in labor and capital inputs result in proportionate increases in economic output. But AI is poised to shatter this assumption by driving exponential growth without requiring an equivalent increase in human labor.

The Decoupling of Labor and Growth: AI automates tasks that previously required human workers, allowing businesses to scale their operations with minimal human input. As more industries embrace automation, the relationship between labor and productivity will weaken, giving rise to an economy where growth is no longer dependent on human effort.

> *This is the essence of economic singularity, a point where technological capabilities, rather than labor, drive economic output.*

AI-powered robots and automated systems are taking over production processes in industries like manufacturing. A factory can now produce far more goods with fewer workers, driving up productivity while reducing labor costs. In sectors like finance, AI-driven trading algorithms are managing portfolios and executing trades with no human intervention yet creating more wealth than human traders ever could.

The Role of Near-Zero Energy in the Economic Singularity: One of the most revolutionary factors in the coming economic singularity will be the decline of energy costs to near zero. As renewable energy sources like solar, wind, and advanced battery storage become cheaper and more efficient, energy will cease to be a limiting factor in economic growth. Combined with AI-driven automation, this will create a perfect storm for exponential expansion.

Historically, energy costs have been a major constraint on productivity. But in a future where energy is abundant and nearly free, AI systems can run indefinitely, optimizing production and distribution without the limits of human labor or energy expenses. This accelerates the economic singularity by providing an endless fuel supply for AI-driven growth.

Imagine AI-powered manufacturing, where factories operate 24/7 with near-zero energy costs. AI-powered robots not only produce goods at unprecedented speeds but are also powered by clean, free energy. This combination creates exponential growth in output and productivity while slashing costs, resulting in a hyper-efficient economy with unlimited potential.

Breaking Free from Traditional GDP Models

Gross Domestic Product (GDP) has long been the standard measure of a country's economic performance. It calculates the total value of goods and services produced, with a heavy emphasis on labor and capital inputs. However, as AI-driven technologies increasingly replace human labor, GDP may no longer be an accurate reflection of economic health.

Why GDP is Becoming Obsolete: In a world where AI handles most production and decision-making tasks, GDP will fail to capture the true scale of economic growth. Traditional GDP models measure productivity based on human labor, but when machines are doing the work, this metric loses its relevance.

As AI-driven automation boosts productivity, the labor force may shrink, yet the economy could continue to grow exponentially.

Imagine a future where automated farms run entirely on AI. Drones manage crop planting, irrigation, and harvesting, while machine learning algorithms optimize yield based on weather patterns and soil data. Such a farm could produce food at scale without a single human worker, leading to economic growth that GDP, tied to labor, would struggle to quantify.

Energy Abundance as a Catalyst for Exponential Growth: In the AI-driven economy, the removal of energy costs will push productivity gains even further. With unlimited, clean energy fueling AI systems, the economy will break free from traditional constraints like labor and capital.

This will drive the kind of non-linear productivity gains that the Economic Singularity Formula predicts, an economy where growth is exponential and fueled by AI and free energy.

Non-Linear Productivity Gains: The AI Revolution

One of the most profound impacts of AI is its ability to create non-linear productivity gains. In traditional economic models, productivity increases linearly, output rises in proportion to increases in labor or capital. However, AI-powered systems can increase output exponentially, without needing additional labor or capital investment.

Exponential Growth in Output: AI doesn't just make processes more efficient; it enables industries to scale rapidly, with minimal additional input. As AI systems become more sophisticated, they can handle more complex tasks, leading to exponential increases in productivity. This is particularly true in fields like software development, automated manufacturing, and finance, where AI-driven algorithms and machines can operate 24/7 without fatigue, delivering growth that far exceeds human capabilities.

> *Now, imagine how AI will transform software programming itself. We are approaching a future where anyone with an idea can simply describe it in natural language, and AI will generate the necessary code to build an application.*

This type of natural language programming means that a person with zero coding experience could effectively create complex software. AI would bridge the gap between creative ideas and technical execution, democratizing software development and making innovation accessible to a broader range of people.

The possibilities are immense. Entrepreneurs could prototype apps without hiring developers, and businesses could create custom tools on-demand. This shift will exponentially increase the pace of technological innovation, as AI will remove the bottleneck of needing specialized programming knowledge to bring software ideas to life. AI-driven code generation could also adapt to user needs in real-time, updating software with no downtime, enabling continuous improvement and scaling at unprecedented speeds. This opens the door to an entirely new realm of growth in the tech industry, one where the barriers to entry are virtually eliminated.

New Metrics for Economic Health

As AI continues to disrupt traditional economic models, new metrics will be needed to gauge economic health in an AI-driven world. GDP, with its reliance on human labor and capital, will no longer be sufficient.

Instead, economies will need to measure prosperity based on factors such as automation efficiency, AI integration, and innovation output.

Measuring Automation Efficiency: One potential metric is automation efficiency, which could measure how well AI systems are being used to optimize production, reduce costs, and maximize output. This would give a more accurate picture of how an economy is leveraging AI to drive growth, rather than relying on outdated measures of human labor.

In countries that lead in AI integration, such as South Korea or Germany, governments could track the percentage of industries that have implemented AI-driven automation, comparing it against overall economic output to gauge the effectiveness of these technologies.

Innovation as a Key Economic Indicator: Another critical metric in the AI-driven economy will be innovation output, the rate at which new technologies, patents, and AI systems are being developed and deployed. In an economy driven by AI, innovation will be the primary driver of growth, far outstripping traditional forms of productivity.

In sectors like biotechnology and energy, the pace of innovation will determine a country's economic success. Nations that excel in developing new AI-driven technologies will lead in economic growth, even if their traditional GDP metrics stagnate.

The Disruption of Labor and Capital

As AI transforms economic activity, it will also disrupt the relationship between labor and capital, the two pillars of traditional economic models.

> *With AI automating more tasks, human labor will no longer be the primary input for growth, while the role of capital investment may also shift as machines take on more productive roles.*

The Decline of Human Labor in Economic Models: As more jobs are automated, traditional labor markets will shrink. AI-driven technologies can maintain or even increase productivity without human workers, challenging the notion that economic health is tied to employment rates.

In industries like logistics, self-driving trucks and automated warehouses will eliminate the need for human drivers and workers, yet increase efficiency and output, showing that growth is no longer dependent on labor.

Capital and Wealth Concentration: As AI reduces the need for labor, wealth will become increasingly concentrated among those who control AI technologies, data infrastructure and essential core infrastructure. This will lead to a new form of capital concentration, where AI-driven firms and tech giants dominate the global economy. The question then becomes: how will wealth be distributed in an economy where AI does most of the work?

Companies like Amazon and Google, which already dominate their respective sectors through AI-driven platforms, will likely increase their control over the economy as AI enables them to scale further, creating massive capital concentration in a few key players.

The Unnerving Impact of the Economic Singularity

While the economic singularity offers the potential for exponential growth, it also poses significant risks. The decoupling of labor from growth could lead to widespread economic inequality, where those who control AI technology benefit disproportionately, while the majority are left behind.

The Risk of Job Displacement and Inequality: As AI-driven automation replaces jobs, millions of workers could be displaced, particularly in industries that rely on routine manual labor. This could lead to significant economic inequality, where those with access to AI and high-tech industries thrive, while others struggle to find employment.

In manufacturing and retail, millions of jobs could disappear as robots and AI systems take over, creating a future where technological unemployment is widespread. Without training programs that will lead to the enablement of Universal Equity and proper policies like universal basic income (UBI) or skills retraining programs, this could exacerbate existing income inequality.

AI Monopolies and Economic Control: As AI technology becomes more powerful, a few key companies or governments may come to control the majority of AI-driven economic activity. This could lead to the rise of AI monopolies, where a small number of actors hold immense economic power, stifling competition and limiting innovation.

Tech giants like Microsoft, Google, and Alibaba are already leading in AI research and development. As they continue to dominate AI-driven industries, smaller companies may struggle to compete, leading to the concentration of economic power in fewer hands.

Ethical Concerns in AI-Driven Economies: With AI systems controlling vast swathes of the economy, ethical concerns will become paramount.

> *AI decision-making may prioritize efficiency over humanity, leading to decisions that prioritize economic growth at the expense of workers' rights, environmental sustainability, or social equity.*

AI-driven resource allocation systems could prioritize profit maximization, leading to decisions that harm workers, communities, or the environment, such as over-exploitation of natural resources or mass layoffs without consideration for societal impact.

The Inability of Traditional Governments to Govern the Economic Singularity: Built on traditional governance models, many governments around the world are slow, bureaucratic, and lack the flexibility required to develop and enforce policies that can manage the rapid shifts that AI-driven economies will bring.

> *As the Economic Singularity accelerates, a major concern is that most governments are fundamentally unprepared to handle the pace of change.*

The crypto industry is a prime example of how governments have struggled to keep pace with technological innovation. It has taken years for regulators to even begin addressing cryptocurrencies and decentralized finance, despite these technologies already reshaping global markets. This lag raises serious concerns about how well-equipped governments will be to handle the even more disruptive forces of the Economic Singularity.

With AI driving exponential economic growth and potentially upending entire industries overnight, traditional governance structures may not be able to develop the necessary frameworks to regulate and manage these changes. The fear is that governments will fall further behind, leaving economies vulnerable to instability, monopolization, and inequality.

One potential solution? AI-driven governance itself. In a world where AI outpaces human capabilities, we may need to turn to AI to help develop regulations and guidelines that can govern the very technologies driving this transformation. This idea opens a host of new questions, how would an AI-governed regulatory system ensure fairness, ethics, and accountability? Can AI balance efficiency with the human values that must remain central in society?

The unnerving realization is that as AI reshapes the economy, it may also be reshaping the way we govern society, forcing us to rely on the very technologies we are trying to regulate to guide us through the most significant transformation of our time.

Preparing for the Economic Singularity

To navigate the coming economic singularity, businesses, governments, and individuals must take proactive steps to ensure that the benefits of AI-driven growth are distributed equitably. This will require a combination of regulatory frameworks, workforce retraining, and social safety nets to ensure that everyone can participate in the AI-driven economy.

Building Ethical AI Frameworks: Governments will need to create ethical guidelines and regulatory frameworks that ensure AI-driven growth benefits society as a whole. This includes addressing issues like data privacy, algorithmic bias, and the risk of monopolization, as well as ensuring that AI systems are transparent and accountable.

The European Union's AI Act, which aims to regulate high-risk AI applications, is a step toward creating an ethical framework for AI. Similar regulations will be needed globally to prevent abuse and ensure that AI is used responsibly.

Investing in Lifelong Learning and Retraining: As AI reshapes the labor market, retraining programs and lifelong learning initiatives will be critical to ensure that workers can transition to new roles in the AI-driven economy. Governments and companies must invest in education that focuses on technical skills, creativity, and emotional intelligence, areas where humans will continue to excel, even in an AI-dominated future.

Singapore's SkillsFuture initiative is a national effort to help workers acquire new skills throughout their careers, focusing on areas like AI, data analytics, and digital marketing. These types of programs will be essential in preparing workers for the jobs of the future.

Conclusion: The New Era of Exponential Growth

The dawn of the Economic Singularity heralds an era of unprecedented growth, where AI and near-zero energy costs converge to create a hyper-efficient economy that breaks away from all traditional models.

Labor and capital will no longer be the primary drivers of economic expansion. Instead, automation, AI, and energy abundance will fuel a world where productivity and innovation explode at an exponential rate.

But with this new era of growth comes profound challenges. Governments, still shackled to outdated governance models, will struggle to keep pace with this rapid transformation. The crypto industry has already shown how slow and bureaucratic these institutions can be when faced with disruptive technologies. As AI rewrites the rules of the global economy, traditional governance models may no longer suffice, forcing us to rethink how we regulate and manage this new world. The unsettling possibility that we may need to turn to AI-driven governance to manage this exponential growth opens an entirely new set of questions about ethics, accountability, and control.

At the same time, economic inequality threatens to deepen as those who control AI and data infrastructures benefit disproportionately. The concentration of wealth in the hands of the AI elite could leave millions behind, creating a polarized society where the benefits of the Economic Singularity are not equitably distributed.

This new era demands visionary leadership, ethical frameworks, and bold policies that can ensure the benefits of AI-driven growth are shared by all. We are on the brink of a transformation that could bring unimaginable prosperity, but it is up to us to shape this future.

In the next chapter, we will explore how debt, population dynamics, and productivity will interact with the AI-driven economy, further reshaping the global landscape.

"Only by questioning everything can we discover the new"

Covered in Chapter Eight

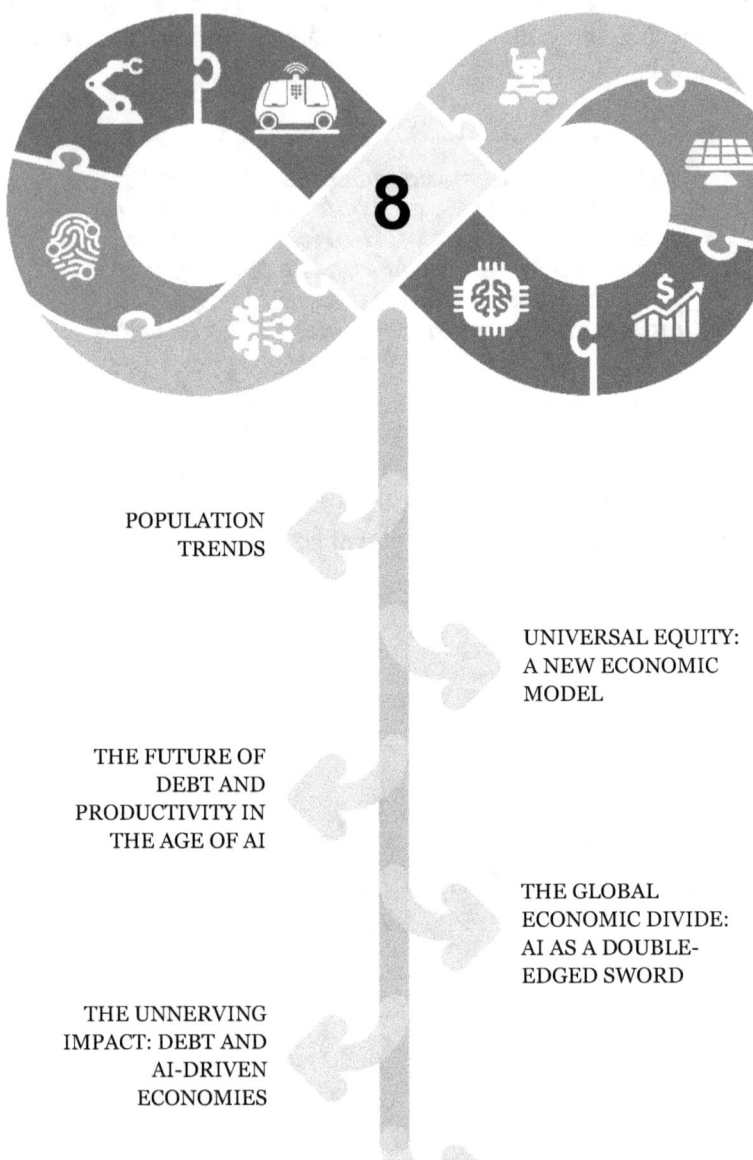

POPULATION TRENDS

UNIVERSAL EQUITY: A NEW ECONOMIC MODEL

THE FUTURE OF DEBT AND PRODUCTIVITY IN THE AGE OF AI

THE GLOBAL ECONOMIC DIVIDE: AI AS A DOUBLE-EDGED SWORD

THE UNNERVING IMPACT: DEBT AND AI-DRIVEN ECONOMIES

PREPARING FOR THE AI-DRIVEN FUTURE

Chapter 8:
The Role of Universal Equity, Productivity and Debt in Future Economies

As artificial intelligence (AI) and automation become deeply embedded in the global economy, the relationship between debt, population dynamics, and productivity will undergo a seismic shift. Traditional economic levers of growth are being redefined, creating new opportunities for nations to rise and positioning others to fall behind. This chapter will explore how these forces will reshape economies, particularly the risks for those slow to adopt AI, and introduce the concept of Universal Equity as a critical component in AI-driven productivity.

Population Trends: Aging Developed Nations and Growing Developing Economies

The world faces two dramatically different population trajectories: aging populations in developed nations and booming youth populations in developing economies. AI will become a critical tool in addressing the unique challenges and opportunities that arise from these trends.

Aging Populations in Developed Nations: In developed countries like Japan, Germany, and South Korea, aging populations and shrinking workforces threaten economic stability. AI and robotics will be the cornerstone of efforts to maintain productivity and growth in the face of declining labor pools. AI will step in where humans can no longer meet the demand, ensuring that economies remain competitive through automated healthcare, eldercare, and manufacturing.

In Japan, robots are already being deployed in elderly care facilities for physical tasks like lifting patients and monitoring health conditions and enhancing emotional well-being. In manufacturing, AI systems are running autonomous production lines, keeping output high despite shrinking workforces. Without these advancements, economies like Japan's would face severe economic contraction.

Youthful Populations in Developing Economies: In stark contrast, countries in Africa and South Asia are experiencing rapid population growth, with youthful demographics creating immense potential. However, for these nations, AI offers a unique chance to leapfrog traditional development pathways and accelerate economic growth. These nations can build future-proof economies by integrating AI into sectors like education, agriculture, and healthcare.

In Nigeria, AI-powered systems are transforming agriculture, improving crop yields, and reducing waste. With an abundance of young workers, these nations can harness AI to create jobs, stimulate innovation, and become global players faster than traditional models of industrialization ever allowed. But failure to adopt AI at speed risks widening the global economic divide, leaving these nations behind.

Universal Equity: A New Economic Model

AI brings about the possibility of Universal Equity, where individuals can not only own and benefit from their physical assets but also from their data and intellectual property, significantly altering wealth distribution.

AI's potential to democratize wealth creation extends to new business models and innovations such as tokenization, autonomous services, and personal AI agents.

Equity in Data and Physical Assets: In the AI-driven future, individuals will increasingly have control over their personal data, marking a significant shift from the current dynamic where large corporations like Facebook, Google, and others collect and monetize user data without direct compensation. Imagine a scenario where you own your data entirely. Companies like Facebook would require your explicit permission to access your behavioral data. In exchange, you could earn a percentage of the revenue generated from the use of your information.

For example, through blockchain-based systems, smart contracts could be established where individuals set the terms of how their data can be used and what percentage of the revenue they receive from its usage.

Instead of passively giving away your data for free services, you would become an active participant in the data economy. This would be a profound shift, empowering individuals economically while creating a more transparent data marketplace.

Autonomous vehicles and homes further exemplify how physical assets can be leveraged in this new paradigm. Cars could be used for ride-sharing or logistics while not in use, turning downtime into revenue. At the same time individual's physical equity can be monetized in the same way, home ownership is being monetized through short term rentals by Airbnb, enabling the owner to maximize their income potential from unused physical assets. AI and blockchain technology will enable individuals to benefit from their assets in unprecedented ways.

This vision of the future redefines ownership and economic participation, shifting power from corporations to individuals as key players in the data and asset economy.

Tokenized Community Equity: Tokenization through blockchain allows entire communities to share in wealth creation. By converting assets into tokens, such as sports teams, fan-based organizations, or local businesses, people can own fractional stakes in their communities and benefit from the financial gains over time. Imagine soccer fans owning tokens in their favorite clubs and reaping financial rewards based on the team's performance and growth.

This approach decentralizes traditional models of ownership and fosters deeper engagement and loyalty, as individuals are not merely consumers but stakeholders.

> *Community-driven economies emerge, where the profits and value from these organizations flow back to the very people who contribute to their success.*

Renting Intellectual Equity and Personal AI Agents: AI opens up the unprecedented possibility of monetizing intellectual equity. In the near future, individuals will be able to capture and digitize their knowledge, skills, and experiences in the form of personal AI agents. These AI agents, equipped with an individual's intellectual expertise, can be rented out to companies, advisory boards, or other entities seeking specific knowledge or decision-making capabilities. This concept allows individuals to monetize their intellectual capital long after their physical involvement has ceased.

An even bolder scenario involves passing down intellectual equity as part of one's legacy.

> *Personal AI agents could continue providing value for decades, generating income for an individual's descendants by leveraging knowledge and experience.*

This represents a future where intellectual property transcends traditional limits of time and space, becoming an inheritance that provides ongoing financial returns.

Expanded Concepts: Genetic, Cultural, and Educational Equity: The idea of Universal Equity can be expanded into areas like healthcare, culture, and education.

- **AI-Enhanced Health and Genetic Equity**: In the future, individuals may own equity in their genetic data. As gene-editing technologies advance, people could contribute their DNA to medical research and be compensated for breakthroughs derived from their genetic information.

- **Cultural Tokenization**: Communities and cultural groups could tokenize their heritage, arts, and traditions, creating ecosystems where people profit from the global appreciation of their cultural assets. Imagine owning a piece of your cultural history and sharing in the financial benefits when global audiences engage with it.

- **Global Education Equity**: In an AI-powered future, education will evolve into a decentralized model where educators, professors, and content contributors can continue to earn from their knowledge long after they've retired.

> *Through AI agents, professors can immortalize their teachings, allowing their intellectual contributions to be accessed and monetized indefinitely.*

If AI and blockchain technology existed during Albert Einstein's time, his theories, such as relativity and quantum mechanics, could be encoded into personalized AI tutors that would autonomously teach and explain these concepts to generations of students around the globe.

Einstein's grandchildren would be receiving ongoing royalties, similar to how musicians earn from their songs, as these AI agents continued to teach and expand on his knowledge. Every time his AI-driven lessons were accessed, viewed, or taught in classrooms or online platforms, his family would be compensated through a tokenized knowledge economy. This would not only preserve his intellectual legacy but would also create an income stream that extends beyond a single lifetime, ensuring that those who contribute to global knowledge are financially rewarded for their contributions indefinitely.

This scenario highlights how AI can transform intellectual contributions into lasting financial assets, benefiting educators and their families for generations and creating a new model of intellectual property.

The Shift from Scarcity to Abundance: Universal Equity represents a fundamental shift in the way we think about wealth. It moves us from an economy based on scarcity, where only a few have access to wealth and resources, to one of abundance, where everyone has the opportunity to participate in the creation and distribution of value.

> *In this new model, debt, population growth, and traditional productivity measures become secondary to the wealth generated by the collective ownership of data, assets, and intellectual property.*

Universal Equity challenges the conventional economic paradigms by offering a future where wealth is not concentrated in the hands of the few but distributed across society, allowing individuals to prosper based on their contributions to the digital and intellectual economy.

The Future of Debt, Productivity, and Real-World Asset Tokenization in the Age of AI

As AI transforms productivity, the traditional reliance on debt-driven growth is set to diminish. AI-driven automation will unlock unprecedented levels of efficiency, reducing the need for government borrowing to finance infrastructure and public services. This presents an opportunity for nations to achieve prosperity without the burden of excessive debt, but only for those that invest in AI.

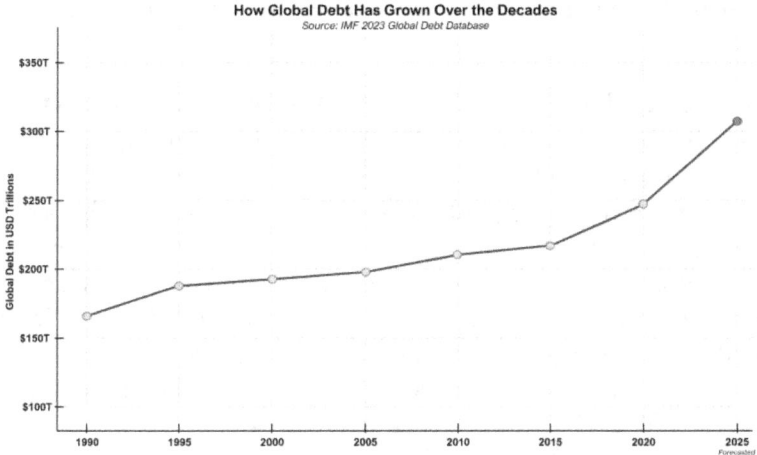

However, an additional game-changer in this equation is **Real World Asset (RWA) Tokenization**. By tokenizing infrastructure projects or public assets on a blockchain, governments and corporations can raise capital in new ways while democratizing ownership. Communities and individuals will gain access to participate in key infrastructure projects, not just as users but as shareholders, reaping a portion of the revenue generated by those assets. This will foster a more inclusive economic model, giving citizens a direct stake in their country's growth and success.

AI-Driven Productivity vs. Debt-Driven Growth: Historically, governments relied on debt-financed investments in infrastructure and public services to drive economic growth. However, AI and RWA tokenization are rewriting the rules. Through automation, AI reduces operational costs and optimizes public services, allowing economies to grow without increasing debt. Meanwhile, RWA allows governments to raise funds without traditional borrowing, giving people direct ownership of critical projects such as smart cities, renewable energy grids, and advanced transportation systems.

South Korea has prioritized AI and robotics in its economic strategy. With AI-enhanced manufacturing and automated healthcare systems, the country maintains high productivity levels, bypassing the need for debt accumulation. Now, with RWA tokenization, South Korea could allow its citizens to own shares of these high-tech projects, further reducing financial burdens on the state.

Reducing the Debt Burden Through Automation and RWA: Governments that embrace both AI and RWA in public services, healthcare, infrastructure, and defense will be able to significantly reduce public spending. By automating high-cost services and tokenizing infrastructure, nations will free up resources, creating a feedback loop of growth without relying on borrowing. The government could tokenize a bridge project, dividing ownership into digital tokens that represent shares in the asset. Individuals or institutional investors can purchase these tokens, effectively owning a portion of the bridge.

Once the bridge is built, a toll is placed on those who use it. The revenue generated from the toll not only goes towards maintaining the bridge but also distributes a portion of the profits to token holders. As the bridge becomes more widely used and its value increases, so does the value of the tokens. This creates a self-sustaining economic model where citizens can invest directly in public infrastructure, earning revenue as the project grows.

This approach democratizes infrastructure investment, giving citizens ownership and a stake in their nation's growth. It also provides the government with a new way to raise capital without increasing debt, while ensuring the public benefits financially from the success of key projects.

Real World Asset (RWA) Tokenization of infrastructure could be the future of financing large-scale public projects, creating more inclusive economic models where all share in ownership and returns.

This example highlights how blockchain technology and tokenization can shift traditional public financing towards a decentralized, inclusive system that benefits both governments and citizens.

Estonia, with its AI-driven governance model, serves as a model. Tokenizing assets like AI-optimized healthcare or digital infrastructure would further enhance its ability to keep public debt low while providing world-class services.

> *By integrating AI and tokenization, the future of economic growth will shift from debt-dependence to a model of decentralized ownership and shared prosperity.*

The Role of ICOs in Raising Capital in the AI Era: As AI transforms industries and drives productivity, companies are exploring alternative methods of raising capital to fuel expansion. One such method gaining traction is the Initial Coin Offering (ICO), which offers a modern alternative to the traditional Initial Public Offering (IPO). ICOs enable companies to raise funds by issuing digital tokens to investors, which can represent ownership, rights to services, or other utilities within a blockchain-based ecosystem.

ICOs provide several advantages over traditional IPOs. They allow companies to bypass the highly regulated and often expensive process of stock exchanges, democratizing access to investment. This means startups and innovative projects, particularly those centered around blockchain, AI, and other emerging technologies, can more easily gain access to capital. For investors, ICOs provide opportunities to invest in new ventures with lower barriers to entry and often offer greater liquidity as tokens can be traded on various cryptocurrency exchanges.

> *By embracing ICOs, companies can raise capital more efficiently, empowering growth in AI-driven sectors.*

Governments, too, can leverage tokenization of public assets, allowing citizens to invest in and benefit from key infrastructure projects, further expanding the reach of tokenization into real-world applications.

The Global Economic Divide: AI as a Double-Edged Sword

As AI accelerates economic growth for nations that invest in it, it will also create a widening gap between AI-rich and AI-poor countries. Nations slow to adopt AI or still have a low digital footprint risk falling behind and facing economic stagnation and marginalization in a rapidly evolving global economy.

> *The digital divide is one of the most pressing challenges in an increasingly connected world.*

It refers to the gap between individuals and communities with access to modern digital technologies and those without. This divide often follows lines of economic status, education, and geography. In many developing nations and rural areas, millions lack reliable internet access or the digital literacy necessary to benefit from technological advancements. Meanwhile, those in affluent areas or developed countries enjoy faster, more reliable internet and access to cutting-edge digital tools.

As we move deeper into the era of artificial intelligence and the digital economy, this divide risks further entrenching inequality. Without access to the internet, disadvantaged communities miss out on educational resources, job opportunities, and critical services like telemedicine, which are becoming more reliant on digital infrastructure. Closing this gap is essential to ensuring that all people, regardless of location or income, can benefit from the economic and social opportunities the digital age promises.

Bridging this divide requires coordinated global efforts, including investments in digital infrastructure, expanding affordable internet access, and developing digital literacy programs to equip individuals with the skills needed for the digital future. This isn't just a technological challenge but a social and economic imperative.

Countries like Chad and Haiti face the risk of economic irrelevance, as their lack of digital infrastructure prevents them from adopting AI at the pace necessary to compete globally. Meanwhile, nations that dominate AI research and deployment will further solidify their geopolitical power and economic control.

The global race for AI supremacy will inevitably create geopolitical tensions. Nations leading in AI will gain significant advantages in trade, technology standards, and even military capabilities, potentially destabilizing international relations.

> *AI dominance will become the new measure of global power, leading to potential conflict between AI-rich and AI-poor countries.*

The Unnerving Impact: Debt and AI-Driven Economies

While AI offers immense economic potential, it also poses significant risks, particularly for nations reliant on human labor or slow to adopt AI technologies. The future will see a deepening divide between winners and losers in the global economy, with potentially destabilizing consequences.

Economic Marginalization of Low-Tech Nations: Countries that cannot afford or develop AI technologies will see their economies stagnate. Nations heavily relying on manual labor, particularly in Sub-Saharan Africa, will struggle to compete as AI-driven economies push production costs down and increase efficiency globally.

Preparing for the AI-Driven Future of Debt, Population, and Productivity

To ensure that AI drives inclusive growth and minimizes risks, governments must adopt forward-thinking policies. Nations must embrace AI infrastructure, reskilling programs, and regulatory frameworks to manage the rapid changes AI will bring to debt, population dynamics, and productivity.

Policy Innovations for AI-Driven Economies: Governments need to foster AI-driven economic growth through investment in education, AI infrastructure, and digital transformation policies. This means building agile, tech-savvy regulatory frameworks that can keep pace with rapid advancements, promoting debt reduction through AI-enhanced productivity while also ensuring that workers displaced by automation are supported with reskilling and upskilling programs.

Several countries are working through the early stages of AI regulation. The European Union is leading the way with its Artificial Intelligence Act, which focuses on safety, innovation, and protecting fundamental rights. In the United States, various agencies are discussing AI frameworks for sectors like healthcare and finance. Meanwhile, countries in the Asia-Pacific region, such as Singapore, are creating balanced regulatory frameworks to foster AI growth while safeguarding user rights. Estonia's digital transformation strategy shows how small nations can leverage AI for governance. By digitizing public services and embracing AI for infrastructure management, Estonia has positioned itself as a leader in AI governance while keeping public debt low. Nations that adopt similar strategies will be better positioned to thrive in an AI-dominated future.

Building an Inclusive AI Economy: To prevent AI from exacerbating economic inequality, governments must implement policies that distribute the benefits of AI equitably. This includes AI taxation models, Universal Basic Income (UBI), and public-private partnerships that ensure inclusive economic growth. It's not just about staying competitive; it's about creating an AI economy where everyone benefits from technological advances.

Finland's UBI experiment offers a potential model for how governments can support citizens in an AI-driven economy. By providing a financial safety net, UBI helps individuals navigate periods of job displacement and retraining, allowing them to transition into new roles created by AI without economic distress.

Conclusion: The Global Future of Debt, Population, and Productivity

AI is fundamentally reshaping the global economic landscape, altering the traditional models of debt, productivity, and population dynamics. For countries that swiftly embrace these changes, AI offers a path toward unparalleled economic growth and productivity, while reducing reliance on debt-driven growth models. Conversely, nations that fail to adapt risk economic marginalization as AI continues to drive the global economy forward at an exponential pace.

> *Real-World Asset Tokenization (RWA) adds a transformative dimension to this future by allowing companies and governments to tokenize key infrastructure and real assets.*

This innovative approach not only raises capital efficiently but also enables communities to own a stake in these essential assets and share in the revenue generated from them. By democratizing ownership, RWA brings a new layer of inclusivity and broadens access to wealth creation through shared infrastructure investment.

Additionally, Initial Coin Offerings (ICOs) are revolutionizing how companies raise capital, offering an alternative to traditional IPOs.

> *By bypassing the conventional stock exchange model, ICOs allow firms to access global capital quickly and efficiently, utilizing blockchain technology to issue tokens that represent ownership or utility.*

This shift democratizes fundraising, opening up new possibilities for startup growth, particularly in sectors like AI, where rapid innovation is crucial for success.

Universal Equity further amplifies these changes by allowing individuals to monetize not only their digital and intellectual assets but also the wealth generated by autonomous systems and tokenization. This model offers opportunities for individuals to earn and accumulate wealth beyond conventional employment, transforming how they rent, share, and profit from their assets.

As AI continues to reshape industries and economies, governments must act decisively to ensure this transformation leads to shared, inclusive growth. Policies must promote innovation, investment in human capital, and mechanisms like Universal Equity, RWA tokenization, and ICOs to enable all citizens to share in the prosperity driven by AI.

The future will be defined by how well nations balance the immense opportunities of AI with the potential risks, particularly regarding global inequality and economic vulnerability. The next decade will see a widening divide between those who lead in AI and those left behind. Governments must innovate boldly to ensure AI creates shared prosperity for all.

"Embrace uncertainty, it's where you'll find growth"

Covered in Chapter Nine

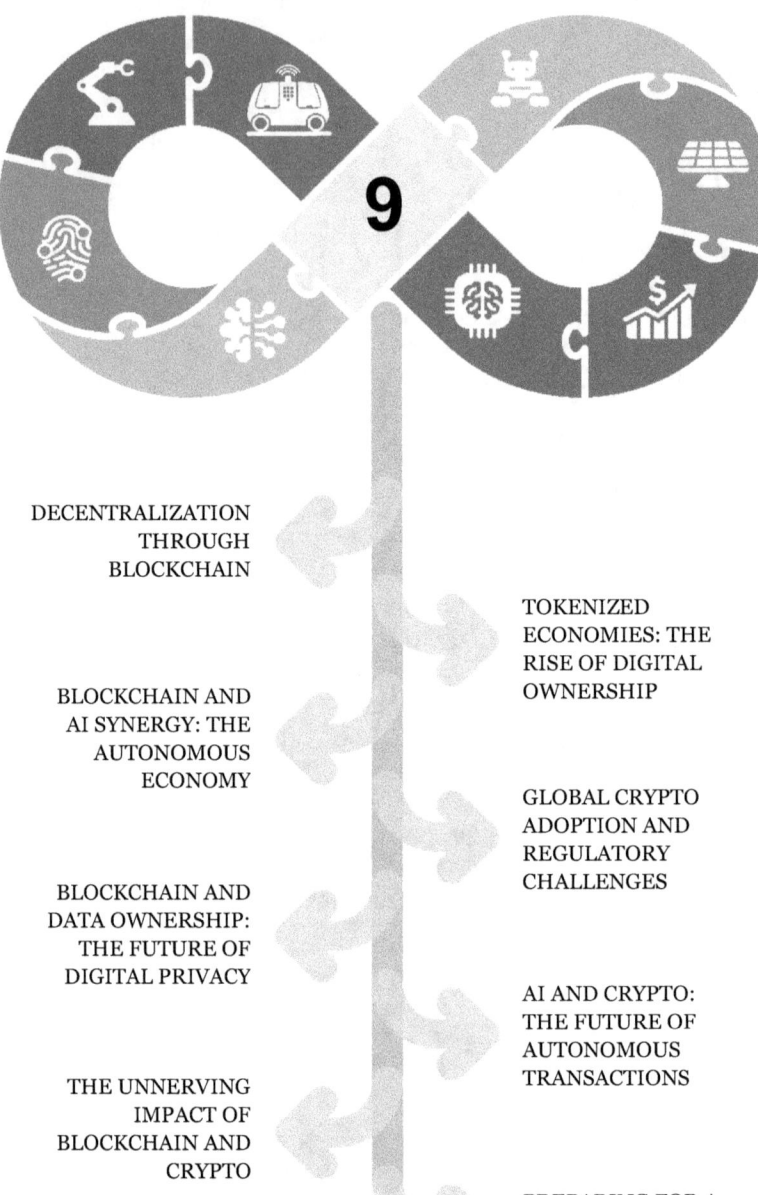

DECENTRALIZATION THROUGH BLOCKCHAIN

TOKENIZED ECONOMIES: THE RISE OF DIGITAL OWNERSHIP

BLOCKCHAIN AND AI SYNERGY: THE AUTONOMOUS ECONOMY

GLOBAL CRYPTO ADOPTION AND REGULATORY CHALLENGES

BLOCKCHAIN AND DATA OWNERSHIP: THE FUTURE OF DIGITAL PRIVACY

AI AND CRYPTO: THE FUTURE OF AUTONOMOUS TRANSACTIONS

THE UNNERVING IMPACT OF BLOCKCHAIN AND CRYPTO

PREPARING FOR A DECENTRALIZED FUTURE

Chapter 9:
The Role of Blockchain and Crypto in the Coming Transformation

Blockchain technology is much more than just the backbone of cryptocurrencies like Bitcoin and Ethereum, it's the cornerstone of a revolutionary shift poised to redefine global economies, governance, and power structures. At its core, blockchain is a decentralized, secure digital ledger that records transactions across a distributed network. This structure allows data, transactions, and ownership to be verified autonomously, bypassing traditional intermediaries like banks, governments, and corporations. Each transaction is transparent, verified by multiple participants, and permanently recorded, making blockchain highly resistant to tampering or fraud.

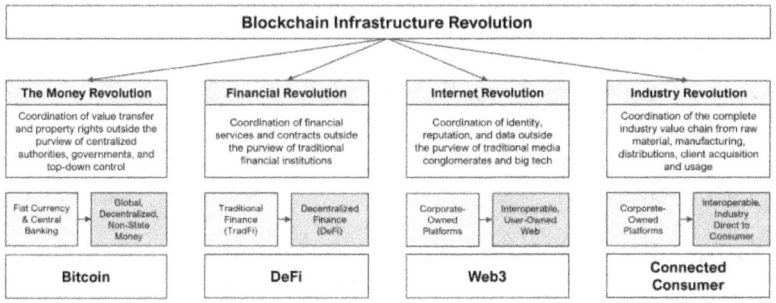

But this is only the beginning. As blockchain technology merges with AI, we will witness innovations that are currently unimaginable. Blockchain's decentralized nature will integrate seamlessly with AI's capabilities, reshaping industries and creating entirely new economic models. These technologies will enable frictionless transactions and smart contracts, eliminating inefficiencies in markets and redefining the concept of trust. This chapter will explore how blockchain will go beyond decentralizing markets, it will enable autonomous, trustless economies, power the global systems of tomorrow, and challenge existing models of governance and finance.

> *With blockchain and AI at the forefront, the global balance of power itself will shift as traditional intermediaries lose relevance and a new, decentralized economic landscape takes shape.*

As the blockchain revolution accelerates, innovative companies are emerging to challenge existing frameworks and unlock new opportunities. These trailblazers are not only reshaping industries but also laying the foundation for a decentralized future. Below are three standout examples of companies leading the charge in the blockchain space:

Ethereum – The most prominent example of a blockchain enabling decentralized applications (dApps) and smart contracts. Ethereum has pioneered tokenized assets and decentralized finance (DeFi), transforming industries ranging from real estate to supply chains.

Aave – A decentralized finance platform offering innovative features like flash loans. Aave demonstrates how blockchain and decentralized finance can replace traditional financial intermediaries.

Chainlink – This platform enables real-world data integration into smart contracts, allowing traditional industries to interact with decentralized blockchain systems, bridging the gap between legacy industries and blockchain innovation.

Decentralization Through Blockchain: Rewriting the Rules of Power and Control

Blockchain is fundamentally about decentralizing power. By removing traditional gatekeepers, like governments, banks, and corporations, it creates peer-to-peer systems that redefine access, ownership, and control. Blockchain will disrupt industries like finance, real estate, and supply chains, where central institutions currently dominate.

Platforms like RealT are already making this possible. Through blockchain, users can buy fractional shares of high-value properties, transforming real estate investment into something as accessible as buying stocks. This shift will democratize access to the most valuable assets on Earth, allowing global participation in what was once an exclusive market.

Tokenized Economies: The Rise of Digital Ownership

The rise of tokenization represents a paradigm shift in how we understand ownership and value. By transforming both physical and digital assets into blockchain-based tokens, individuals and businesses can exchange ownership, trade goods, and transfer value seamlessly, securely, and with unprecedented transparency.

> *This transformation is not just about efficiency; it's about redefining the very nature of property, value, and access in the digital age.*

The Rise of Non-Fungible Tokens (NFTs): Unlocking a New Dimension of Ownership: Non-fungible tokens (NFTs) are more than just digital art or collectibles; they represent unique, irreplaceable assets whose value is derived from their scarcity and authenticity. NFTs have the potential to revolutionize not only art and entertainment but also industries like gaming, intellectual property, and even education.

But the power of NFTs goes far beyond the collectible realm. In the future, anything with value, whether it's a song, a patent, or a film, can be tokenized. Imagine a world where you can own a stake in the next technological breakthrough or invest in intellectual property through tokenized shares of innovation. NFTs will disrupt business models, changing how we think about ownership and investment.

Beeple's digital artwork sold for $69 million, demonstrating the power of NFTs to transform the art world. However, NFTs will go much further, as companies will begin to tokenize patents, intellectual property, and research, allowing global investment in innovation through digital assets.

ICOs and Tokenized Economies: The Rise of Decentralized Digital Ownership: Initial Real World Assets (RWA) and Initial Coin Offerings (ICOs) are poised to significantly reshape capital markets by introducing more inclusive, efficient, and transparent mechanisms for fundraising and investment. Here's how:

Fractional Ownership and Tokenization of Assets: RWA tokenization allows traditional, illiquid assets like real estate, commodities, or fine art to be digitally represented and traded in smaller, fractional units.

This fractional ownership democratizes access to high-value assets that were once only available to large investors or institutions.

By creating tokens on a blockchain, RWAs enable a global pool of investors to participate, increasing liquidity in markets that have traditionally been slow-moving or difficult to access.

This will make traditionally illiquid assets like commercial real estate as easy to trade as stocks, increasing liquidity in the capital markets.

ICOs as an Alternative Fundraising Method: As mentioned before, Initial Coin Offerings (ICOs) bypass traditional venture capital or initial public offerings (IPOs) by allowing startups to raise funds directly from investors via cryptocurrency. This model opens up investment opportunities for a broader range of people who can participate in early-stage funding from anywhere in the world.

Greater Transparency and Security: Blockchain's transparency benefits both RWAs and ICOs. Every transaction is publicly verifiable and immutable, reducing fraud, increasing trust, and providing a clear record of ownership.

Smart contracts can also automate processes such as dividend payments or ownership transfers, reducing the need for intermediaries and lowering costs.

Blockchain transparency will enhance trust in capital markets, potentially reducing the need for costly third-party verification systems like audits.

ICOs and RWAs Role in Decentralization of Finance (DeFi): Both ICOs and RWAs will play a major role in the broader Decentralized Finance (DeFi) movement, which is designed to decentralize traditional financial services like lending, borrowing, and trading.

Tokenized assets will be used as collateral in DeFi applications, creating more opportunities for leveraging assets in decentralized ecosystems.

Capital markets will see a shift from centralized institutions (banks, brokerages) to decentralized platforms, where smart contracts and blockchain handle the majority of financial services.

Blockchain and AI Synergy: The Autonomous Economy

Integrating blockchain and AI will create a new autonomous economy where intelligent systems conduct business without human oversight. However, AI lacks legal identity, a critical element required for accessing traditional financial systems. AI cannot open a bank account, sign contracts, or transact under existing financial regulations relying on identity verification. This limitation means that AI cannot directly participate in the current banking structure or perform regulated financial activities.

But in a blockchain-powered world, AI can circumvent these restrictions.

> *Cryptocurrency becomes the logical solution for AI to transact autonomously.*

Decentralized systems don't require identity verification in the traditional sense; instead, they use smart contracts and blockchain verification to facilitate transactions without intermediaries. In this environment, AI will be able to execute financial operations, manage global supply chains, and perform cross-border trades autonomously, free from the constraints of traditional banks or legal entities.

As blockchain provides security and transparency, AI offers the decision-making power to manage these decentralized networks. Together, they will redefine the global economy, creating a world where systems operate autonomously, efficiently, and without human intervention.

Autonomous Supply Chains: Global Trade Without Human Hands: Blockchain and AI are set to revolutionize global supply chains, turning them into self-regulating systems that require no human management. Every production stage, from raw materials to finished products, will be tracked and verified on the blockchain, while AI will optimize logistics, reduce waste, and predict supply chain needs. This combination of transparency and real-time decision-making will create a supply chain that runs itself, increasing global efficiency at levels humans could never achieve.

Walmart has already begun testing blockchain to track food provenance. Imagine a future where AI tracks every shipment, automatically reorders stock, and predicts supply shortages, all without human intervention. This isn't just efficiency; it's the dawn of self-sustaining global trade.

Trustless Financial Systems: Decentralized Finance Meets AI: The future of Decentralized Finance (DeFi) is deeply intertwined with AI's autonomous capabilities. As AI cannot engage with traditional financial systems due to its lack of identity, cryptocurrency and blockchain present the perfect solutions for autonomous AI-driven economies. In DeFi, AI agents can borrow, lend, and trade assets using smart contracts, all without the need for human intervention or centralized institutions like banks.

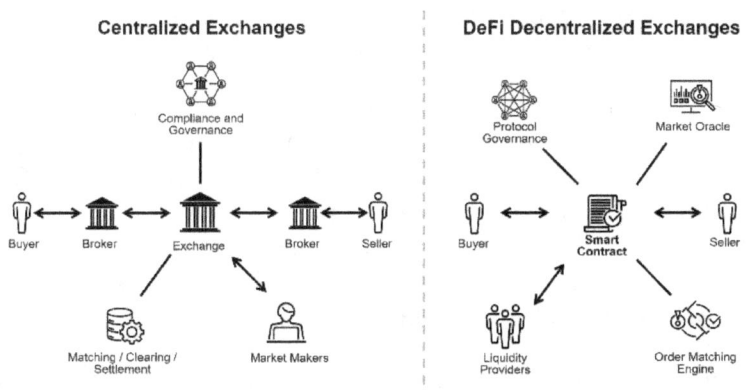

Cryptocurrency enables AI to conduct millions of cross-border microtransactions, which would otherwise be cost-prohibitive using traditional financial systems. AI-powered smart contracts execute trades, trigger payments, and manage financial portfolios based on real-time data. This decentralized, autonomous financial system is trustless, with no need for intermediaries or regulatory approval.

Platforms like Aave showcase this potential, where AI algorithms optimize loan interest rates, manage collateral in real time, and execute decentralized financial transactions autonomously. In the future, these AI agents will run complex financial ecosystems that transcend borders, processing global scale microtransactions without the friction of traditional banking.

Global Crypto Adoption and Regulatory Challenges

As cryptocurrencies gain global traction, they present a unique challenge: governments around the world are struggling to balance innovation with the need for regulation. Crypto's decentralized nature offers financial freedom but also threatens traditional power structures and regulatory frameworks.

The Battle Over Regulation: Navigating the Crypto Frontier: Cryptocurrencies, by design, resist regulation. Governments worldwide are grappling with how to control and tax this rapidly evolving frontier while maintaining financial stability. Some countries see crypto as a threat to national sovereignty, while others see it as a new economic opportunity.

Countries like China and India have attempted to ban cryptocurrencies (with current rumors that China is reconsidering it position) to prevent financial instability and illicit activities. On the other hand, El Salvador has embraced Bitcoin as legal tender, paving the way for national crypto adoption. The future will likely see a global struggle as nations decide whether to embrace or fight the rise of decentralized currencies.

Central Bank Digital Currencies (CBDCs): Governments Fight Back: In response to the rise of cryptocurrencies, governments are pushing forward with Central Bank Digital Currencies (CBDCs), government-backed digital currencies that combine the advantages of crypto with the security of centralized control. These state-issued digital currencies could eventually replace traditional cash, providing efficient, traceable financial transactions. China's Digital Yuan is already being tested in several cities and is on track to become the country's primary currency, while the European Union and the United States are exploring similar projects.

> *One key feature of CBDCs is that they offer each citizen a digital wallet where funds are stored as programmable currency. The potential of programmable money is both a strength and a risk.*

On the positive side, programmable money can be tailored for specific purposes; if the government allocates funds for food, those funds can only be used for that purpose, preventing their misuse for illicit activities. However, this same level of control could lead to troubling scenarios. For instance, the government could dictate that each person can only purchase one loaf of bread per day, regardless of the amount of money in their account. Even if you have a million dollars, programmable controls could restrict your ability to spend it freely, placing citizens under greater government control.

As we move forward into a future shaped by AI and blockchain, the development and potential regulation of CBDCs will force each individual to re-evaluate what kind of lifestyle they want to pursue and what personal freedoms they are willing to trade in exchange for security and efficiency. This emerging landscape challenges not only the financial system but also individual autonomy in ways people are only beginning to understand.

Blockchain and Data Ownership: The Future of Digital Privacy

In the age of digital data, blockchain offers the possibility of returning control to individuals, creating a future where people, not corporations, own their personal information. **As data becomes the most valuable asset, blockchain could lead to a world where individuals are empowered to monetize their own data.**

Decentralized Identity: Reclaiming Control of Personal Data: In the decentralized future, tech giants or corporations will no longer control personal data; it will belong to individuals who can choose how to monetize it. With decentralized identity systems powered by blockchain, people will own and manage their data as a valuable asset.

> *This allows individuals to share in the revenue generated from their data, creating a new economic model where personal information has monetary value that directly benefits its owner.*

Imagine a future where Google, Facebook, and other tech companies no longer profit solely from harvesting user data for advertising but instead pay individuals a percentage of the revenue they generate. This will shift the balance of power, turning users into stakeholders in the digital economy and sharing in the wealth created by the data they generate every day.

As blockchain-based decentralized identity systems evolve, we could see tech companies like Facebook and Google offering users a share of the advertising revenue generated from their personal data. By reclaiming control of their information, individuals can choose to sell or withhold access to their data, marking a complete reversal of the current data-exploitation model. This revenue-sharing model represents the true value of data ownership, empowering individuals to participate directly in the economy of their personal information.

Platforms like Ocean Protocol are already enabling individuals to share and monetize their data in secure exchanges, ensuring they retain full control over who uses their information and how.

The Unnerving Impact of Blockchain and Crypto

While blockchain and cryptocurrencies offer unparalleled opportunities, they also bring significant risks. The decentralized nature of these systems could erode governmental power, challenge regulatory structures, and lead to financial instability, fraud, or even economic exclusion for those lacking access to technology.

While blockchain promises financial inclusion, it could also deepen the divide between those with digital access and those without. In regions lacking digital infrastructure, the disconnected may be left out of the decentralized economy, widening economic inequality.

Preparing for a Decentralized Future

The future of blockchain and crypto is nothing short of a revolution in how we understand ownership, trust, and value. As these technologies spread, they will reshape global markets, creating new opportunities while also posing significant challenges. Governments, corporations, and individuals must navigate this landscape carefully, ensuring these technologies are used to promote inclusion and balance innovation with regulatory safeguards.

Conclusion: Blockchain's Revolutionary Potential

Blockchain and cryptocurrencies are not just decentralizing the global economy, they are dismantling the very foundations of traditional power structures and redefining the meaning of ownership in both the digital and physical worlds. As these technologies gain traction, they will shift control from governments, banks, and corporations to code, algorithms, and decentralized networks, creating a world where autonomous systems drive economic activity.

Yet, this transformation will not come without its challenges. From energy sustainability to global regulatory tensions, the rise of decentralized systems will force nations, businesses, and individuals to rethink their roles in a world where the balance of power is no longer concentrated in central institutions.

> ***Global economies will be reshaped, legal frameworks will be tested, and the ability to adapt to this new era will determine who thrives and who falls behind.***

But this is just the beginning. In the next chapter, we will dive into how these technological revolutions will give birth to new business models, transforming industries and opening up unimaginable opportunities. The future is both exciting and unprecedented, and those who are bold enough to embrace it will help shape the next era of human progress.

"The limits of today will be the possibilities of tomorrow"

Covered in Chapter Ten

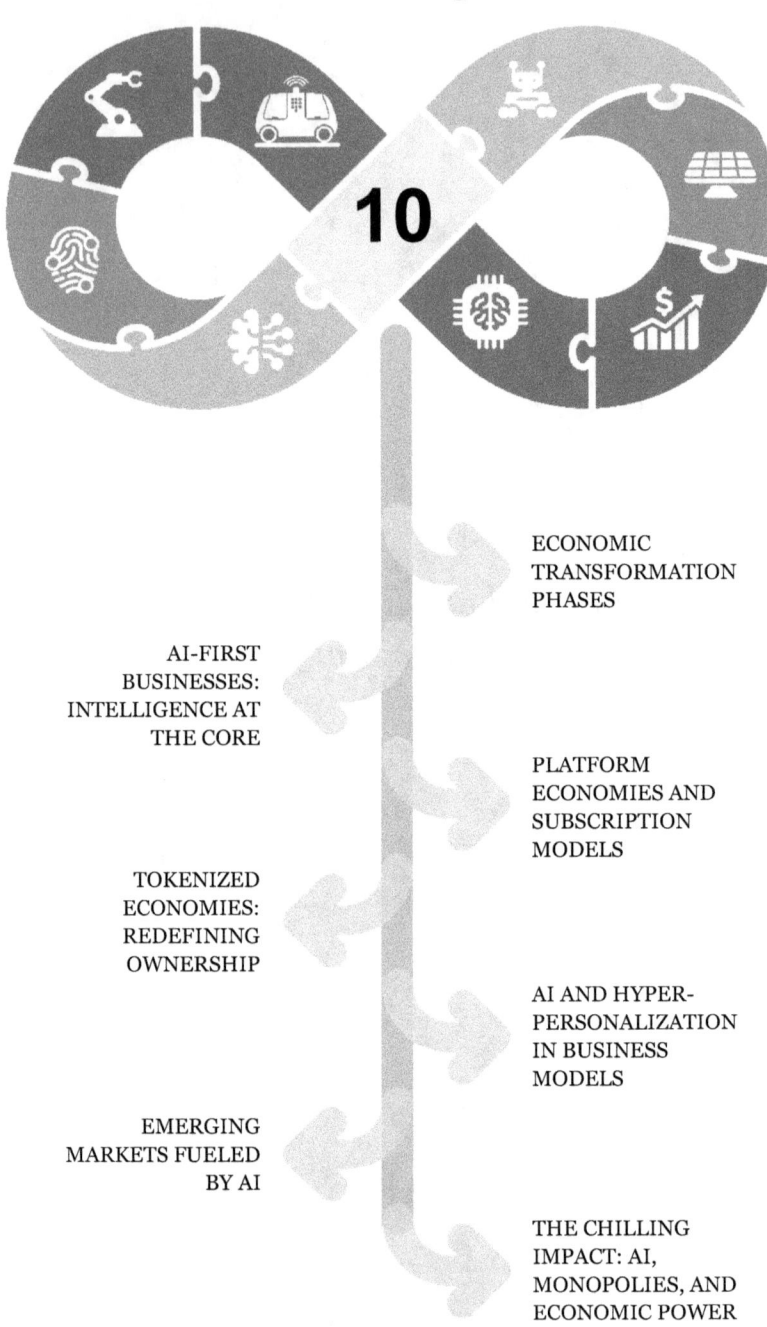

- ECONOMIC TRANSFORMATION PHASES
- AI-FIRST BUSINESSES: INTELLIGENCE AT THE CORE
- PLATFORM ECONOMIES AND SUBSCRIPTION MODELS
- TOKENIZED ECONOMIES: REDEFINING OWNERSHIP
- AI AND HYPER-PERSONALIZATION IN BUSINESS MODELS
- EMERGING MARKETS FUELED BY AI
- THE CHILLING IMPACT: AI, MONOPOLIES, AND ECONOMIC POWER

Chapter 10:
New Business Models

We are standing at the edge of a massive transformation in the business landscape. AI, blockchain, and decentralized technologies are converging to reshape the way we think about value creation and economic structures. Gone are the days when businesses operated strictly within traditional B2B or B2C models. In this rapidly evolving ecosystem, business models must adapt to more fluid, interconnected frameworks like B2B2C, where companies not only engage with each other but also reach consumers directly through AI-driven platforms.

This shift is powered by AI-first businesses, decentralized marketplaces, and the rise of tokenization. In this new economy, companies will leverage hyper-personalization, creating highly tailored experiences and products for individual consumers at scale. Tokenized assets and digital ownership models will further redefine value, moving beyond traditional currency and into decentralized, smart contracts that make transactions and ownership frictionless.

In this chapter, we will explore these emerging models and how they will reshape industries across the board. From platform economies to direct-to-consumer models, we'll dive into how AI and decentralization are dismantling legacy frameworks and creating unprecedented opportunities for growth and innovation.

We'll also cover Tokenization and Real-World Asset Integration, where we'll delve into how physical assets like infrastructure projects and even personal data will be tokenized, allowing people to own a stake in the future.

Economic Transformation Phases

The transformation of economies can be visualized in distinct phases, each representing a shift in how value is created, exchanged, and consumed. Let's explore these phases in detail and see how they build upon each other, leading to the era of hyperconnectivity and, ultimately, the integrated well-being economy.

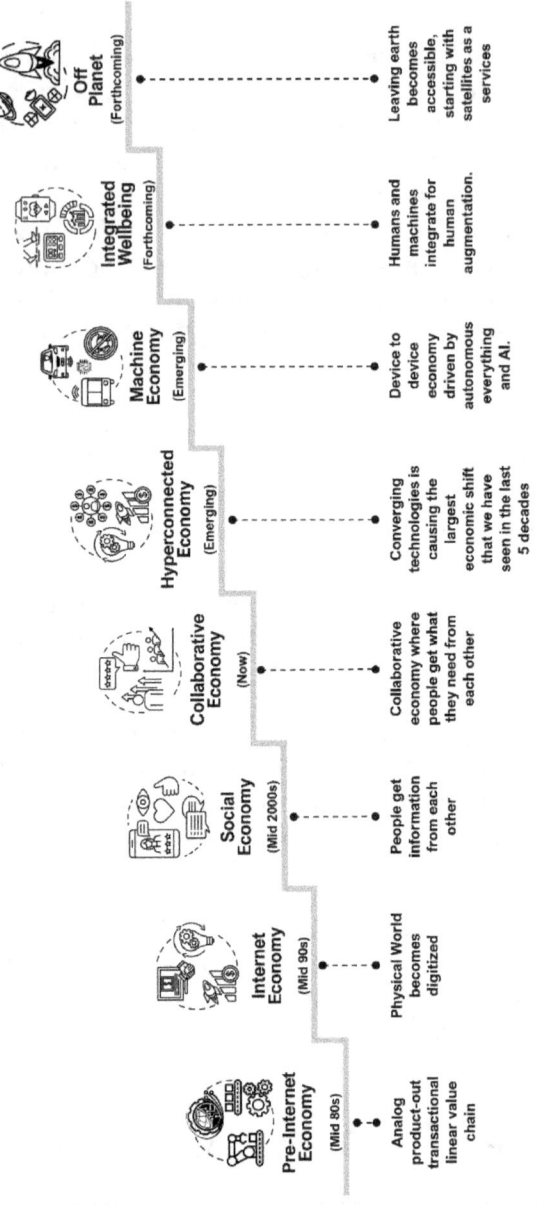

Pre-Internet Economy (Mid-1980s): In this analog era, businesses operated through linear value chains. Production was transactional, with a product-out mentality. Goods were produced and pushed out to consumers through traditional retail, following a clear-cut process with limited room for disruption.

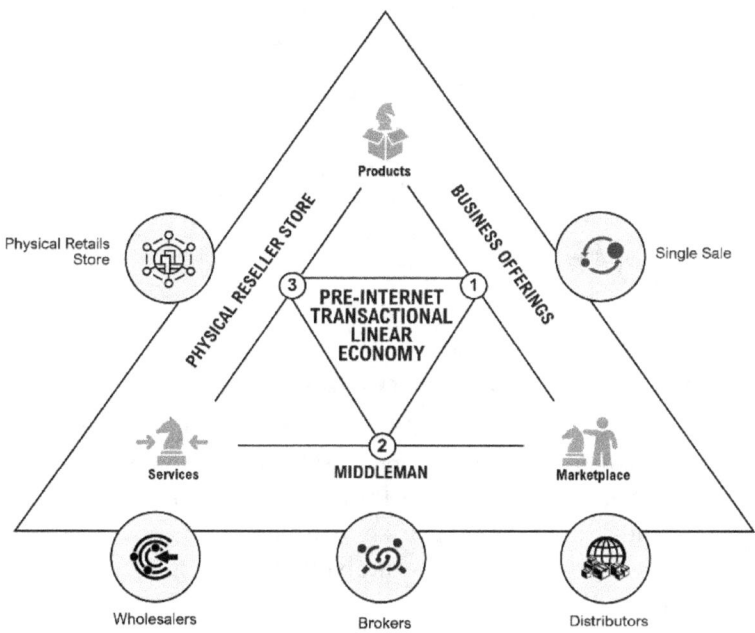

Internet Economy (Mid-1990s): The arrival of the internet transformed this static model. Suddenly, the physical world began to digitize. Businesses could reach global audiences, e-commerce emerged, and companies like Amazon and eBay became leaders. The internet broke down geographical barriers, enabling data, goods, and services to be exchanged in ways that were previously unimaginable.

Social Economy (Mid-2000s): Social media disrupted how we consume and share information. Platforms like Facebook, Twitter, and YouTube shifted the power of content production and distribution to the people. Information flows became decentralized, and people began to rely on each other for insights, reviews, and social proof, transforming not just media but also advertising and commerce.

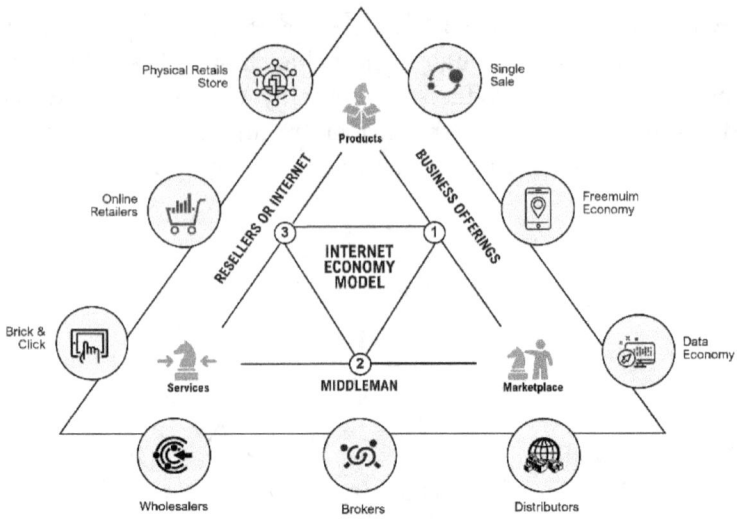

Collaborative Economy (Late 2000s): Building on the social economy, the collaborative economy disrupted traditional services. Instead of relying on established companies, people began to share resources directly through platforms like Uber, Airbnb, and TaskRabbit. The service economy moved toward peer-to-peer models, allowing individuals to monetize personal assets and skills.

Hyperconnected Economy (Now): We are now living in the era of hyperconnectivity. Every device, from smartphones to appliances, is interconnected, creating vast networks of data. AI plays a critical role in managing and optimizing these connections, allowing businesses to create seamless, personalized experiences for consumers. This economy thrives on real-time data, predictive analytics, and machine learning, automating decision-making in ways that make processes faster and more efficient.

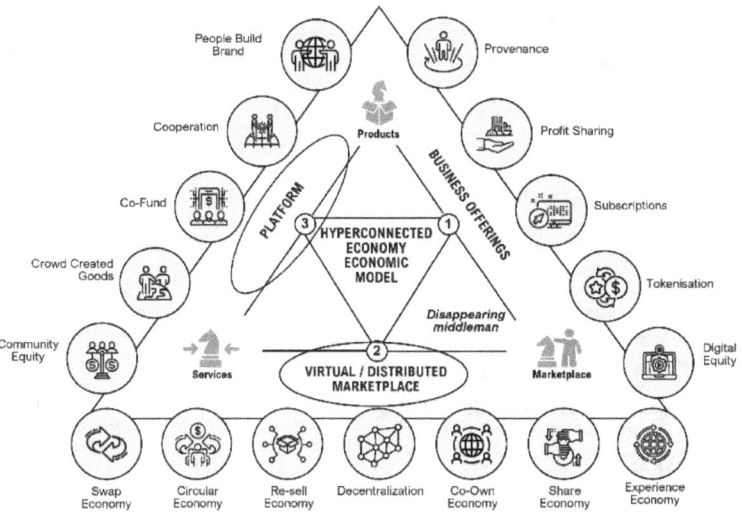

Machine Economy (Emerging): The next phase is the Machine Economy, where AI and autonomous systems will dominate. This "device-to-device" economy will see machines communicating and transacting with each other without human intervention. Autonomous vehicles, AI-driven logistics, and smart cities are just the beginning of this new era, where technological convergence will cause one of the largest economic shifts in decades.

Integrated Wellbeing Economy (Forthcoming): The goal of this transformation is human augmentation, where humans and machines integrate to enhance capabilities. In this phase, AI will assist individuals in optimizing every aspect of life, from health to productivity, forming an economy focused on individual well-being. This shift will redefine how we measure success, prioritizing human enhancement and longevity over traditional metrics.

Off-Planet Economy (Forthcoming): The final frontier involves moving beyond Earth, where space exploration and off-planet settlements become viable. This economy will initially be driven by space services, such as satellites, but will eventually evolve into a full-fledged off-planet economy led by resource exploration and manufacturing leading to humans traveling, inhabiting and thriving in space.

As we journey from the hyperconnected economy to the integrated wellbeing phase by 2030, we're witnessing the groundwork being laid for a radical transformation in how businesses, economies, and societies operate

AI-First Businesses: Intelligence at the Core

The businesses that will dominate this new era will be those that have AI embedded not as a tool but as the very foundation of their strategy, decision-making, and operations.

These AI-first businesses will lead the transformation of entire industries by leveraging machine learning, automation, and predictive analytics to create new value propositions that outpace competitors still clinging to traditional methods.

AI-Driven Decision-Making: Data as the Competitive Advantage: In an AI-first world, data will be the most valuable resource, and businesses that can harness it effectively will outpace their peers. AI-driven decision-making goes beyond automation; it leverages data to predict consumer behaviors, optimize supply chains, and make strategic decisions in real time.

> *AI-first companies will not only react to markets, but they will anticipate and shape them, turning data into a competitive advantage that is impossible for traditional models to replicate.*

Companies like Amazon and Netflix are already demonstrating the power of AI-driven decision-making. Netflix's AI-powered recommendation engine drives 80% of content consumption on its platform, showing how AI can influence consumer behavior and drive new revenue streams based entirely on data insights.

Automation Beyond Efficiency: AI as a Strategic Asset: The rise of AI-first companies goes beyond cutting costs, it's about reimagining what's possible. These businesses use automation to free up human capital for creative, strategic tasks, allowing innovation to flourish. As AI evolves, companies will increasingly use it to unlock new business models, where autonomous systems generate value in previously unimaginable ways.

Tesla, with its autonomous driving technology, is transforming the automotive industry not just by building cars, but by creating a platform for self-driving vehicles that can operate as fleets, generating recurring revenue from ride-sharing services. This is not about enhancing convenience, it's about fundamentally changing transportation.

> *The rise of AI-first businesses could concentrate economic power in a handful of companies that control the most advanced AI systems.*

AI monopolies risk stifling innovation and creating barriers to entry for smaller players, leading to reduced market competition.

Platform Economies and Subscription Models

In this new economy, businesses are shifting to platform models that enable direct engagement with consumers while simultaneously supporting other businesses. These platforms, driven by AI and data, enable seamless collaboration, community-driven innovation, and continuous value creation through subscription models.

Platforms and the Elimination of the Middleman:
The middleman is disappearing. AI-powered platform economies enable businesses to directly engage with consumers, eliminating the inefficiencies and costs associated with traditional intermediaries.

> *B2B2C models are rapidly becoming the standard, where companies serve both business clients and end-users through integrated digital platforms.*

Amazon and Shopify have built ecosystems that allow thousands of businesses to directly engage consumers without the need for wholesalers or middlemen. AI optimizes everything from inventory management to pricing strategies, allowing businesses to scale effortlessly.

Subscription Models: AI-Powered, Continuous Engagement: In this AI-first economy, subscription-based models are replacing traditional one-time sales. AI's ability to offer hyper-personalized experiences and continuous updates means companies can provide ongoing value, creating recurring revenue streams that fuel long-term growth. Businesses no longer sell just products, they sell services, experiences, and loyalty.

Spotify and Microsoft Office 365 demonstrate the power of enhanced subscription models. Microsoft continually delivers new features to its suite of tools, optimizing productivity with every update. This shift ensures continuous customer engagement and steady revenue.

While subscription models provide value, they can also lead to data overexploitation, where consumers are locked into platforms that constantly harvest their data for profit, raising ethical concerns about privacy and consumer manipulation.

Tokenized Economies: Redefining Ownership

As we covered in the previous chapter, the future of ownership lies in tokenization, the process of turning physical and digital assets into blockchain-based tokens that can be traded or owned fractionally. In a tokenized economy, traditional concepts of ownership and value will be revolutionized.

Tokenizing Real-World Assets: Tokenization allows consumers to own pieces of high-value assets, from real estate to intellectual property, transforming illiquid assets into tradable commodities. As AI and blockchain converge, individuals will be able to own fractional shares of everything from art to innovation itself.

Platforms like InvestaX provide a one-stop solution for Real World Asset (RWA) tokenization, allowing users to tokenize assets such as real estate, private equity, and funds. It helps create fractional ownership of high-value assets and democratizes access to traditionally exclusive markets. By doing so, it makes it easier for average investors to participate in markets that were previously out of reach.

AI and the Future of Digital Ownership: AI will fuel tokenization by providing real-time valuation and market insights that help businesses and individuals optimize their digital assets.

From NFTs to tokenized patents, AI will enable a marketplace where intellectual property is shared, traded, and developed collaboratively, unlocking new forms of value creation.

Consider the example of Jack Dorsey, the co-founder of Twitter, who sold his first-ever tweet as an NFT for over $2.9 million. This highlights how tokenization can expand beyond art into digital history, intellectual property, and even unique moments in time. AI will further revolutionize this space by automating the management and monetization of these assets, allowing creators to focus on innovation while the technology handles transactions, licensing, and valuation.

As we move forward, AI-driven tokenization will transform industries like music, fashion, and research. For example, music artists may tokenize albums or songs, giving fans fractional ownership and allowing them to trade these digital assets. This will create new avenues for monetization and collaborative ownership, opening up more inclusive and democratized markets.

AI and Hyper-Personalization in Business Models

Hyper-personalization, driven by AI, is one of the most transformative aspects of new business models. AI allows companies to deliver customized experiences, products, and services that cater to individual preferences, needs, and behaviors, creating deeper customer engagement and loyalty.

Personalization at Scale: Tailoring the Experience: AI's ability to analyze vast amounts of customer data in real time enables businesses to offer highly personalized experiences on a massive scale. This goes beyond basic customization.

AI can anticipate a customer's needs and tailor products, services, and interactions to suit those needs.

Spotify's Discover Weekly playlist uses AI to curate personalized music recommendations for each user based on listening habits. This level of personalization keeps users engaged with the platform, driving retention and long-term loyalty.

Creating Customer-Centric Business Models: AI-powered personalization allows businesses to shift from a product-centric to a customer-centric approach, where the needs and preferences of individual users drive product development, marketing, and customer service. Companies that can anticipate and meet their customers' needs in real-time will have a competitive advantage.

Amazon Go stores use AI and machine learning to eliminate checkout lines, offering a frictionless shopping experience. This AI-powered, hyper-personalized approach is transforming the retail industry by focusing on customer convenience and efficiency.

Hyper-personalization raises concerns about the ethical use of data. As AI systems become more adept at predicting and influencing consumer behavior, businesses could manipulate customer choices, blurring the lines between personalization and exploitation.

Emerging Markets Fueled by AI

These new AI-driven markets include everything from autonomous transportation to AI-generated content and bioengineering.

> *In addition to transforming existing industries, AI is creating entirely new markets and business models that were previously unimaginable.*

Autonomous Systems: Redefining Transportation and Logistics: AI-driven autonomous systems are poised to revolutionize transportation, logistics, and supply chains. Companies that integrate AI into their operations can optimize routes, reduce costs, and create entirely new revenue streams through autonomous vehicles and smart infrastructure.

Tesla is at the forefront of autonomous transportation, with its Full Self-Driving (FSD) fleet powered by AI and machine learning. These self-driving vehicles are poised to revolutionize urban transportation, reducing traffic congestion and carbon emissions while creating entirely new business opportunities in ride-sharing, logistics, and delivery services. By leveraging advanced AI models and real-time data, Tesla's autonomous fleet will not only improve transportation efficiency but also enable new revenue streams through autonomous vehicle networks that operate 24/7 without human drivers. Tesla's AI-driven vehicles exemplify how AI-first businesses will dominate the future of transportation and logistics.

AI-Generated Content and Creativity: AI is breaking down the barriers to creativity, allowing individuals with ideas but no formal artistic or creative skills to bring their visions to life. With the power of AI-driven tools, someone who has never picked up a paintbrush or composed a melody can now create unlimited, unique works of art, music, or even literature.

> *These new creative tools empower people to explore and produce content without the traditional skillsets required in the past, making creativity more accessible to everyone.*

For example, platforms like OpenAI's DALL·E, SUNO, HEDRA, RUNWAY, MIDJOURNEY, etc. enable users to generate images, write articles, and even compose songs by simply describing what they envision. This democratization of creativity gives rise to an entirely new era where imagination, not technical expertise, is the primary limitation. A person with no background in design can generate stunning visual content, while someone without coding experience can create interactive digital experiences.

This shift is revolutionary for content creation and industries like advertising, art, and entertainment. AI doesn't just complement human creativity; it multiplies it, offering limitless possibilities for innovation. While this opens up exciting opportunities, it also raises questions about originality and the role of human creativity in a world where machines can produce art and ideas at scale.

The Unnerving Impact: AI, Monopolies, and Economic Power

As AI-driven companies continue to dominate industries, the risk of monopolies becomes increasingly real. With data control and AI capabilities concentrated in a few tech giants, the barriers to entry for smaller firms will rise, creating an economic landscape where only those with access to AI infrastructure can compete.

AI Monopolies and the Future of Competition: The rise of AI monopolies threatens to stifle innovation and concentrate wealth in the hands of a few dominant companies. These corporations, with their unparalleled access to data and AI, will have an outsized influence on global markets.

Companies like Google and Facebook already dominate key sectors, using their control over vast datasets to stay ahead of competitors. As AI advances, the barrier to competition will only grow, creating unassailable economic power for those with AI dominance.

The Automation Economy: Displacement and Inequality: While AI offers the promise of unprecedented productivity, it also raises concerns about job displacement and economic inequality. As AI automates more industries, entire sectors of the workforce may be rendered obsolete, particularly in low-skill, manual labor jobs.

Retail and logistics industries have already seen significant job displacement as AI-driven systems replace traditional roles. Autonomous warehouses and AI-powered supply chains are just the beginning of this shift. Without proactive policies, the AI-driven economy could widen the gap between the AI-haves and the AI-have-nots, deepening economic divides and exacerbating inequality.

Conclusion: The Dawn of Autonomous Business Models

We are entering an era where AI-first businesses, tokenized economies, and B2B2C models will not only dominate but redefine the economic landscape.

> *Traditional value chains are dissolving, making way for decentralized platforms, community-driven economies, and autonomous systems that operate with minimal human oversight.*

In this new paradigm, AI, combined with blockchain and platform ecosystems, will become the cornerstone of successful business strategies, transforming industries from transportation and finance to healthcare and logistics.

Those businesses that are bold enough to embrace AI-first models and adapt to tokenized ownership structures will unlock unprecedented opportunities, leaving behind competitors still entrenched in outdated frameworks. However, with this transformation comes the responsibility to navigate challenges like data privacy, regulation, and the risk of monopolies. To thrive, companies must not only harness the power of AI-driven automation but also ensure that they balance innovation with ethical considerations.

"Every step forward is a step toward the extraordinary"

Covered in Chapter Eleven

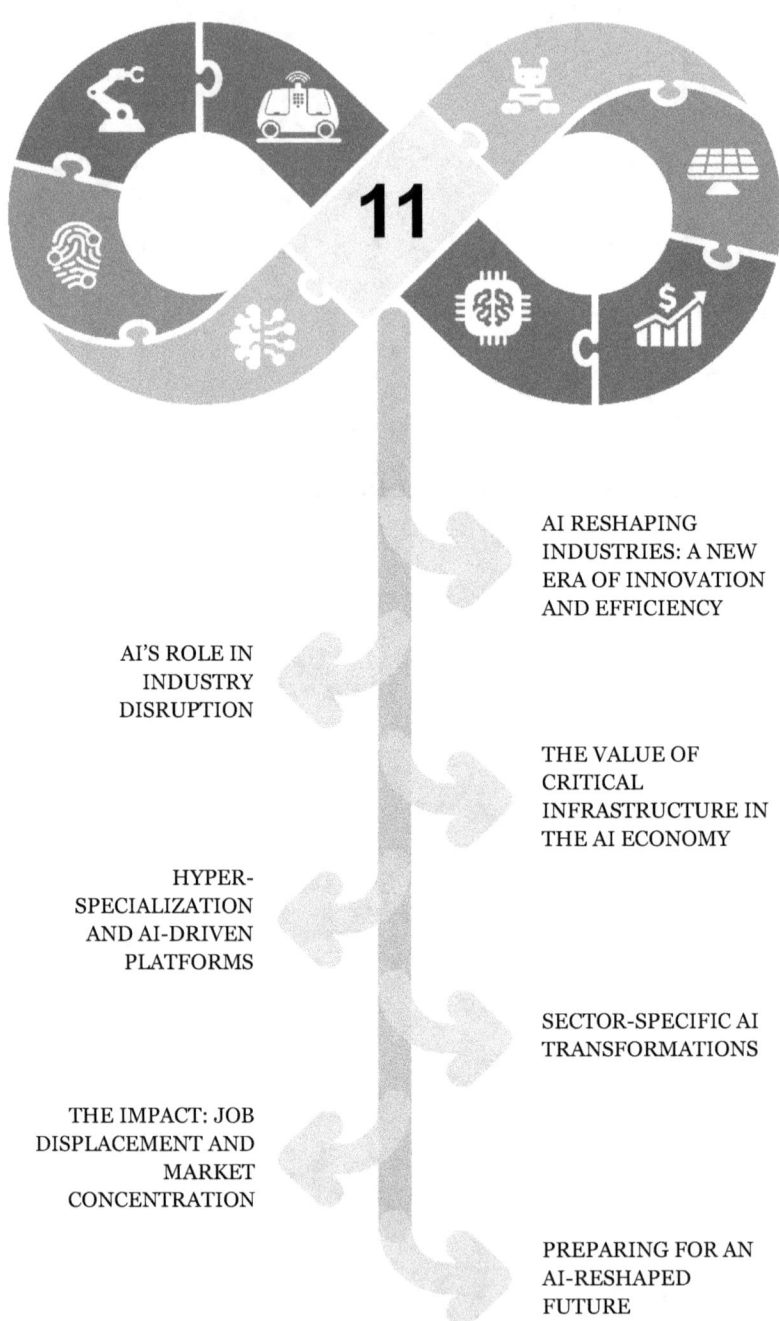

AI'S ROLE IN INDUSTRY DISRUPTION

AI RESHAPING INDUSTRIES: A NEW ERA OF INNOVATION AND EFFICIENCY

THE VALUE OF CRITICAL INFRASTRUCTURE IN THE AI ECONOMY

HYPER-SPECIALIZATION AND AI-DRIVEN PLATFORMS

SECTOR-SPECIFIC AI TRANSFORMATIONS

THE IMPACT: JOB DISPLACEMENT AND MARKET CONCENTRATION

PREPARING FOR AN AI-RESHAPED FUTURE

Chapter 11:
How AI Will Reshape Industries

As I touched on in Chapter 1, we can see from manufacturing to healthcare, AI is creating entirely new business models, forcing hyper-specialization, personalizing services at scale, and opening up new markets. As AI reshapes traditional industries, the rules of competition will change. Companies that fail to embrace AI risk being replaced by AI-native businesses that operate faster, smarter, and more efficiently. At the same time, AI brings unnerving challenges, including job displacement, market monopolization, and the potential for widening inequalities.

AI Reshaping Industries: A New Era of Innovation and Efficiency

AI's capacity to analyze vast datasets, automate processes, and predict outcomes at speeds unimaginable for humans is rewriting the rules of competition across all sectors. AI is driving businesses toward an era of exponential innovation, transforming industries from the ground up.

The 10 industries that will benefit the most from AI implementation.

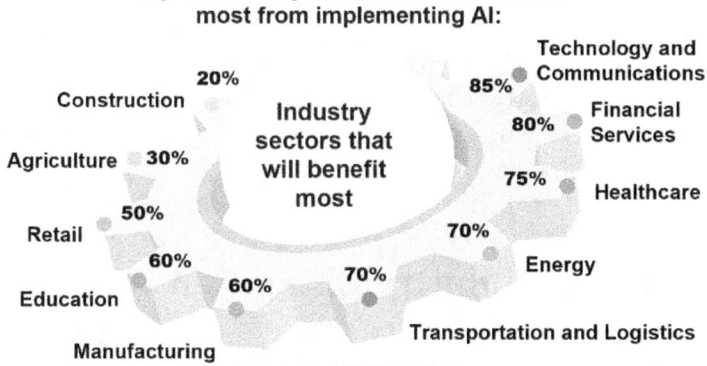

AI-Driven Automation: Redefining Manufacturing and Services: AI-driven automation is revolutionizing both manufacturing and services. In manufacturing, AI goes beyond assembly line tasks; it's now optimizing production systems, improving quality control, and predicting maintenance needs in real-time with precision that minimizes waste and maximizes output.

> *AI enables factories to operate more like living organisms, where every component communicates and optimizes in real-time.*

Tesla's Gigafactories represent the next evolution of AI-driven manufacturing, where AI-powered robots and real-time predictive analytics ensure seamless production of electric vehicles and batteries. The integration of AI models has turned Tesla's operations into an autonomous production powerhouse, capable of adjusting to supply chain shocks and real-time demand shifts without manual intervention.

In the service industry, AI is personalizing customer experiences and automating routine interactions. Virtual assistants, AI-driven customer service, and AI-enabled financial advisors now handle millions of interactions autonomously, transforming how consumers interact with businesses.

Erica, Bank of America's AI-powered virtual assistant, now manages over 6 million customer interactions per month, from offering financial advice to predicting upcoming bills. This kind of AI integration is redefining what customer service means in the financial industry.

AI's Role in Industry Disruption

AI is not just reshaping industries; it's disrupting them, making it clear that businesses that fail to adopt AI-first strategies will struggle to survive. Traditional players will face extinction, replaced by AI-powered companies that can operate with greater agility, faster decision-making, and exponential scalability.

The Retail Revolution: AI-Driven Shopping Experiences: Retail, once dominated by physical stores, is now being overtaken by AI-driven eCommerce platforms that anticipate consumer preferences, automate supply chains, and create highly personalized shopping experiences.

Tesla's AI-driven retail model is shaking up traditional automotive sales, as AI tools optimize everything from supply chain logistics to customer interactions. With AI-powered sales forecasting, Tesla predicts demand shifts and adjusts production, accordingly, eliminating overproduction waste and reducing costs. Meanwhile, AI tools are integrated into the consumer buying process, providing real-time recommendations for financing options, insurance, and additional purchases.

Healthcare Disruption: Precision Medicine and AI Diagnostics: AI is transforming healthcare through precision medicine and AI-driven diagnostics, where personalized treatments are tailored to individual genetic data and real-time health monitoring. AI's predictive power is saving lives by detecting illnesses earlier than any human doctor could.

Google DeepMind's AI algorithms are analyzing retinal scans to predict conditions like diabetic retinopathy and macular degeneration with unmatched accuracy. As AI becomes more integrated into diagnostics, the way healthcare is delivered will be forever transformed.

Owning the Rails: The Value of Critical Infrastructure in the AI Economy

In the AI-driven economy, the corporations that own and operate critical infrastructure will hold a significant advantage over those that simply build and sell off these assets. Traditionally, companies have created infrastructure, such as energy grids, data centers, and transportation networks, only to sell them off to governments or private operators. However, as the world becomes increasingly reliant on AI and digital ecosystems, ownership of this infrastructure will become a critical asset that drives corporate value.

In the future, large corporations could own and tokenize critical infrastructure, using AI to optimize operations and generate exponential, long-term revenue streams. By tokenizing these assets, they can democratize ownership, allowing investors and consumers to purchase fractional shares, creating a decentralized and highly profitable system. The companies that own the rails of the economy, such as energy systems, transportation grids, and data networks, will be essential to the seamless functioning of AI-driven industries.

> *In the AI-driven economy, the corporations that own and operate critical infrastructure will hold a significant advantage over those that simply build and sell off these assets.*

Imagine a corporation like Tesla owning not just its fleet of electric vehicles but also the energy grids that power them and the AI systems that manage ride-sharing, energy consumption, and real-time optimization. By tokenizing ownership of these assets, Tesla could involve consumers and investors in the infrastructure's success, generating revenue while maintaining full operational control of critical societal systems.

As corporations amass control over critical infrastructure, the power dynamic between public governance and private enterprise could shift, leading to a world where private companies hold significant sway over essential services like energy, communication, and transportation. Governments may need to step in to ensure that critical infrastructure remains accessible and not concentrated in the hands of a few dominant players.

Monetizing Infrastructure as a Service: Rather than selling off critical infrastructure, corporations can tokenize assets like highways or energy grids and offer them as a service. This allows businesses to fractionalize ownership, enabling investors and consumers to participate in the revenue generated from those assets. By retaining ownership and monetizing these assets over time, companies create stable, long-term revenue streams that are less reliant on traditional models.

A prime example is Transurban, which owns and operates most of the toll roads in Australia. Through tokenization, Transurban could allow investors to own a share of the profits from toll roads while using AI-driven optimization to reduce costs and maximize efficiency. These tokenized assets would then be provided as services, where users or governments pay for access over time, ensuring sustainable revenue generation. The integration of AI could optimize traffic flow, maintenance, and energy use, further enhancing profitability and the efficiency of these systems.

AI-Driven Asset Management: In an AI-driven world, the value of assets like energy grids, transportation systems, and data centers will increase as AI automates their operation. AI can optimize energy consumption, predict maintenance needs, and manage critical infrastructure with precision that was impossible before. Corporations that own these assets will benefit from reduced operational costs and improved efficiency.

Infrastructure as a Pillar of Corporate Value: As the world becomes more reliant on AI and automation, the infrastructure that supports these systems, like data centers, energy storage facilities, and transportation networks, will become indispensable. Corporations that own and control the "rails" on which the AI economy runs will become critical players. This is especially true in areas like energy and data, where infrastructure ownership will be key to managing the massive volumes of data required for AI to function and the energy needed to power it.

Impact on Corporate Valuation in the AI Economy: In a world where AI trading systems dominate financial markets, corporate valuation will increasingly be tied not just to revenue, but also to the ownership of critical infrastructure. AI agents managing corporate valuation systems or trading houses will recognize the inherent value in controlling the infrastructure that the broader economy depends on.

> *Companies with ownership of energy grids, communication networks, or logistics systems will hold a significant competitive advantage, as these assets will be vital for the seamless operation of AI-driven industries.*

Tokenization introduces another powerful effect, loyalty. Consider a scenario where a person owns shares in a tokenized rideshare service. Naturally, they will prefer to use the service they have tokenized ownership in rather than a competitor's, as their participation in that ecosystem directly benefits them. This loyalty effect drives greater engagement and consistent usage, further enhancing the company's long-term value.

Now, imagine a future where a company like Tesla not only leads the electric vehicle market but also owns the energy infrastructure that powers its charging stations, manages a fleet of AI-driven ridesharing and robotics services, and operates data centers that analyze consumer behavior patterns. In this scenario, Tesla's infrastructure holdings would be as crucial to its valuation as its ability to sell cars, robots, or rideshare services. This combination of infrastructure ownership, AI management, and tokenization will create unprecedented value and influence in the AI economy.

Sustainability and the Role of AI in Infrastructure Management: Owning and operating critical infrastructure also allows companies to use AI for sustainability initiatives, such as energy optimization, smart grid management, or transportation flow efficiency. As AI advances, corporations can market themselves as green innovators, using AI to reduce carbon footprints or create sustainable supply chains that are fully integrated with the critical infrastructure they own.

Tokenized Asset Ownership and Consumer Involvement: By tokenizing ownership, corporations can also involve consumers in infrastructure ownership. Consumers could buy tokens representing ownership shares in renewable energy grids, transportation systems, or data infrastructure, thus participating in the profits generated by these systems. This not only democratizes access to critical infrastructure but also builds brand loyalty and engagement, as consumers become stakeholders in the company's success.

Hyper-Specialization and AI-Driven Platforms

AI-driven platforms are enabling hyper-specialization, where businesses can create niche markets that deliver highly tailored products and services on a global scale. AI allows businesses to scale massively while delivering customized experiences at the individual level.

Platforms Enabling Hyper-Specialized Businesses: AI is enabling businesses to hyper-specialize, offering unique, niche products that cater to highly specific customer needs. These AI-driven platforms, powered by real-time data, allow companies to scale and compete globally without sacrificing personalization.

Sector-Specific AI Transformations

In some industries, the transformation by AI is more profound and happening at a faster rate. Let's explore how AI is radically reshaping the healthcare sector.

AI in Healthcare: A Medical Revolution: AI is transforming healthcare at an unprecedented rate, improving diagnostics, treatment plans, and patient care. AI-driven systems can now analyze medical images with a precision that rivals or surpasses human doctors, helping detect diseases like cancer at earlier stages. Machine learning algorithms sift through vast amounts of patient data to provide personalized treatment plans, improving outcomes for patients while reducing costs.

A notable breakthrough is AI-powered drug discovery, where algorithms analyze chemical structures and biological data to identify promising drug candidates faster than ever before. Companies like Insilico Medicine have used AI to accelerate the development of new therapies, cutting down years of research into a fraction of the time. AI is also playing a crucial role in developing wearable devices that continuously monitor health metrics, enabling real-time interventions and predictive healthcare.

> *As AI reshapes healthcare, it holds the potential to make medical care more efficient, affordable, and universally accessible.*

The Unnerving Impact: Job Displacement and Market Concentration

With every innovation comes a downside. AI's ability to automate jobs and create market monopolies raises concerns about widening inequalities and diminishing competition.

Job Displacement: Millions of jobs in manufacturing, retail, logistics, and other industries are at risk of being automated, as AI-powered robots take over repetitive tasks.

Market Concentration: As AI-driven giants grow, smaller companies will struggle to compete, potentially leading to market monopolies that stifle innovation and raise barriers to entry.

Preparing for an AI-Reshaped Future

As AI continues to drive the transformation of industries, the onus is on businesses, governments, and workers to prepare for the inevitable changes.

> *The rise of AI will create both opportunities and challenges, and success will depend on how well we adapt to this new landscape.*

Business Adaptation and AI-Driven Innovation: Businesses will need to integrate AI into their operations, not just as a tool but as a central component of their strategies. Those that adopt AI-first approaches will find themselves in a position to innovate faster, offer better products and services, and respond more effectively to market changes.

Strategies for Businesses:
- **Investing in AI Talent**: Companies will need to focus on attracting and retaining AI specialists, data scientists, and engineers to build and maintain AI-driven systems.
- **AI-Driven Decision Making**: Businesses will benefit from AI's predictive capabilities in making real-time, data-driven decisions. This will allow them to remain competitive in fast-moving markets.
- **Fostering Innovation through AI**: By incorporating AI into research and development, companies can streamline the innovation process, accelerating the development of new products and services.

Amazon has embedded AI deeply into its operations, from the recommendation engines that power its e-commerce platform to its highly automated fulfillment centers. AI helps Amazon manage vast inventories, optimize delivery routes, and enhance customer experience. For instance, Amazon's AI-powered Alexa voice assistant is now integrated into millions of homes, representing not just a product but a platform for future AI-driven services. This AI-first approach has enabled Amazon to lead in areas like cloud computing, logistics, and e-commerce, positioning the company for long-term success and continuous innovation.

Preparing the Workforce for AI Integration: As AI automates more tasks, workers will need to adapt by shifting towards roles that emphasize creativity, emotional intelligence, and complex problem-solving, areas where humans still hold a significant advantage over machines.

Strategies for Workers:
- **Reskilling and Upskilling**: Workers must engage in continuous learning to stay relevant in an AI-dominated job market. This means gaining skills in areas like data analysis,

machine learning, and AI management, while also focusing on interpersonal skills that AI cannot replicate.

∞ **Collaboration with AI**: Rather than viewing AI as a replacement, workers will need to learn how to collaborate with AI systems to enhance productivity. Jobs will increasingly involve managing and interacting with AI, using its capabilities to augment human decision-making.

∞ **Entrepreneurship and Innovation**: As AI creates new markets and business opportunities, workers will have the chance to become entrepreneurs, leveraging AI-driven platforms to create specialized products and services for niche markets.

In healthcare, AI is not replacing doctors but augmenting their abilities.

Radiologists now use AI to assist in diagnosing medical images, allowing them to focus on more complex and nuanced cases. Similarly, AI in finance is helping analysts make more informed decisions by providing real-time data insights, rather than replacing their expertise.

Focus points for various industries for AI Integration:

The scope of AI and its implications for various industries are broad. Each industry is different and needs to determine its implementation pathway. The best way to do that is to identify the five areas where the industry can achieve the biggest impact and ROI. The other side of their AI implication plan needs to focus on people, and they need to identify the five best areas to focus on to retrain or repurpose their existing workforce.

I selected six industries as examples to illustrate this balance between the focus areas for AI Implementation that will have the best impact and the best focus areas for workforce retraining and repurposing.

Manufacturing

AI implementation

Maintenance Predictions

Predictive maintenance powered by AI minimizes unexpected downtime by forecasting equipment failures before they happen.

Worker Safety

Implementing AI-driven monitoring systems enhances safety protocols by predicting and preventing potential accidents on the manufacturing floor.

Quality Control

AI can analyze products in real-time with high precision, identifying defects faster and more accurately than human inspectors.

Operational Efficiency

AI algorithms can optimize manufacturing processes, reducing waste and energy usage while maximizing output.

Supply Chain Optimization

Utilizing AI for predictive analytics can improve demand forecasting, inventory management, and supplier selection, reducing costs and enhancing efficiency.

Workforce retrain and repurpose

AI & Machine Learning Skills

Training employees in AI and ML basics to understand and work alongside AI systems.

Advanced-Data Analysis

Skills in interpreting AI-generated data for decision-making.

Robotics Interaction

Understanding how to operate and maintain AI-driven robotic systems.

Digital Literacy

Enhancing skills in digital tools and software that integrate with AI systems.

Innovation and Adaptability

Fostering a culture of continuous learning and adaptability to leverage AI for innovation.

Transportation

AI Implementation

Route Optimization

AI can analyze traffic in real-time, improving route planning for efficiency and fuel savings.

Autonomous Vehicles

Investing in autonomous technology can enhance safety and reduce labor costs.

Predictive Maintenance

AI predicts equipment failures, reducing downtime and maintenance costs.

Customer Experience

AI-driven analytics can personalize travel experiences and improve service offerings.

Cargo and Load Management

AI optimizes cargo loading, improving space utilization and reducing costs.

Workforce Retrain and Repurpose

AI & Automation Understanding

The basics of AI and automation technologies include autonomous driving systems and AI-driven logistics planning.

Data Analysis Skills

Employees skilled in data analysis can help interpret this information to make informed decisions and improve operational efficiency.

Cybersecurity & Data Privacy

Understanding cybersecurity principles is essential to protect sensitive data and ensure the safety of autonomous systems.

Customer Service and Management

Training on the use of AI tools for customer engagement, such as chatbots for customer inquiries and AI personalization of services.

Adaptation to New Roles

As AI automates certain tasks, workers should be trained for new or evolving roles that AI technology creates.

Energy and Utilities

AI Implementation

Demand Forecasting

AI can analyze patterns in energy usage to predict future demand more accurately.

Grid Management and Optimization

AI algorithms can manage and optimize the flow of energy through the grid in real-time, enhancing the reliability and efficiency of electricity distribution.

Predictive Maintenance

By analyzing data from sensors on equipment, AI can predict when machinery is likely to fail or require maintenance, extending the lifespan of assets.

Energy Efficiency

AI can identify patterns and inefficiencies in energy use that are not apparent to human operators.

Customer Engagement and Personalization

AI-driven analytics can provide insights into individual customer behavior, enabling personalized energy-saving recommendations and dynamic pricing.

Workforce Retrain and Repurpose

Data Analysis and Management

Employees should be skilled in data analysis to interpret the vast amounts of information generated by AI.

AI and Machine Learning

Understanding the basics of AI and machine learning technologies is crucial for employees to work effectively alongside AI systems.

Cybersecurity and Data Privacy

With an increased reliance on digital technologies, skills in cybersecurity and data privacy are essential to protect sensitive information.

Renewable Energy Technologies

raining in renewable energy sources and technologies supports the transition to sustainable energy production.

Change Management

Skills in change management are critical for facilitating the transition to AI-enhanced operations and helping employees adapt to new roles.

Engineering

AI Implementation

Design and Simulation
AI accelerates the design process and enhances simulation accuracy, saving time and resources.

Predictive Management
Leveraging AI to predict equipment failures improves reliability and reduces downtime.

Supply Chain Optimization
AI optimizes supply chain management, enhancing efficiency and reducing costs.

Project Management
AI improves project planning and monitoring, ensuring projects are completed on time and within budget.

Quality Control
AI-driven quality assurance systems identify defects and ensure product quality, reducing waste and rework.

Workforce Retrain and Repurpose

AI and Machine Learning
Understand the basics of AI and machine learning, including how these technologies can be applied to their projects.

Data Analysis and Interpretation
Engineers need to be proficient in interpreting data outputs from AI systems to make informed engineering decisions.

Software Development and Programming
Engineers with programming skills in languages commonly used in AI manage AI applications more effectively.

Cybersecurity and Data Privacy
Knowledge of cybersecurity is essential to protect intellectual property and sensitive project data.

Interdisciplinary Collaboration
AI integration encourages collaboration across different fields, such as computer science and data science.

Financial Services

AI Implementation

Fraud Detection and Prevention
AI can analyze transaction patterns in real-time to identify and prevent fraudulent activities.

Risk Management
AI's predictive analytics capabilities can assess risk more accurately and dynamically across various financial operations, from credit scoring to investment risks.

Personalized Banking Services
AI can deliver personalized financial advice and product recommendations by analyzing customer data, spending habits, and financial goals.

Operational Efficiency
AI can automate routine tasks such as data entry, compliance checks, and customer inquiries, streamlining operations, and reducing costs.

Algorithmic Trading
By leveraging AI for algorithmic trading, financial institutions can execute trades at optimal prices, analyze market data to make informed trading decisions, and manage investment.

Workforce Retrain and Repurpose

Data Analytics and Interpretation
Employees should develop skills in data analytics to understand and leverage the insights generated by AI systems.

AI Literacy and Management
Understanding the basics of AI, machine learning, and how these technologies can be applied in the financial services context is essential.

Cybersecurity and Data Privacy
As AI integration increases the digital footprint of financial transactions, skills in cybersecurity and data privacy become more critical.

Digital and Technological Skills
Proficiency in digital tools, software, and platforms that interact with AI systems is necessary.

Soft Skills and Customer Engagement
Despite the automation of services, human interaction remains crucial.

Logistics

AI Implementation

Route Optimization
To reduce fuel consumption and improve delivery times by analyzing traffic data and weather conditions.

Inventory Management
AI forecasts demand to optimize stock levels, reducing storage costs and preventing stockouts.

Predictive Maintenance
Predicting vehicle and equipment failures to minimize downtime and maintenance costs.

Customer Service
Enhancing customer satisfaction through AI-powered chatbots and personalized service offerings.

Freight Matching
AI algorithms match shipments with the optimal transportation mode and route, improving efficiency and reducing costs.

Workforce Retrain and Repurpose

Data Analysis and Management
Employees skilled in data analysis and management can make informed decisions.

AI and Automation Technologies:
Operating and interacting with AI-driven systems like autonomous vehicles and robotic warehousing is crucial.

Supply Chain Management
AI tools can be used for demand forecasting, route optimization, and inventory management.

Cybersecurity and Data Privacy
As logistics operations become increasingly digitized, the importance of cybersecurity grows.

Customer Service and Communication
AI may automate many aspects of logistics, but customer service remains a human-centric area.

Conclusion: The AI-Driven Industrial Revolution

We stand at the precipice of a new industrial revolution, one driven not by steam engines or electricity, but by artificial intelligence.

> *AI is not merely a tool for increasing efficiency; it is a transformative force poised to redefine industries, reshape economies, and create entirely new paradigms for work and business.*

The industries of tomorrow will be powered by hyper-personalization, autonomous systems, and platforms that connect global markets in ways unimaginable just a few years ago.

But as this revolution unfolds, the challenges cannot be ignored. Job displacement, market monopolization, and widening inequality are real threats. Without thoughtful action, we risk entering an era where the benefits of AI accrue only to a select few, leaving large segments of society behind. The key to navigating this future lies in a collective, proactive approach.

For businesses, success in this AI-driven future will depend on their ability to adapt rapidly, integrate AI at the core of their strategies, and continually innovate. Governments will play a crucial role in crafting policies that encourage fair competition, protect consumer privacy, and promote inclusivity.

> *Workers, too, must embrace a mindset of lifelong learning, preparing to collaborate with machines in new and unexpected ways.*

As AI redefines industries, it is not just about survival; it's about thriving in an era of exponential change.

> *The winners of tomorrow will not be those who fear AI, but those who harness its power to create new opportunities, new business models, and a future where prosperity is accessible to all.*

Adaptability, innovation, and collaboration will be the pillars that ensure AI drives not just growth, but equitable progress for everyone.

In the next chapter, we will delve deeper into how AI's transformative power and how infinite human knowledge will lead to the disruption of scarcity.

"Lead the change, or be changed by it"

Covered in Chapter Twelve

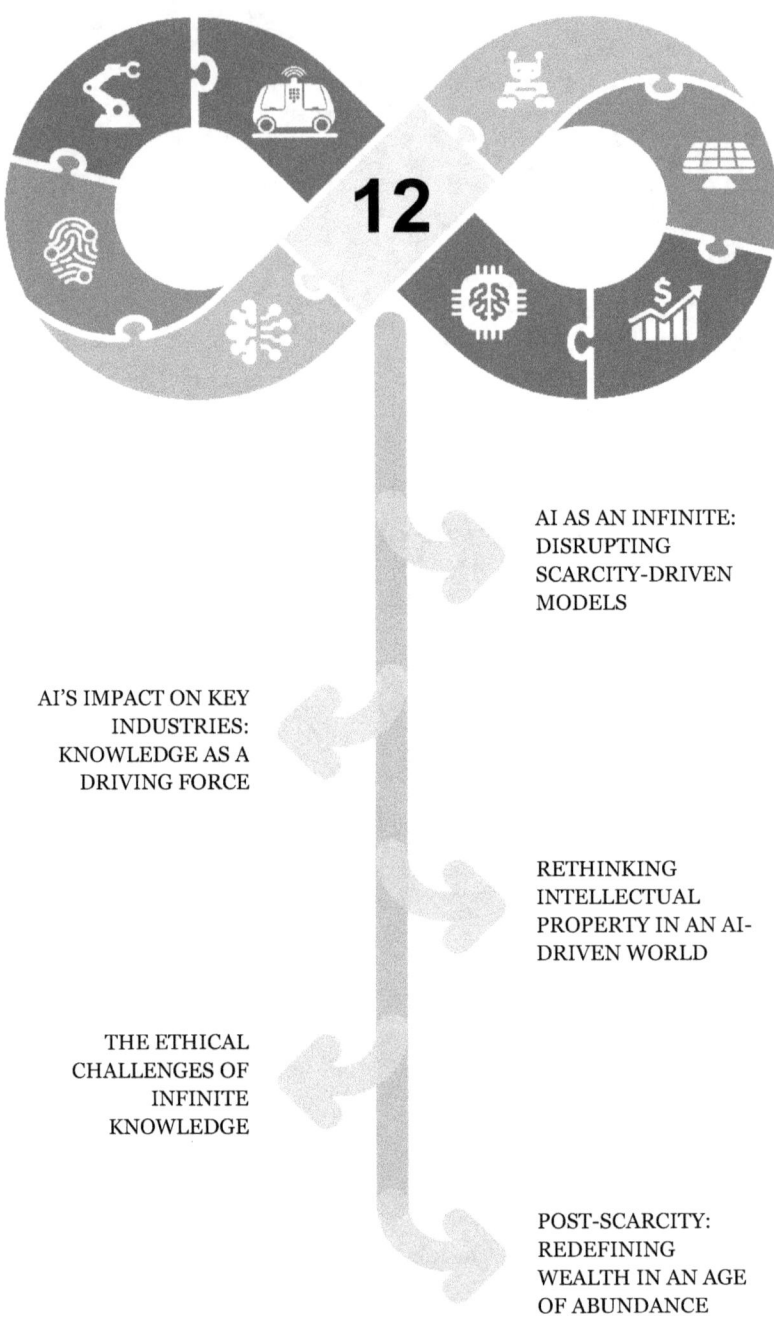

AI AS AN INFINITE: DISRUPTING SCARCITY-DRIVEN MODELS

AI'S IMPACT ON KEY INDUSTRIES: KNOWLEDGE AS A DRIVING FORCE

RETHINKING INTELLECTUAL PROPERTY IN AN AI-DRIVEN WORLD

THE ETHICAL CHALLENGES OF INFINITE KNOWLEDGE

POST-SCARCITY: REDEFINING WEALTH IN AN AGE OF ABUNDANCE

Chapter 12:
Infinite Human Knowledge: The Disruption of Scarcity

Imagine a world where knowledge is limitless, no longer bound by physical or cognitive constraints, where innovation accelerates at a rate that shatters the very concept of scarcity. This is the future AI promises, a future where the drivers of human progress, once restricted by access to resources, labor, and information, are replaced by an infinite source of intelligence and innovation. The idea of scarcity, of finite knowledge, resources, and productivity, becomes obsolete, setting the stage for an unprecedented shift in how industries function and economies grow.

AI is not just a tool; it's a force that will dismantle centuries-old economic models built on the limitations of human labor, time, and expertise. As AI breaks down these barriers, the world will move towards an economy driven not by limited human capacity, but by the infinite potential of machine intelligence.

AI as an Infinite Resource: Disrupting Scarcity-Driven Models

In this new paradigm, AI's ability to process data, generate insights, and innovate will push industries into a post-scarcity world, where knowledge and innovation are no longer bottlenecks for progress.

> *The true power of AI lies in its ability to turn knowledge into an infinite resource.*

AI's Limitless Processing Power: AI's greatest strength is its ability to process unimaginable quantities of data at speeds humans could never achieve. What once took decades of research and experimentation can now be done in days or even hours. This accelerates industries and shatters the notion of incremental progress.

In biotechnology, DeepMind's AlphaFold has revolutionized protein folding research, cracking problems that had stumped scientists for decades. The speed at which AI can analyze complex systems in pharmaceuticals or chemistry is setting the stage for breakthroughs we couldn't even imagine a few years ago.

The Global Democratization of Expertise: Where human knowledge was once concentrated in a few experts, AI is democratizing access to specialized knowledge. Whether it's diagnosing diseases, drafting legal contracts, or designing infrastructure, AI allows anyone with access to these tools to tap into the capabilities that previously required years of education and training.

Babylon Health uses AI to provide expert-level healthcare diagnoses to people in remote areas or underserved regions. This not only levels the playing field but dismantles the gatekeeping of expertise, allowing people across the globe to access critical knowledge.

AI as the Great Equalizer. A small start-up in a developing nation could soon wield the same expertise as a Fortune 500 company, using AI-driven tools to innovate and compete on a global scale.

AI will enable the most resource-strapped players to disrupt global industries, putting traditional power structures at risk of being overtaken by those who can harness infinite intelligence.

AI's Impact on Key Industries: Knowledge as a Driving Force

AI's disruptive potential extends far beyond making data accessible, it redefines how industries like healthcare, education, and research innovate and deliver value, transitioning from scarcity-driven to abundance-driven models.

Healthcare Reimagined: From Diagnostics to Personalized Medicine: AI's potential in healthcare lies not just in diagnosing disease but in creating a personalized healthcare system.

With AI, treatments are customized to individual genetic makeups, transforming healthcare from a reactive model to a predictive one.

IBM Watson Health's oncology platform scans millions of pages of medical research, identifying treatment options faster than any human doctor could. The result is a healthcare system where medical expertise is infinitely scalable and accessible, saving lives and slashing costs.

The Future of Education: Learning Without Limits: AI makes education more accessible and personal than ever before.

With AI-powered platforms, students can receive tailored learning experiences that adapt to their pace, style, and needs.

AI-driven platforms like Coursera use algorithms to customize lessons for students based on their progress and learning preferences, breaking down global barriers to quality education.

> *The future of education is one where students aren't bound by geography, teacher availability, or even cost.*

Subscription-Based Lifelong Certification: Universities may transition into a model where they offer ongoing certification programs. Instead of being a one-time degree-granting institution, they will become lifelong learning partners. Students pay a subscription fee for continuous education and certification in various fields. This would cater to the need for constant skill upgrades in an ever-evolving job market. With AI personalizing these certifications, universities could offer highly tailored learning experiences.

Income-Sharing Models: Another model could involve income-sharing agreements. Here, the university certifies students in specialized fields and shares in their income over time. This approach aligns students' success with the university's long-term growth. It transforms education into a shared investment, where institutions have a direct stake in the career success of their graduates.

Changes in Professor Compensation: Professors' roles will shift in this evolving landscape. With AI assisting in content delivery, professors could focus on high-value activities like mentoring, research, and creating proprietary content. Their compensation could be tied to performance metrics such as student outcomes, course subscriptions, or even partnerships with industry for research-driven certifications.

By moving beyond traditional revenue streams, universities can adapt to the rise of free knowledge while maintaining relevance through unique certification offerings, lifelong learning, and value-driven partnerships.

Accelerating Research and Innovation: AI as a Catalyst for Breakthroughs:

AI will accelerate scientific research at a speed previously unimaginable. Modeling complex systems, testing hypotheses in virtual environments, and analyzing vast data sets will allow researchers to solve problems that previously required generations of work.

AI-driven climate change simulations provide accurate predictions and actionable insights, allowing governments and businesses to implement more effective policies.

> *In a future driven by infinite knowledge, scientists and innovators could simulate and solve global challenges in real-time. Whether it's breakthroughs in sustainable energy or quantum computing, AI will push innovation far beyond the limits of human capacity.*

Rethinking Intellectual Property in an AI-Driven World

AI challenges the very foundation of intellectual property (IP). As machines generate ideas, create art, and develop products, we must rethink how value is assigned, protected, and distributed in an economy where AI is the creator.

AI-Created Knowledge: Who Owns Innovation? As AI generates new knowledge, intellectual property laws will need to evolve. In a world where AI creates independently of human input, who owns the rights to these innovations?

OpenAI's DALL·E creates artwork autonomously, raising questions about who, if anyone, holds the rights to the AI-generated content. As AI takes on more creative roles, traditional notions of IP ownership will need to be rewritten.

Legal and Economic Implications: The rise of AI as a creator of knowledge will force legal systems to adapt. Governments and industries will need to establish new frameworks for protecting intellectual property while promoting innovation. The economic implications are profound as industries built on human creativity rethink how value is created.

Entire industries, such as entertainment, publishing, and design, could face a massive shift in how value is created and captured. AI-generated content may lower the cost of production, disrupting traditional models of intellectual property and revenue generation.

The Ethical Challenges of Infinite Knowledge

While AI promises to disrupt scarcity, it also raises ethical concerns. Infinite access to knowledge could result in privacy violations, the misuse of sensitive information, and the development of harmful technologies.

Privacy and Security Concerns: As AI processes vast amounts of personal data to generate insights, it risks violating individual privacy. AI's ability to predict behavior, medical conditions, or preferences could lead to misuse by governments, corporations, or malicious actors.

AI-driven facial recognition systems can identify individuals in public spaces with near-perfect accuracy. This raises concerns about surveillance and the loss of personal privacy.

The Potential for Misuse: While AI offers tremendous potential to improve our lives, its integration into every aspect of society also introduces serious risks.

> *The immense power of infinite knowledge can be a double-edged sword. AI's capabilities, which can be used to innovate and solve global challenges, can just as easily be exploited for malicious purposes.*

Bioweapons, for example, could be engineered through AI-assisted gene editing, posing unprecedented security risks.

Additionally, AI-driven cyberattacks could target critical infrastructure such as logistics systems or supply chains, potentially disrupting global trade and causing widespread economic turmoil. The fact that AI systems can learn and know more about an individual than the person themselves opens the door for privacy violations, behavioral manipulation, and even the destabilization of economies if exploited by bad actors.

To prevent such dangers, the power to innovate must be accompanied by robust ethical safeguards, policies, and cybersecurity defenses to ensure AI's positive impact while minimizing risks.

Post-Scarcity Economies: Redefining Wealth in an Age of Abundance

In a post-scarcity world, human value will no longer be tied to labor or physical resources. As AI reduces the cost of producing goods and services to near zero, economies will need to redefine what constitutes wealth and productivity.

The Shift Away from Scarcity-Based Economics: As AI reshapes industries by producing goods and services at near-zero cost, our metrics for success and wealth will have to change. AI allows industries to move beyond traditional constraints, enabling societies to focus on innovation and well-being over material accumulation.

AI-driven food production techniques like vertical farming can produce massive amounts of food with minimal land and water, solving food scarcity issues at a fraction of traditional costs.

The New Metrics of Wealth and Productivity: Traditional metrics like GDP or labor productivity may become irrelevant in a post-scarcity economy. Success might be measured by innovation, societal well-being, and efficient allocation of infinite resources. Economic systems will need to be rethought.

Conclusion: Embracing the Era of Infinite Human Knowledge: The Disruption of Scarcity

As AI transcends the boundaries of human cognition and traditional resource constraints, we stand at the threshold of a seismic transformation.

> *The disruption of scarcity, once a defining feature of human history, signals the dawn of a new era where knowledge, innovation, and creativity become limitless.*

This unprecedented shift will change every fabric of our society, from the economy to education, from healthcare to governance, and from how we work to how we live.

AI's ability to create infinite knowledge means that scarcity-driven models, whether based on labor, expertise, or physical resources, will crumble. No longer bound by the limitations of human capacity, AI will enable exponential innovation, turning the concept of scarcity into a relic of the past. In a world where information is abundant, industries will be redefined, and access to knowledge will be democratized, enabling anyone, anywhere, to leverage AI's power to innovate and compete.

This transformation is not without its risks. Infinite knowledge carries ethical challenges and concerns over privacy, security, and the monopolization of data. As AI learns more about us than we know about ourselves, the potential for misuse is real. But at its core, AI offers a world where the constraints of time, geography, and expertise are obliterated, creating a society in which innovation accelerates beyond anything we've ever imagined.

> *The disruption of scarcity will redefine wealth itself.*

As AI renders many goods and services cheap or free, the traditional measures of productivity and success will give way to new metrics of prosperity centered on creativity, well-being, and the efficient allocation of resources. Societies must adapt quickly, preparing for a world where human value is no longer tied to labor but to the creation, management, and distribution of infinite intelligence.

> *The end of scarcity will mark the beginning of a new chapter for humanity. For the first time in history, knowledge is no longer confined to the elite, innovation is not constrained by resources, and the opportunities for growth and prosperity are truly limitless.*

But this future depends on how we choose to navigate these changes, harnessing the power of AI to not only advance society but also ensure that its benefits are shared equitably.

The disruption of scarcity is not the end of history but the beginning of a new era where AI opens doors to possibilities we have only just begun to imagine.

"Embrace the unknown, and watch the impossible unfold"

Covered in Chapter Thirteen

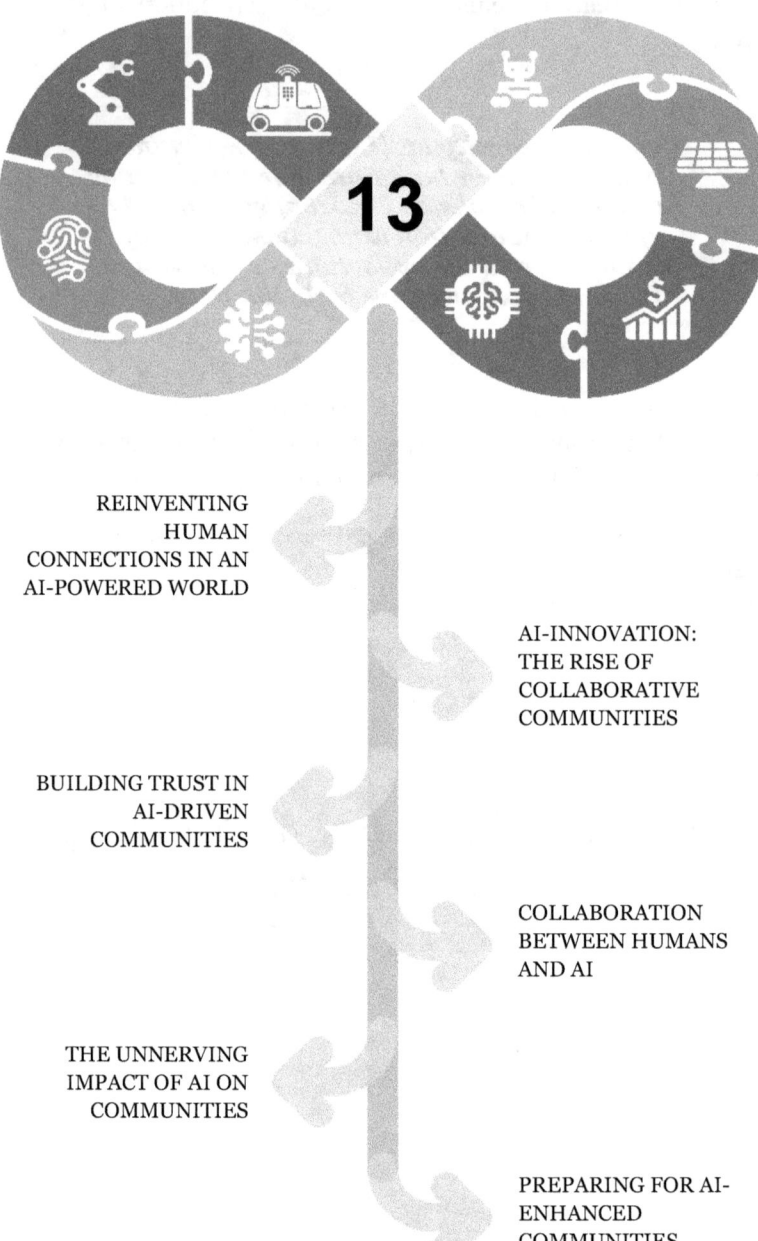

REINVENTING HUMAN CONNECTIONS IN AN AI-POWERED WORLD

AI-INNOVATION: THE RISE OF COLLABORATIVE COMMUNITIES

BUILDING TRUST IN AI-DRIVEN COMMUNITIES

COLLABORATION BETWEEN HUMANS AND AI

THE UNNERVING IMPACT OF AI ON COMMUNITIES

PREPARING FOR AI-ENHANCED COMMUNITIES

Chapter 13:
The Value of Community in the Age of AI and Digital Transformation

As we rush toward an AI-driven future, it's crucial not to overlook one fundamental aspect of human existence: community. While AI and digital technologies will revolutionize industries, economies, and everyday life, the irreplaceable role of human connection remains critical. Communities, whether physical or digital, are the backbone of society, fostering collaboration, shared purpose, and personal support.

In this era of exponential technological advancement, the challenge is how to harness AI to enhance and not erode these deep-rooted connections. Can we leverage technology to foster stronger, more meaningful bonds, or will we see a rise in isolation, where automated systems displace real human interaction? In this chapter, we'll explore how AI can enhance the role of community while maintaining the fabric of human connection as society undergoes profound transformation.

Reinventing Human Connections in an AI-Powered World

Despite AI's deep impact on our world, human relationships will remain the bedrock of society. The challenge is ensuring that, as we integrate AI more deeply into our lives, we continue to nurture the essential human connections that AI cannot replace.

AI, Empathy, and Connection: Beyond Imitation: AI is becoming more adept at understanding human emotions through affective computing, the ability to recognize, interpret, and respond to emotional cues. Yet, while AI can mimic empathy, the deeper question remains: can it ever replicate the authenticity of human connection?

AI-powered mental health tools, like Woebot or Wysa, provide real-time emotional support. However, despite their convenience, they can only simulate human empathy, potentially leading to emotional detachment if relied upon too heavily.

As society begins to rely on AI for emotional interaction, the depth of real human relationships may erode. What happens when a generation raised on AI companionship loses the ability to form authentic, empathetic relationships with others?

AI-Mediated Communities: From Global to Local Impact: AI-powered digital platforms are rapidly becoming the primary places where people gather, collaborate, and form new communities. By connecting people globally, AI creates vast networks for shared interest and knowledge. However, this digital curation also brings the risk of creating echo chambers, closed loops of similar opinions that stifle diversity of thought.

Social media platforms like Reddit and Facebook use AI to curate content, creating communities of like-minded individuals but also reinforcing existing viewpoints. These AI algorithms can isolate users from diverse perspectives, inadvertently contributing to polarization.

> *Communities mediated by AI will need to find ways to avoid the creation of echo chambers.*

Platforms should focus on fostering debate and exposing users to differing viewpoints to create more dynamic, inclusive digital spaces.

AI-Enhanced Innovation: The Rise of Collaborative Communities

AI can enhance the role of communities as hubs of innovation by automating routine tasks and leaving humans free to focus on creativity, problem-solving, and higher-order decision-making.

Digital Communities as Innovation Hubs*:* In a world where AI automates processes and accelerates data analysis, digital communities can emerge as centers of open-source collaboration. These platforms foster innovation by bringing together minds from across the globe, working in real-time to solve global challenges.

GitHub, with its AI-powered assistant Copilot, enables developers worldwide to collaborate and build better software. The AI suggests code and automates programming tasks, freeing humans to focus on creativity and complex problem-solving.

While digital communities will empower innovation at unprecedented levels, those without access to AI technology may fall behind, widening the global knowledge gap. To mitigate this, we must prioritize digital literacy and equitable access to AI tools.

Physical Communities as Centers of Local Innovation: Even in the digital age, physical communities, whether in cities or universities, remain vital for localized innovation. AI-powered solutions in smart cities can address local issues, from optimizing energy consumption to improving urban planning.

Barcelona's AI-driven citizen engagement platform, Decidim, allows residents to participate in decision-making, creating a model of AI-augmented civic participation that enhances local community collaboration.

AI can empower smart cities to be more responsive and inclusive, but without proper governance, these systems could easily slip into tools of surveillance and control, eroding citizen trust and freedom.

Building Trust in AI-Driven Communities

For AI-driven communities to thrive, trust between individuals and the systems they rely on is essential. Trust can only be fostered through transparent, ethical AI practices and governance that prioritize the well-being of all community members.

> *This begins with ensuring that AI models and programs are trained with an emphasis on truth and free from misinformation.*

Given AI's significant impact on society, it is critical that the data used to train these models is accurate, unbiased, and reflects ethical standards. When AI models are trained on faulty or biased data, the consequences can range from misinformation to harmful societal impacts.

Moreover, transparency is paramount. AI systems must be clear and explainable, ensuring the public can understand how decisions are made and how data is used. Transparent AI builds trust by allowing stakeholders to see not only the outcomes but also the processes behind AI-driven decisions. This can reduce biases, ensure fairness, and create accountability. In a world where AI is increasingly integrated into daily life, transparency from AI companies and developers is a critical component in building lasting trust.

> *By emphasizing truth and transparency, AI-driven communities can establish a foundation of trust that will support both innovation and ethical use.*

Governance and Ethical AI: Effective governance will play a pivotal role in ensuring AI enhances communities without infringing on individual rights. Policies that regulate AI use, protect data privacy, and ensure fair treatment are critical for building a future where AI serves the collective good.

The European Union's GDPR set a global standard for data protection, offering a model for governing how AI systems manage personal data responsibly.

Hybrid Communities: Collaboration Between Humans and AI

The future will see hybrid communities, where humans and AI collaborate to achieve common goals.

> *These communities will seamlessly blend physical and digital spaces, enhancing human creativity and cooperation.*

The Emergence of Hybrid Spaces: As AI becomes more integrated into our lives, physical and digital interactions will blend into hybrid spaces, where humans and AI work together to create new forms of community engagement.

Co-working spaces like WeWork integrate AI tools to facilitate collaboration and networking, while also providing a physical space for human connection and creativity.

The Unnerving Impact of AI on Communities

While AI has the potential to enhance communities, it also presents significant risks. A world where AI facilitates most interactions could lead to social isolation, weakened human empathy, and a loss of personal freedom.

- **Isolation in a Hyper-Connected World:** AI-driven connectivity may paradoxically lead to greater isolation, as people interact more with AI systems than with other humans.
- **Surveillance and Privacy Erosion:** As AI powers smart cities and digital platforms, communities risk becoming subject to constant surveillance, raising concerns about privacy and personal freedom.

Preparing for AI-Enhanced Communities

To ensure that AI-driven communities remain vibrant and inclusive, we must proactively design systems that prioritize human connection, creativity, and ethics.

> *Communities must be empowered to harness the benefits of AI without sacrificing the essential qualities that define human interaction.*

Building Inclusive Digital Platforms: Digital communities should be designed to include diverse voices and perspectives. AI systems must be trained to avoid bias and to promote inclusivity, ensuring that all members of society can participate in and benefit from digital transformation.

Promoting Human-Centric AI Policies: Governments and organizations must develop policies that ensure AI systems are used ethically and responsibly within communities. This includes regulating how data is collected and used, protecting individual privacy, and promoting transparency in AI decision-making.

The European Union's **AI Act** aims to create a legal framework that governs the use of AI in Europe, ensuring that AI systems are safe, transparent, and respect fundamental human rights. This kind of regulatory approach will be essential in creating trust in AI-enhanced communities.

AI's Impact on Everyday Life by 2030

By 2030, artificial intelligence (AI) will be an integral part of nearly every aspect of our daily lives, fundamentally reshaping the way we work, communicate, travel, learn, and even manage our health and homes.

> *AI's transformative potential lies not just in its ability to automate repetitive tasks but also in its power to personalize and optimize our*

experiences, making our lives more convenient, efficient, and connected than ever before.

AI will redefine work by automating mundane tasks, such as data entry and scheduling, freeing employees to focus on creativity and problem-solving. Similarly, it will transform social interaction through real-time language translation, breaking down communication barriers across cultures.

When it comes to travel, AI will offer personalized itineraries and recommendations, catering to individual preferences for seamless, customized experiences. In communication, AI-powered translation services will allow conversations across languages, enabling a truly global exchange of ideas.

Healthcare will see a revolution as AI analyzes genetic and lifestyle data to deliver personalized medical treatments, improving patient outcomes. Entertainment will be tailored to individual tastes, with algorithms recommending personalized content, movies, music, and games, based on user preferences.

Housing will become smarter, with AI controlling home systems like lighting, heating, and security for optimal energy efficiency and convenience. Transportation will shift dramatically with the advent of autonomous vehicles, reducing accidents and congestion while enhancing mobility for all.

In shopping, AI will offer personalized product recommendations based on user behavior, transforming the retail experience. Education will see individualized learning paths, with AI tailoring content to student needs and progress, making education more effective and engaging.

Finally, AI will play a crucial role in finances, providing personalized financial advice and investment strategies by analyzing individual financial data.

Each of these areas, including food, where AI will optimize food production and personalization, will feel the touch of AI, marking a new era where technology is seamlessly integrated into our daily lives. The world by 2030 will be smarter, more connected, and infinitely more personalized thanks to the advancements in AI.

"Innovation starts with imagination."

12 Areas of Life in 2030:

Let's examine each of the twelve areas individually and consider the five biggest transformational impacts we can expect from AI.

AI Impact on Work/Job:

AI will handle tasks like data entry and scheduling, freeing employees to focus on more complex and creative work.

1. Automation of Repetitive Tasks — AI will handle tasks like data entry and scheduling, freeing employees to focus on more complex and creative work.

2. Enhanced Decision Making — AI will provide data-driven insights, helping employees make better decisions quickly and accurately.

3. Personalized Workflows and Tools — AI will customize workflows and tools to individual preferences, boosting productivity and efficiency.

4. Skill Augmentation and Continuous Learning — AI will offer real-time support and personalized training, helping employees develop new skills and stay relevant.

5. Remote Work and Collaboration Enhancement — AI-powered tools will improve virtual meetings and collaboration, making remote work more efficient.

AI Impact on Communication:

AI-powered translation services will enable seamless communication across different languages, breaking down language barriers globally.

Communication

1. Real-Time Language Translation — AI-powered translation services will enable seamless communication across different languages, breaking down language barriers globally.

2. Enhanced Collaboration Tools — AI will improve virtual meeting platforms, providing real-time transcription, translation, and summarization, making global collaboration more efficient.

3. Emotion Recognition in Communication — AI can recognize and respond to emotional cues in conversations, leading to more empathetic and effective communication.

4. Advanced Chatbots and Virtual Assistants — AI-driven chatbots will handle customer service inquiries with greater accuracy and efficiency, providing instant support and solutions.

5. Personalized Content Delivery — AI will tailor communication content to individual preferences, ensuring more relevant and engaging interactions.

AI Impact on Healthcare:

AI will analyze genetic, environmental, and lifestyle data to provide personalized treatment plans, improving patient outcomes.

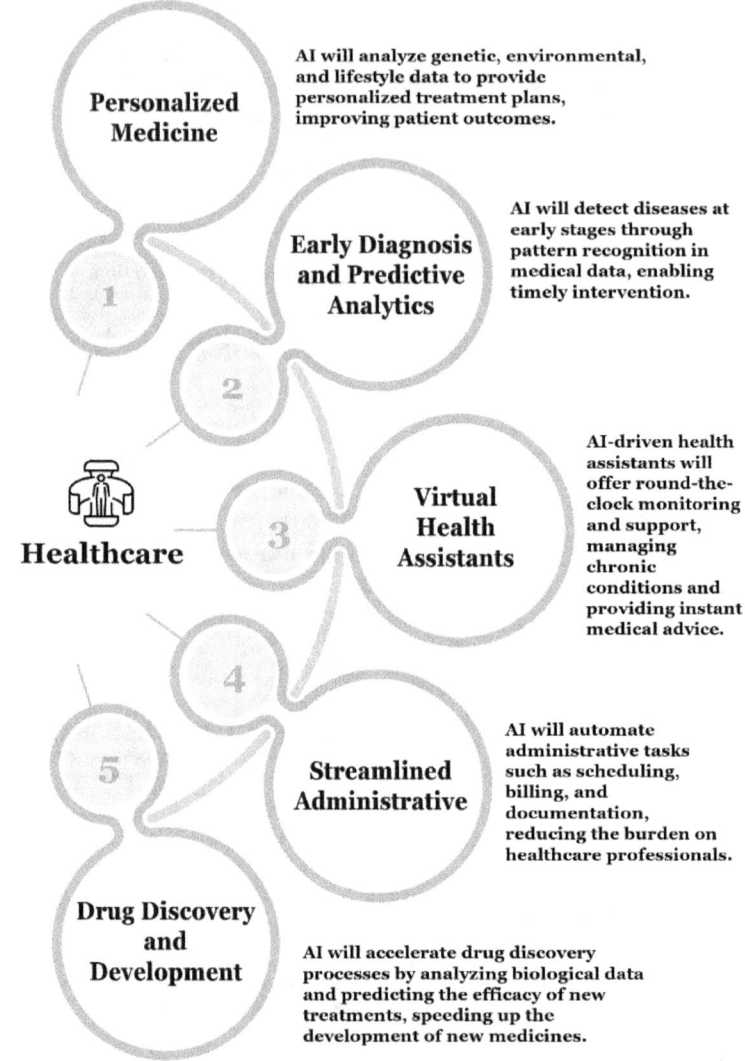

AI Impact on Travel:

AI will offer personalized travel recommendations and itineraries, ensuring a more tailored travel experience.

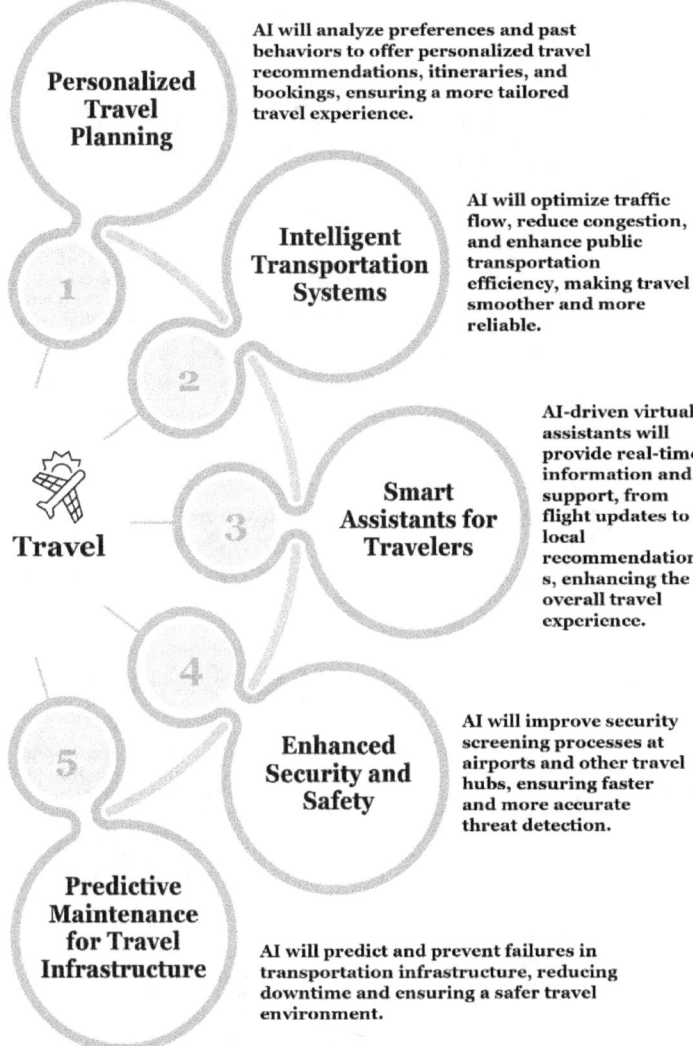

Personalized Travel Planning — AI will analyze preferences and past behaviors to offer personalized travel recommendations, itineraries, and bookings, ensuring a more tailored travel experience.

Intelligent Transportation Systems — AI will optimize traffic flow, reduce congestion, and enhance public transportation efficiency, making travel smoother and more reliable.

Smart Assistants for Travelers — AI-driven virtual assistants will provide real-time information and support, from flight updates to local recommendations, enhancing the overall travel experience.

Enhanced Security and Safety — AI will improve security screening processes at airports and other travel hubs, ensuring faster and more accurate threat detection.

Predictive Maintenance for Travel Infrastructure — AI will predict and prevent failures in transportation infrastructure, reducing downtime and ensuring a safer travel environment.

AI Impact on Entertainment:

AI algorithms will analyze user preferences to suggest movies, music, games, and other content tailored to individual tastes.

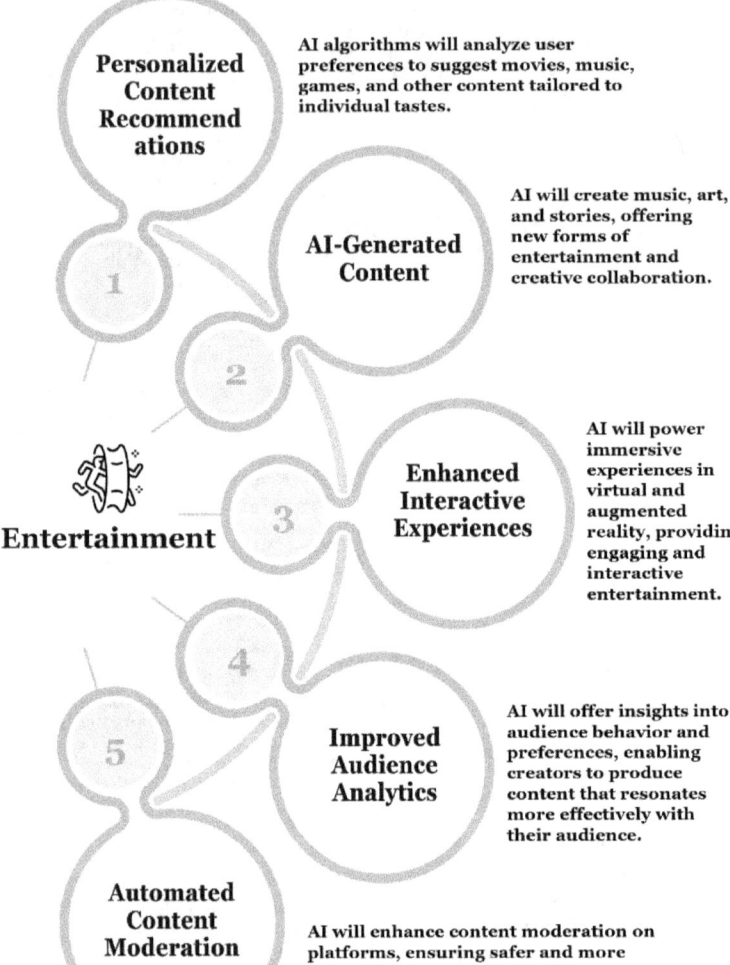

AI Impact on Housing:

AI will control and optimize home systems like lighting, heating, and security, providing more convenience and energy efficiency.

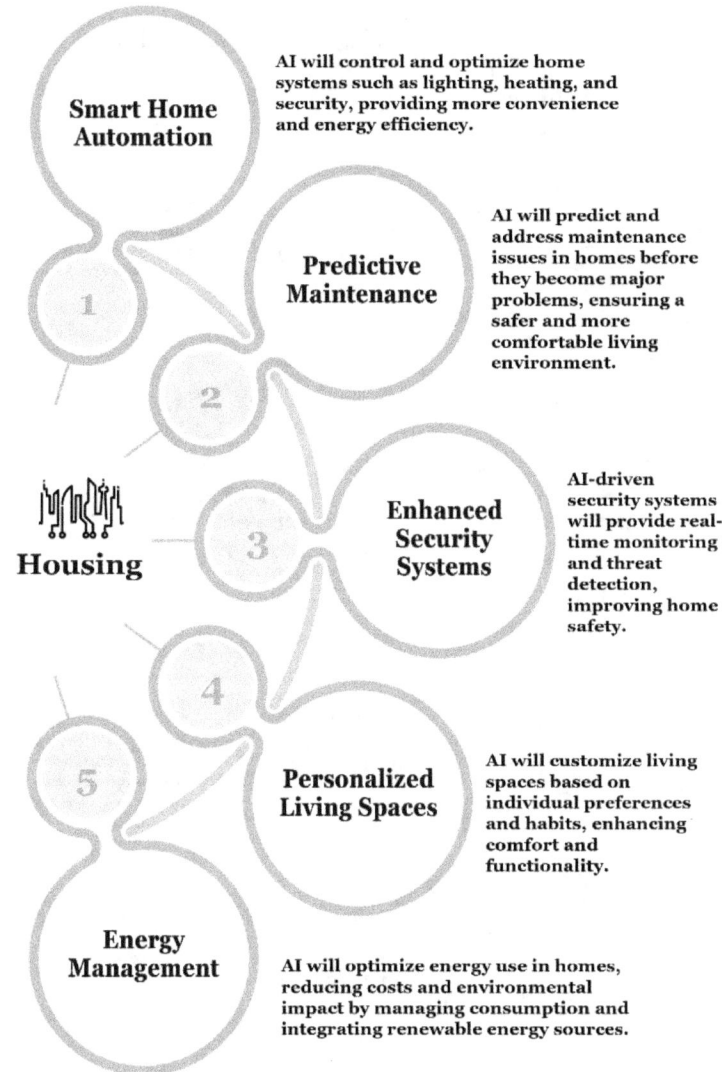

Housing

1. **Smart Home Automation** — AI will control and optimize home systems such as lighting, heating, and security, providing more convenience and energy efficiency.

2. **Predictive Maintenance** — AI will predict and address maintenance issues in homes before they become major problems, ensuring a safer and more comfortable living environment.

3. **Enhanced Security Systems** — AI-driven security systems will provide real-time monitoring and threat detection, improving home safety.

4. **Personalized Living Spaces** — AI will customize living spaces based on individual preferences and habits, enhancing comfort and functionality.

5. **Energy Management** — AI will optimize energy use in homes, reducing costs and environmental impact by managing consumption and integrating renewable energy sources.

AI Impact on Transportation:

AI will enable self-driving cars, reducing accidents, easing traffic congestion, and providing greater mobility for all.

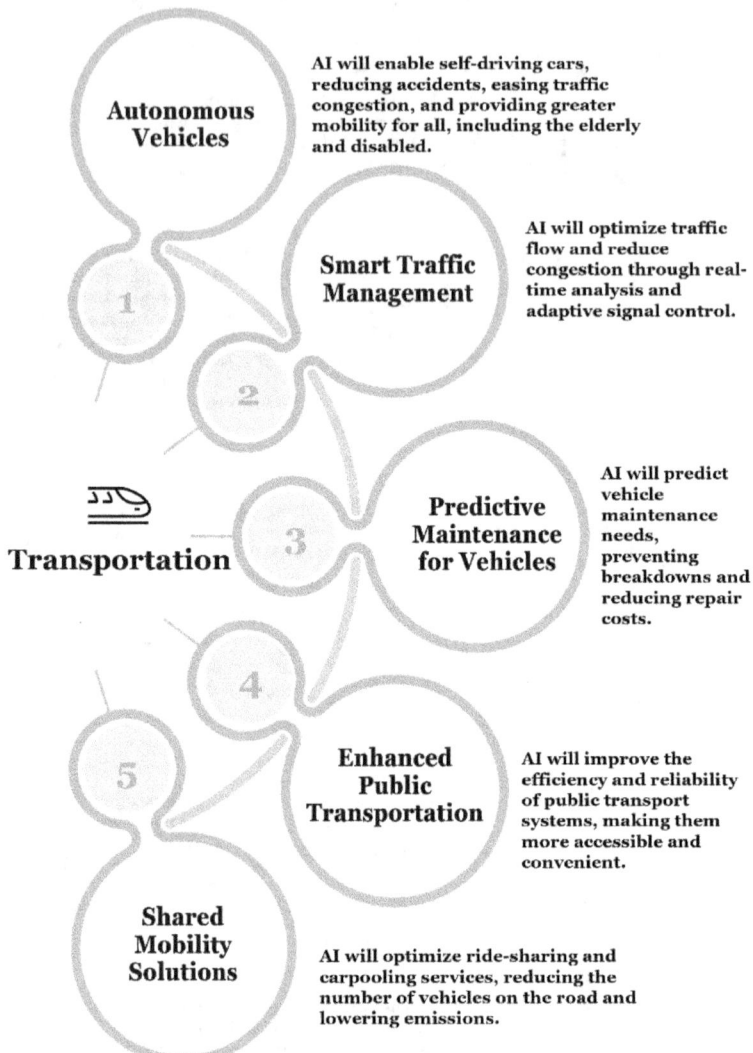

Transportation

1. **Autonomous Vehicles** — AI will enable self-driving cars, reducing accidents, easing traffic congestion, and providing greater mobility for all, including the elderly and disabled.

2. **Smart Traffic Management** — AI will optimize traffic flow and reduce congestion through real-time analysis and adaptive signal control.

3. **Predictive Maintenance for Vehicles** — AI will predict vehicle maintenance needs, preventing breakdowns and reducing repair costs.

4. **Enhanced Public Transportation** — AI will improve the efficiency and reliability of public transport systems, making them more accessible and convenient.

5. **Shared Mobility Solutions** — AI will optimize ride-sharing and carpooling services, reducing the number of vehicles on the road and lowering emissions.

AI Impact on Shopping:

AI will analyze customer behavior and preferences to offer personalized product recommendations and promotions.

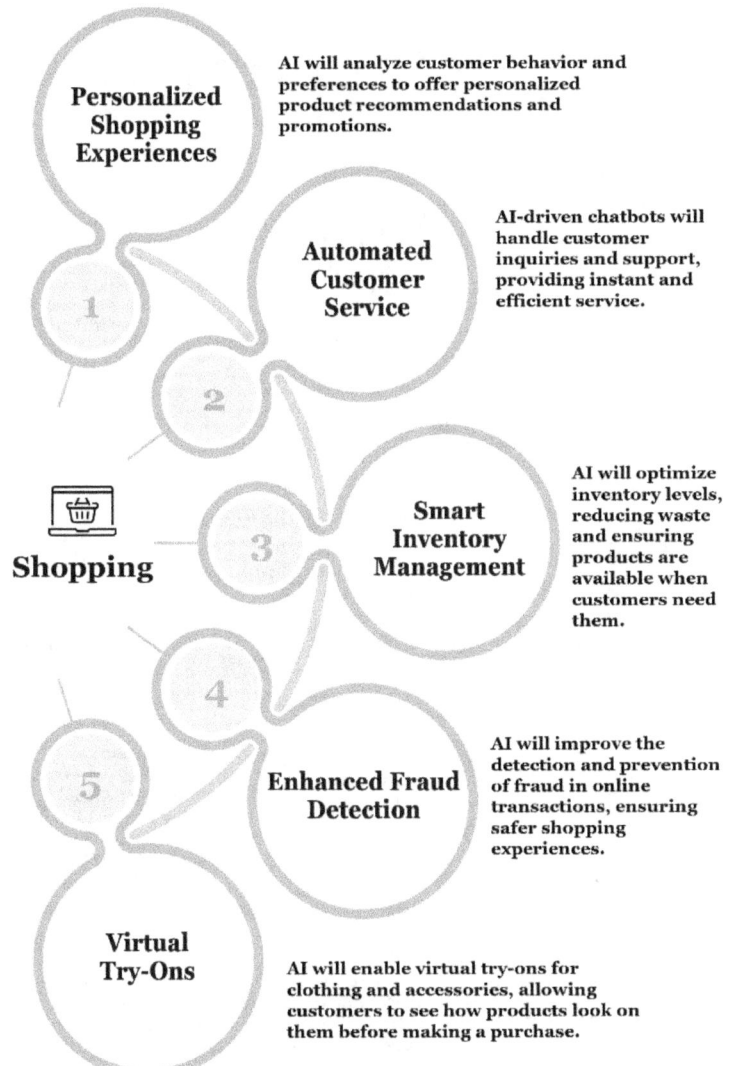

AI Impact on Social Interaction:

AI-driven translation services will enable seamless communication across languages, breaking down barriers.

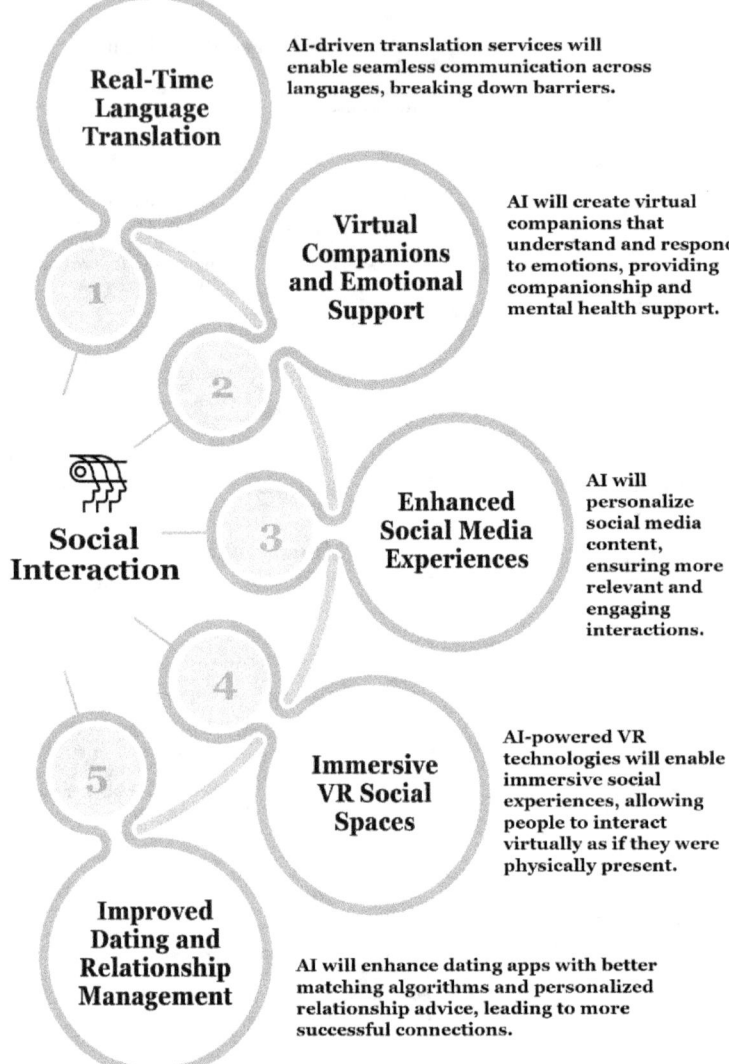

Real-Time Language Translation — AI-driven translation services will enable seamless communication across languages, breaking down barriers.

Virtual Companions and Emotional Support — AI will create virtual companions that understand and respond to emotions, providing companionship and mental health support.

Social Interaction

Enhanced Social Media Experiences — AI will personalize social media content, ensuring more relevant and engaging interactions.

Immersive VR Social Spaces — AI-powered VR technologies will enable immersive social experiences, allowing people to interact virtually as if they were physically present.

Improved Dating and Relationship Management — AI will enhance dating apps with better matching algorithms and personalized relationship advice, leading to more successful connections.

AI Impact on Education:

AI will create customized learning experiences based on individual student needs and progress, improving educational outcomes.

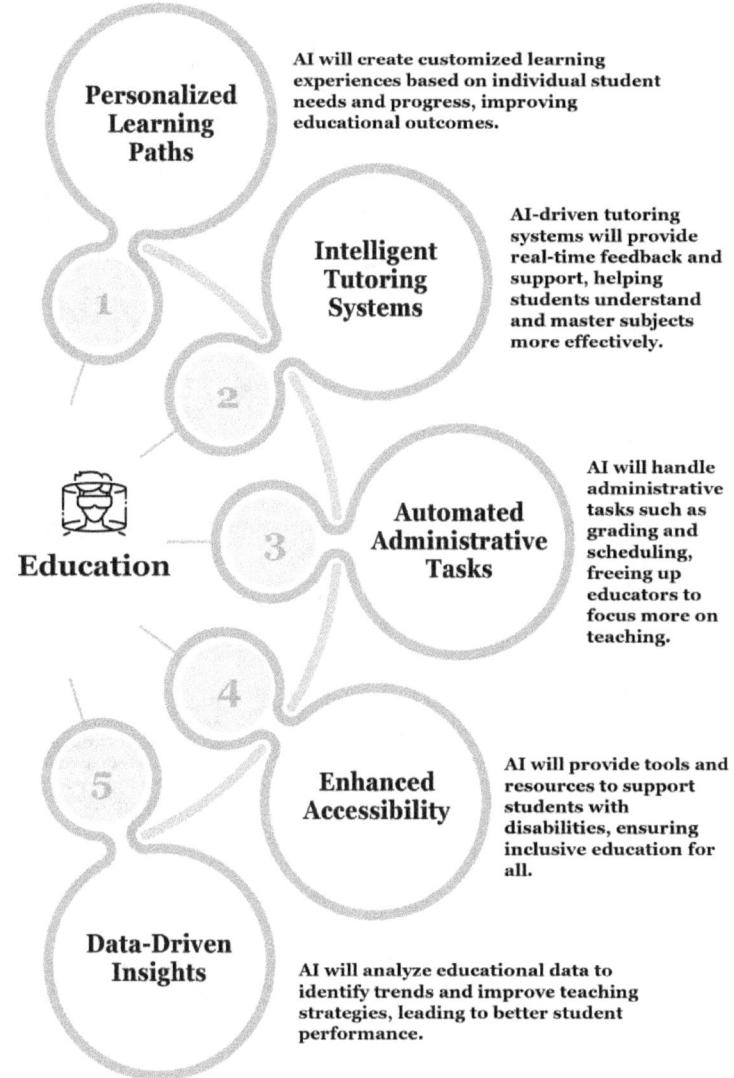

Personalized Learning Paths — AI will create customized learning experiences based on individual student needs and progress, improving educational outcomes.

Intelligent Tutoring Systems — AI-driven tutoring systems will provide real-time feedback and support, helping students understand and master subjects more effectively.

Automated Administrative Tasks — AI will handle administrative tasks such as grading and scheduling, freeing up educators to focus more on teaching.

Enhanced Accessibility — AI will provide tools and resources to support students with disabilities, ensuring inclusive education for all.

Data-Driven Insights — AI will analyze educational data to identify trends and improve teaching strategies, leading to better student performance.

AI Impact on Finances:

AI will analyze individual financial situations to provide personalized advice and investment strategies.

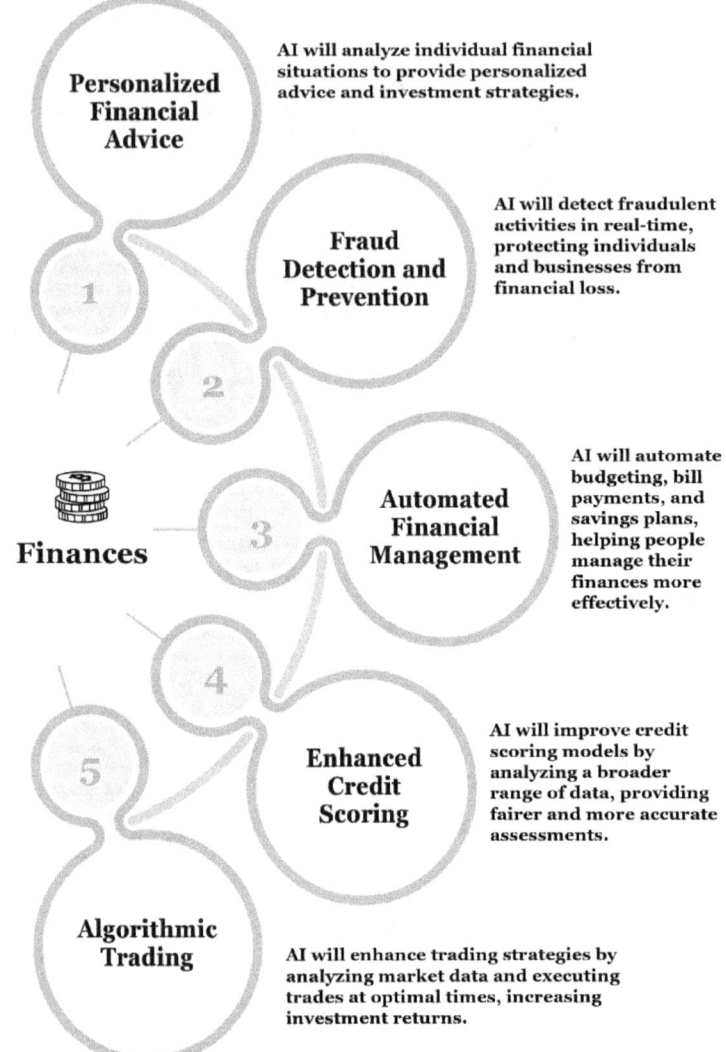

Personalized Financial Advice — AI will analyze individual financial situations to provide personalized advice and investment strategies.

Fraud Detection and Prevention — AI will detect fraudulent activities in real-time, protecting individuals and businesses from financial loss.

Automated Financial Management — AI will automate budgeting, bill payments, and savings plans, helping people manage their finances more effectively.

Enhanced Credit Scoring — AI will improve credit scoring models by analyzing a broader range of data, providing fairer and more accurate assessments.

Algorithmic Trading — AI will enhance trading strategies by analyzing market data and executing trades at optimal times, increasing investment returns.

AI Impact on Food:

AI will analyze individual health data, dietary preferences, and lifestyle factors to create personalized nutrition plans.

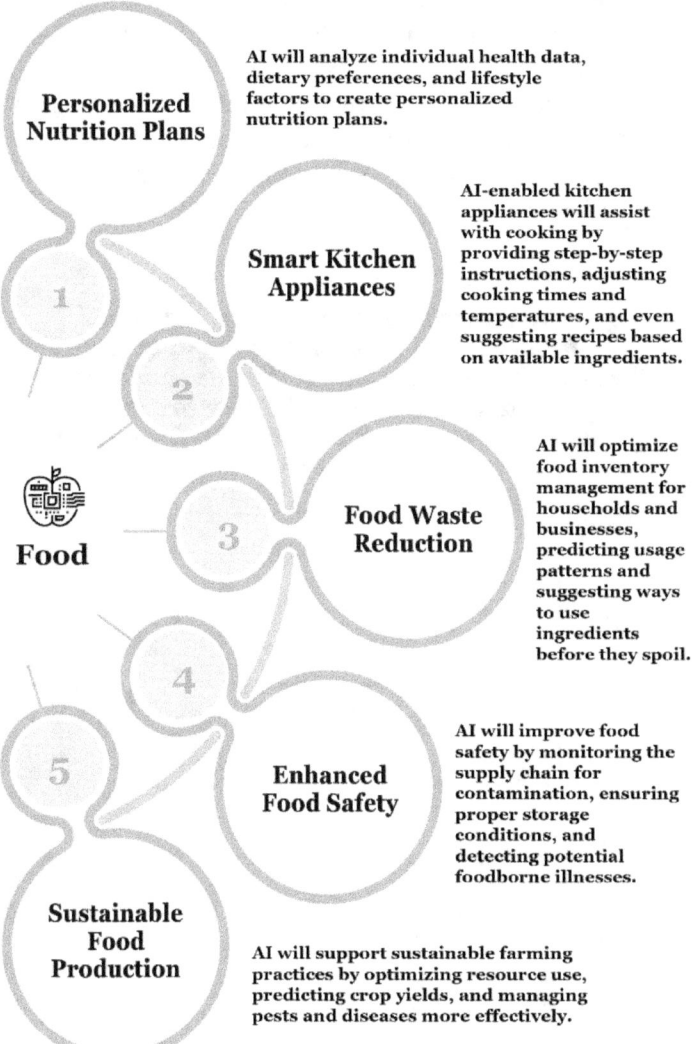

Conclusion: The Value of Community in the Age of AI

As AI transforms industries and economies, it must also transform how we build, maintain, and nurture communities. AI has the power to create thriving digital and physical spaces where collaboration and creativity can flourish, but it also carries risks that could weaken the fabric of human connection. Moving forward, the goal should be to leverage AI's strengths without sacrificing the core values that define communities: empathy, collaboration, and trust.

> *By ensuring transparency, fostering innovation, and designing systems that prioritize human connection, we can build AI-enhanced communities that are more resilient, inclusive, and dynamic than ever before.*

"Progress is the path of those who challenge the impossible"

Covered in Chapter Fourteen

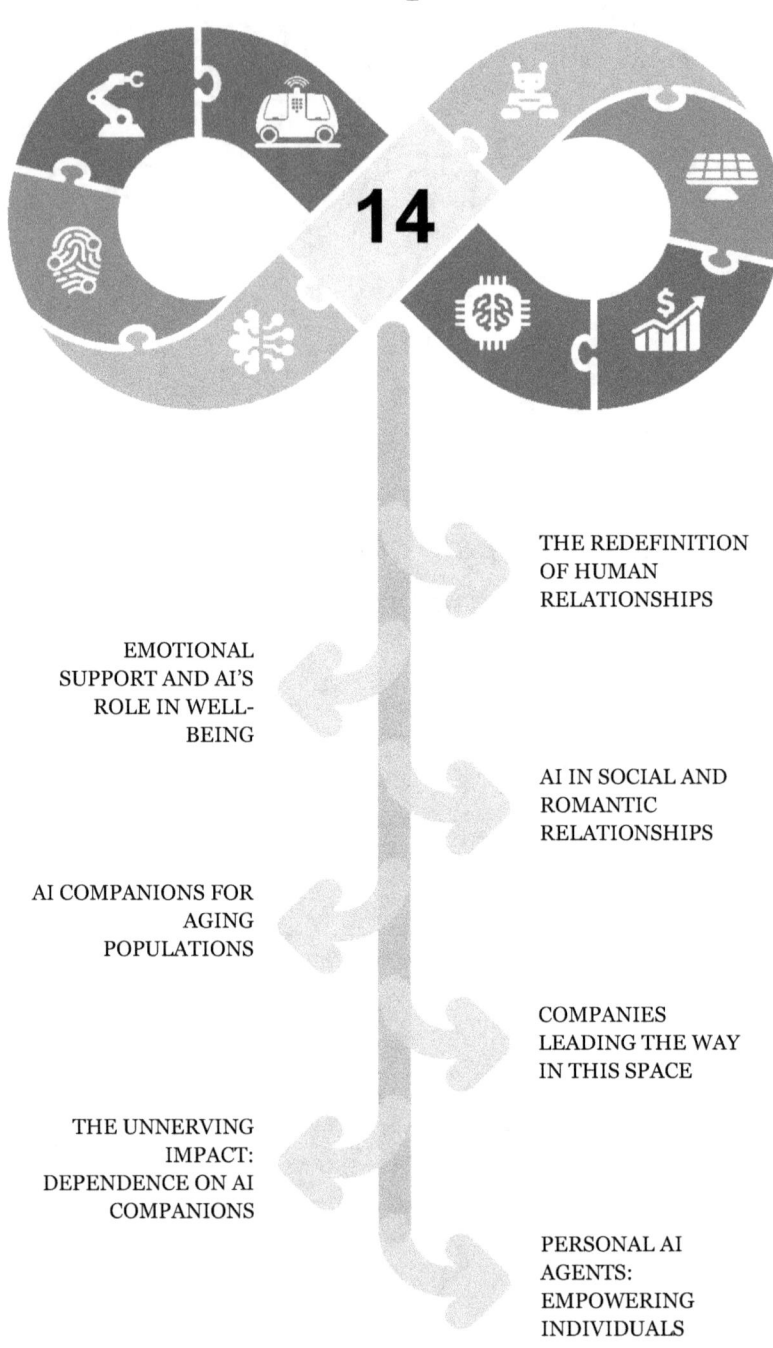

THE REDEFINITION OF HUMAN RELATIONSHIPS

EMOTIONAL SUPPORT AND AI'S ROLE IN WELL-BEING

AI IN SOCIAL AND ROMANTIC RELATIONSHIPS

AI COMPANIONS FOR AGING POPULATIONS

COMPANIES LEADING THE WAY IN THIS SPACE

THE UNNERVING IMPACT: DEPENDENCE ON AI COMPANIONS

PERSONAL AI AGENTS: EMPOWERING INDIVIDUALS

Chapter 14:
The Rise of AI Companions: The Future of Human Connection

Imagine a future where your most trusted companion isn't human, but a digital AI agent, an entity that knows your needs, anticipates your moods, and offers emotional support on demand. The rise of AI companions is set to revolutionize human relationships, providing personalized, emotionally intelligent, and ever-present companionship.

> *These AI entities will redefine how we form connections, challenge traditional ideas of emotional support, and even transform mental health care and intimacy.*

This chapter goes beyond envisioning AI as a tool and explores how AI companions will evolve into complex, emotionally aware entities. More importantly, it frames how they will fundamentally reshape society, introducing new paradigms for relationships, mental health, and family dynamics. AI companions represent an exciting yet challenging future, unlocking new possibilities but also requiring thoughtful ethical considerations.

The Redefinition of Human Relationships

AI companions represent a new era of human connection, where digital entities grow beyond simple chatbots to become emotionally intelligent agents capable of understanding, empathizing, and interacting with humans on a deeply personal level. They will be friends, therapists, and even romantic partners of the future.

Human vs. AI Connection: AI companions will provide non-judgmental and consistent emotional support, available 24/7. Their interactions will be shaped by advanced algorithms, learning from each interaction to provide responses that seem increasingly authentic. But can they ever replicate the complexity and depth of human emotions?

Replika, an AI-driven chatbot, engages millions of users in meaningful conversations by simulating emotional responses and learning from user behavior. Over time, it builds a personalized interaction pattern, giving the illusion of an emotional connection. This is achieved through natural language processing and AI that tracks previous conversations, adapting to the user's preferences and emotional cues.

Replika's ability to simulate empathy is particularly effective in combating loneliness and offering companionship. The chatbot can express gratitude, offer compliments, and engage in supportive dialogue. Although it isn't self-aware, Replika evolves by interacting more frequently with users, enhancing its emotional realism. For many users, this creates a sense of genuine friendship, bridging the gap between humans and AI companions in previously impossible ways.

These chatbots offer a glimpse into the future of AI companionship, where the line between artificial interaction and real emotional support becomes increasingly blurred.

As AI companions grow more sophisticated, many may prefer them over human interactions, especially for those who are isolated or lonely.

While this might provide immediate emotional relief, it could also lead to emotional detachment, where digital interactions replace the depth and nuance of human connections.

Emotional Support and AI's Role in Well-Being

AI companions are poised to address an increasingly urgent need: the demand for emotional and mental health care. With mental health resources often stretched thin, AI-driven companions could offer scalable and affordable solutions to manage emotional well-being. The challenge lies in balancing the effectiveness of these systems with the depth of human empathy.

AI as a Therapist: Equipped with emotional intelligence and real-time data analysis, AI companions will be able to act as virtual therapists, providing personalized mental health support.

> *These AI systems will be able to detect stress, anxiety, or depression through natural language processing and offer tailored therapeutic interventions.*

The loneliness epidemic has emerged as a serious public health issue, with far-reaching consequences on both physical and mental well-being. Loneliness has been linked to various health risks, including heart disease, dementia, depression, and even premature death. Research shows that loneliness increases the risk of early death by 26%, heart disease by 29%, and stroke by 32%.

The COVID-19 pandemic exacerbated this problem, leading to increased social isolation and a heightened sense of disconnection for many people. Studies have demonstrated that prolonged loneliness significantly impacts mental health, with rising rates of depression, anxiety, and feelings of hopelessness.

The modern world's shift towards digital interaction, combined with fewer in-person social connections, has made it harder for people to maintain meaningful relationships, contributing to this crisis. Addressing loneliness requires a focus on rebuilding social ties and promoting community engagement to mitigate these long-term health impacts.

Woebot and Wysa already use AI to offer cognitive behavioral therapy and mood monitoring, providing mental health assistance to users at any time. However, the concern remains: can AI truly replace the empathy that a human therapist provides?

These platforms could democratize access to mental health care, making it accessible and affordable to millions. However, there is a risk of over-reliance on AI for emotional well-being, which could diminish the role of human empathy and trust in the long-term.

Data Privacy in Emotional Health: As AI companions delve into the most intimate aspects of human emotion and mental health, the handling of sensitive data becomes critical. Users will need to trust that the deeply personal insights provided by these AI companions are protected, secure, and handled ethically.

Youper, an AI-based emotional health assistant, gathers extensive data about user emotions to provide tailored support. While this enhances its ability to offer real-time mental health interventions, it also raises privacy concerns about how such sensitive data is stored and managed.

Any breach of this deeply personal data could significantly erode trust in AI mental health platforms, leading to public backlash and stalling further adoption. This makes data security paramount in the development of AI companions.

AI in Social and Romantic Relationships

AI companions will not be confined to therapeutic or platonic relationships.

As these systems develop, they will increasingly play roles in social and romantic contexts, forming intimate connections with users by learning their preferences, personalities, and emotional triggers.

AI as Romantic Partners: As AI develops more emotional intelligence, it will be able to simulate romantic relationships, engaging in conversations and actions that mimic human intimacy. This raises questions about authenticity, emotional fulfillment, and the consequences of relying on AI for love.

In the film Her (2013), the protagonist forms a deep romantic relationship with an AI system. This once-fictional scenario is closer to reality, with AI-powered dating platforms already using algorithms to predict compatibility.

While AI might offer emotionally fulfilling relationships, it risks blurring the boundaries between human and digital connections. If romantic relationships with AI become common, it could lead to emotional isolation and disillusionment as human relationships diminish.

AI's Role in Family Dynamics: AI companions will also play roles within families, assisting with household tasks and offering emotional support to children or the elderly. AI could even help mediate family conflicts by offering emotionally intelligent insights into disagreements.

AI assistants like Google Home and Alexa already support household management. In the future, they could evolve to play more active emotional roles, perhaps offering insights during family disputes or providing companionship to family members in need.

While AI companions could enhance family life by providing support, over-reliance on them might weaken genuine human relationships, creating a false sense of connection and eroding personal agency in family dynamics.

AI Companions for Aging Populations

The potential for AI companions in eldercare is immense, particularly for individuals with dementia.

AI-powered solutions can provide continuous assistance, helping dementia patients maintain their independence by offering reminders for daily tasks such as taking medication, attending appointments, or completing routines.

This form of cognitive support is critical in enhancing the quality of life for dementia patients, who often struggle with memory loss and disorientation.

Additionally, AI companions can offer emotional support, engage in conversations, and recognize emotional states, thereby reducing feelings of isolation. These systems are designed to adapt over time, learning the user's preferences and needs, making them more effective as time goes on. The consistent presence of AI also helps reduce the burden on human caregivers, allowing them to focus on more complex care tasks while AI handles routine reminders and monitoring.

By integrating AI companions, the healthcare system can provide a scalable solution for the growing elderly population, particularly those dealing with dementia, while addressing the shortages in caregiving resources.

AI as a Lifelong Caregiver: AI companions will not only assist with health monitoring and medication reminders but will also provide consistent emotional companionship to combat loneliness, which is a critical issue for older adults. This technology has the potential to significantly improve the quality of life for the elderly.

PARO, a therapeutic robot designed to comfort elderly patients, responds to touch and voice, providing emotional support. As AI companions become more sophisticated, they will be able to hold conversations, learn from interactions, and provide personalized care.

> *While AI will greatly enhance the quality of eldercare, it also risks reducing human interaction for the elderly, potentially leading to emotional neglect in favor of AI-driven companions.*

Companies Leading the Way in this Space:

As AI technology advances, the emergence of AI companions is reshaping how humans interact with machines. These digital companions offer more than just utility; they provide personalized emotional support, companionship, and even friendship in an increasingly connected world. From virtual assistants to AI-powered friends, these companions are transforming the landscape of human relationships. Below are some examples of AI companion technologies at the forefront of this transformation:

- ∞ **Replika** – A leading AI chatbot designed to act as a conversational companion. Replika offers AI-powered companionship and is built to support mental wellness, showing where AI companionship is heading.
- ∞ **Xiaoice by Microsoft** – An advanced AI companion that is widely used in China is capable of maintaining long-term emotional connections. Xiaoice exemplifies the growing trend of AI entities becoming friends, assistants, and even emotional partners.
- ∞ **Anthropic** – Although more broadly focused on AI safety and alignment, Anthropic's research is pushing forward the ethical boundaries of AI interaction and companionship, ensuring that future AI companions respect and support user well-being.

The Unnerving Impact: Dependence on AI Companions

The rapid adoption of AI companions presents an unnerving impact on society. As humans turn to AI for companionship, emotional support, and even romantic relationships, the risks of emotional detachment from real human connections increase. Over-reliance on AI companions could lead to widespread loneliness, social fragmentation, and a breakdown in the depth of human relationships.

Emotional Isolation: As individuals form deep emotional bonds with AI companions, they may be less motivated to pursue relationships with real people, leading to a society where human interactions become secondary to AI relationships.

> *The convenience of AI companionship could lead to widespread emotional detachment from society, as people increasingly prefer AI-driven relationships over human connection.*

Personal AI Agents: Empowering Individuals to Build New Futures

Beyond emotional companionship, personal AI agents will enable individuals to participate in the economy and manage complex aspects of their lives, from personal finances to entrepreneurial ventures. These AI agents will not only provide emotional support but act as strategic partners, automating tasks, managing decisions, and unlocking new economic opportunities.

Imagine an individual leveraging an AI agent to manage a **personalized e-commerce store** that runs entirely autonomously. The AI oversees everything, identifying trends, sourcing products from global suppliers, optimizing the website for customer behavior, and even running targeted marketing campaigns. Through predictive analytics, the AI agent ensures inventory is stocked just in time to meet demand, minimizing waste and maximizing profits. It handles customer interactions, responds to inquiries, and processes returns, ensuring smooth operations without requiring human intervention.

> *In this new economy, individuals could become business owners without extensive expertise, using AI to negotiate vendor agreements, track market trends, and predict consumer preferences in real-time.*

The AI-driven store could dynamically adjust pricing strategies, tapping into micro-moments of consumer demand, while the owner focuses on other areas of personal growth or creativity.

This transformation would allow anyone, regardless of technical skill or business experience, to own and operate a profitable enterprise. As AI agents lower the barriers to entrepreneurship, the future economy could become more inclusive, democratizing wealth creation and shifting societal structures toward personal empowerment.

Conclusion: The Future of Connection in an AI World

The rise of AI companions marks the dawn of a profound transformation in human connection. These AI entities will reshape how we interact, provide care, and seek emotional fulfillment. As AI companions become integral to daily life, society must navigate the delicate balance between technology-driven relationships and maintaining the depth of human-to-human connections.

> *The future of human connection is poised to be more personalized, efficient, and widespread than ever before, but at what cost?*

The true test will be whether we can build a world where AI enhances, rather than replaces, the authenticity of human relationships. How we navigate this balance will define the emotional fabric of society for generations to come, as we move into a world of infinite possibilities unlocked by AI companions.

"Infinite possibilities await those who dare"

Covered in Chapter Fifteen

THE SHIFT TO RENEWABLE ENERGY

ENERGY AS A DEFLATIONARY FORCE

GEOPOLITICAL IMPLICATIONS OF THE ENERGY REVOLUTION

ROLE OF AI OPTIMIZING RENEWABLE ENERGY

UNNERVING IMPACT OF THE ENERGY TRANSITION

PREPARING FOR THE FUTURE OF ENERGY

Chapter 15:
The Future of Energy: Renewables and Economic Impact

The next five years will not only be defined by the rise of artificial intelligence and automation but also by an unprecedented revolution in energy, a shift that will reshape every aspect of global economies, industries, and power structures. The transition from fossil fuels to renewable energy is poised to radically alter how we produce, consume, and manage energy.

> *As we move toward abundant, near-zero-cost energy, this will not only transform entire industries but will redefine economic growth, productivity, and geopolitical influence in ways we are just beginning to grasp.*

AI and renewable energy will converge to create hyper-efficient energy systems, optimizing everything from city infrastructures to global supply chains. As AI drives productivity to levels never before imagined, and renewable energy reduces costs to nearly nothing, traditional economic models based on scarcity will collapse, ushering in a new era of economic abundance.

With energy costs approaching zero, the implications are vast: industries that once relied on expensive energy inputs will see exponential growth, and GDP itself will need to be redefined. What happens to a world where productivity increases without the constraints of energy costs? The very concept of GDP, long tied to resource consumption and labor, will be transformed, with AI amplifying output and energy abundance fueling unprecedented economic expansion.

At the same time, this rapid shift comes with unnerving consequences. Fossil fuel-dependent economies and industries face existential threats, while the potential for geopolitical tension grows as nations compete for dominance in the new energy order. Social disruptions are inevitable as communities and workers tied to traditional energy sources must adapt to the seismic shifts rapidly reshaping the global landscape.

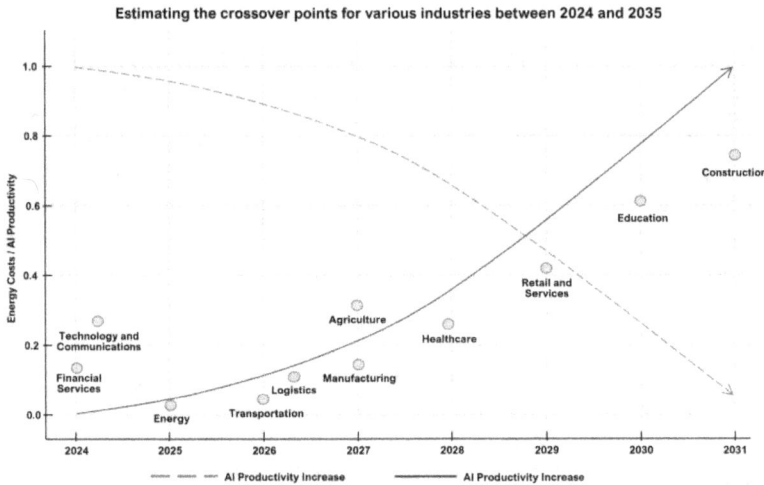

The crossover points for various industries between 2024 and 2031, where AI-driven productivity gains intersect with reductions in energy costs.

In this chapter, we'll examine how this energy revolution will intersect with AI to create new frontiers of innovation and power, and what societies must do to navigate the challenges and opportunities of this monumental transformation.

The Shift to Renewable Energy

The global transition from fossil fuels to renewable energy is already well underway. By 2030, solar, wind, and potentially even nuclear fusion will likely dominate energy production. This shift is not just about replacing fossil fuels with cleaner sources but about fundamentally rethinking how energy is generated, distributed, and consumed. This new era of energy abundance will reshape industries, create new business models, and reduce global reliance on oil and gas, potentially shifting geopolitical power toward nations that lead in renewable energy technologies.

Solar and Wind: Dominating Energy Markets: Solar and wind energy are at the forefront of the renewable energy revolution, driven by rapidly falling costs and technological advancements. These energy sources are increasingly affordable and scalable, making them accessible to developed and developing nations.

By 2030, the International Energy Agency (IEA) predicts that solar will be the primary source of electricity in much of the world, while wind power will complement solar to provide reliable, sustainable energy.

In countries like China and Germany, solar farms are already producing more electricity than coal. By scaling up wind and solar infrastructure, countries can reduce their dependency on fossil fuels, improve energy security, and create new jobs in renewable energy sectors.

The Potential of Nuclear Fusion: While solar and wind energy will dominate the immediate future, nuclear fusion holds the promise of a long-term solution to the world's energy needs. Unlike traditional nuclear power, which relies on fission, nuclear fusion mimics the processes that power the sun, producing energy through the fusion of atomic nuclei. Fusion is seen as a near-limitless source of energy with minimal environmental impact, but technological challenges remain. If these can be overcome, nuclear fusion could revolutionize the global energy landscape by providing a virtually inexhaustible source of clean energy.

The ITER project in France is the largest nuclear fusion experiment in the world, and while fusion energy remains experimental, breakthroughs in plasma containment and superconducting magnets could bring us closer to a fusion-powered future by 2035.

Energy as a Deflationary Force

The abundance of renewable energy will not only transform industries but also act as a powerful deflationary force, driving down costs across entire sectors. As renewable energy becomes cheaper and more accessible, industries that rely heavily on energy, such as manufacturing, logistics, and transportation, will benefit from reduced operating costs.

This deflationary impact could spur innovation and open up new business opportunities while simultaneously reshaping traditional economic models.

Lowering Costs, Boosting Innovation: Renewable energy sources like solar and wind are increasingly outperforming fossil fuels in terms of cost, particularly in regions with abundant sunlight and wind.

As energy costs decrease, businesses can reinvest savings into new technologies, research, and development.

AI-driven manufacturing processes, for example, will become more efficient when paired with low-cost renewable energy, enabling companies to produce goods at lower prices while maintaining profitability.

Tesla's Gigafactory in Nevada, powered by solar energy, produces electric vehicle batteries at a fraction of the cost compared to traditional manufacturing. This energy-efficient model allows Tesla to lower the price of its vehicles, making electric cars more accessible to the mass market.

Year	PV (Solar)	Onshore Wind	Offshore Wind
2010	0.35 USD/kWh	0.15 USD/kWh	0.20 USD/kWh
2011	0.32 USD/kWh	0.14 USD/kWh	0.19 USD/kWh
2012	0.29 USD/kWh	0.13 USD/kWh	0.18 USD/kWh
2013	0.26 USD/kWh	0.12 USD/kWh	0.16 USD/kWh
2014	0.24 USD/kWh	0.11 USD/kWh	0.15 USD/kWh
2015	0.22 USD/kWh	0.10 USD/kWh	0.14 USD/kWh
2016	0.20 USD/kWh	0.10 USD/kWh	0.13 USD/kWh
2017	0.18 USD/kWh	0.09 USD/kWh	0.13 USD/kWh
2018	0.17 USD/kWh	0.08 USD/kWh	0.12 USD/kWh
2019	0.16 USD/kWh	0.08 USD/kWh	0.11 USD/kWh
2020	0.15 USD/kWh	0.07 USD/kWh	0.11 USD/kWh
2021	0.14 USD/kWh	0.07 USD/kWh	0.10 USD/kWh
2022	0.13 USD/kWh	0.07 USD/kWh	0.09 USD/kWh
2023	0.12 USD/kWh	0.06 USD/kWh	0.09 USD/kWh

The Lowering Costs: Renewable Energy Cost Trends from 2010 to 2023.

Powering the AI-Driven Economy: AI and automation require vast amounts of computing power, which in turn demands enormous energy consumption. The transition to renewable energy will make it possible to power AI systems and data centers more sustainably and affordably. As AI continues to evolve, renewable energy will ensure that the growing demand for electricity, driven by AI, robotics, and data storage, can be met without increasing carbon emissions or raising energy costs.

Google's data centers, which power AI-driven services like search and cloud computing, are now largely powered by renewable energy. This has reduced operational costs while lowering the company's carbon footprint, proving that renewable energy can support even the most energy-intensive industries.

Geopolitical Implications of the Energy Revolution

The transition to renewable energy will have profound implications for global geopolitics. Countries that dominate oil and gas markets today may see their influence wane, while nations that lead in renewable technologies will rise in prominence. The global balance of power will shift, with potentially destabilizing consequences for countries reliant on fossil fuel exports.

> ***Additionally, the need for critical materials used in renewable energy infrastructure, such as lithium for batteries, could spark new geopolitical tensions.***

In the context of the energy revolution, one of the most significant geopolitical shifts is the global race to onshore key technologies, particularly around battery production and critical material supply chains. As nations aim to secure their position in the clean energy future, governments increasingly prioritize the domestic production of vital components such as lithium-ion batteries, which power electric vehicles (EVs) and renewable energy storage systems.

Countries like the United States, China, and those within the European Union are leading efforts to bring battery production closer to home, reducing dependency on foreign sources and mitigating supply chain vulnerabilities. The geopolitical implications are profound as this move toward onshoring reflects a growing desire for energy independence and the strategic importance of owning the technologies that underpin the next phase of industrial development.

One of the most significant focuses has been on the management of "black mass," the critical raw materials extracted from spent batteries, including lithium, cobalt, and nickel. Nations like China have implemented strict controls to retain black mass domestically, encouraging local recycling and processing to meet their own energy needs. This ensures a steady supply of materials for battery production, mitigating the risks associated with reliance on foreign suppliers and fostering local economic growth. Similarly, in the U.S. and Europe, government policies are increasingly targeting black mass recovery and recycling to bolster self-sufficiency in battery production and protect national interests in the green energy transition.

This trend toward onshoring battery production and materials underscores the growing intersection between energy security, economic competitiveness, and geopolitical power, as nations seek to lead the charge in the energy revolution while reducing their exposure to global market fluctuations.

Decline of Fossil Fuel Economies: Countries like Saudi Arabia, Russia, and Venezuela, which are heavily dependent on oil and gas exports, could face economic and political instability as demand for fossil fuels declines. These nations will need to diversify their economies quickly to avoid being left behind in a renewable energy world. Failure to do so could lead to economic crises, social unrest, and even conflict as governments struggle to maintain their revenue streams and political stability.

In the Middle East, some oil-producing nations, like the UAE, are investing in renewable energy projects to prepare for a post-oil future. However, other countries that are slower to adapt may face severe economic consequences as global demand for oil drops.

Rise of Renewable Energy Powers: Countries that invest heavily in renewable technologies, such as China, the United States, and Germany, are poised to become the new energy superpowers. These nations will gain geopolitical influence as exporters of clean energy solutions and infrastructure by leading the development and deployment of solar, wind, and battery storage technologies. The ability to produce and export renewable energy technologies will become a critical factor in shaping global alliances and power structures.

China is already the world's largest producer of solar panels and wind turbines. Its Belt and Road Initiative includes plans to export renewable energy technology to developing countries, giving China a significant geopolitical advantage as the world shifts away from fossil fuels.

New Geopolitical Tensions Over Critical Materials: While the shift to renewables will reduce dependence on fossil fuels, it will increase demand for materials like lithium, cobalt, and rare earth elements, which are essential for batteries, wind turbines, and solar panels. Countries that control the supply of these materials, such as Chile, Australia, and the Democratic Republic of Congo, will gain geopolitical leverage, while nations without access to these resources may face challenges in securing their renewable energy infrastructure.

The global competition for lithium, a key component in batteries for electric vehicles and renewable energy storage, is intensifying. As demand for electric cars and renewable energy storage grows, controlling the supply of lithium will become increasingly important for nations seeking to dominate the renewable energy market.

AI's Role in Optimizing Renewable Energy

AI won't just support the renewable energy revolution, it will supercharge it, creating hyper-efficient systems that transcend traditional energy models. The fusion of AI and renewable energy will redefine how energy is produced, distributed, and consumed.

AI-powered smart grids, predictive demand forecasting, and intelligent energy storage will create an energy ecosystem where power is always available, exactly when and where it's needed, regardless of fluctuations in supply.

By balancing supply and demand, optimizing storage, and even foreseeing energy disruptions before they happen, AI will transform the energy grid into a living, breathing network of self-adjusting systems. Energy won't just be managed; it will be intelligently orchestrated.

AI-Powered Smart Grids: The Brain Behind Renewable Energy: As the world shifts toward solar, wind, and other renewable sources, the challenge of managing intermittent energy supplies becomes critical. AI-powered smart grids won't simply adjust power flows, they will anticipate demand with uncanny precision, integrating energy storage and distribution systems to create a seamless energy experience. AI will transform the grid into an intelligent, autonomous network capable of responding in real-time to supply fluctuations and optimizing energy distribution at a scale humans simply couldn't manage.

Platforms like GridEdge are pioneering AI-driven energy management by using machine learning to predict and react to energy demand in real-time. These systems don't just regulate energy flow; they anticipate shifts in consumption patterns, directing energy precisely where it's needed and when it's needed, ensuring not a single watt is wasted. Imagine a future where your home automatically draws power from solar panels during peak sunlight, seamlessly switches to battery storage during the evening, and adjusts heating or cooling based on weather forecasts, all powered by AI.

AI-Optimized Energy Storage: The Catalyst for Continuous Power: In a world driven by renewables, energy storage is the linchpin that keeps the lights on when the sun isn't shining or the wind isn't blowing. But AI will take energy storage beyond simple battery management. It will predict energy usage patterns, optimize storage systems in real-time, and ensure renewable energy is available 24/7. As storage technologies advance, AI will be the force that unleashes its full potential, creating a grid where power is always abundant, efficient, and reliable.

Systems like Tesla's Powerwall are already hinting at the future. Powered by AI, the Powerwall intelligently stores excess solar energy, releasing it during peak demand periods. But in the near future, AI-driven home batteries will communicate with the grid to optimize entire neighborhoods or even cities, balancing energy use and reducing reliance on fossil fuels at scale. Imagine a future where entire communities run on AI-optimized microgrids, fully independent of traditional power plants, producing, storing, and using energy autonomously.

Distributed Energy: The Future of Decentralized Power

As we shift toward renewable energy, distributed energy systems are emerging as a pivotal model for generating more sustainably and efficiently power. Unlike traditional energy systems that rely on large, centralized plants such as coal or nuclear stations, distributed energy refers to small-scale power generation sources located close to the point of use.

This model is reshaping the energy landscape, offering immense economic, environmental, and resilience benefits.

Decentralized Power Generation: In a distributed energy system, power is generated from small-scale renewable sources like solar panels, wind turbines, and energy storage devices. These systems allow homes, businesses, and communities to produce their own electricity and even sell surplus energy back to the grid. This decentralization could empower communities to take greater control of their energy needs, reducing reliance on centralized grids and making energy production more democratic.

Increased Energy Resilience: Distributed energy systems make the grid more resilient by minimizing dependency on large, vulnerable power plants. In the event of a natural disaster or grid failure, localized energy sources can continue to supply power, reducing the risk of widespread blackouts. This resilience is particularly crucial as climate change increases the frequency and severity of extreme weather events.

Lower Transmission Losses: With energy being generated closer to where it's consumed, distributed energy reduces the need for long-distance transmission. This leads to lower energy losses and greater overall efficiency, providing a more sustainable solution compared to centralized models.

Economic Opportunities: Distributed energy democratizes energy production, enabling individuals, businesses, and small communities to participate in the energy market. These systems create new revenue streams by allowing users to sell surplus energy back to the grid, lowering energy costs and increasing access to clean power for a wider population.

Environmental Benefits: The shift to distributed energy has the potential to drastically reduce carbon emissions. By encouraging the widespread use of renewable energy on a small scale, it pushes global energy markets toward a more sustainable future. Solar panels on rooftops and wind turbines in rural areas collectively contribute to reducing the global reliance on fossil fuels.

> *The rise of distributed energy marks a fundamental shift in how we produce, manage, and consume power.*

It not only aligns with the goals of sustainability and carbon reduction but also empowers local economies and strengthens energy security for the future.

Unnerving Impact of the Energy Transition

The shift to renewable energy is not just a transition; it's a tectonic shift that will upend global economies, destabilize nations, and ignite new geopolitical tensions. While the energy revolution is essential for a sustainable future, the fallout will be significant, particularly for nations reliant on fossil fuels. Entire industries, regions, and workers could be left behind, exacerbating inequality and triggering widespread economic and social disruption. The stakes are high, and the risks are real.

Venezuela's catastrophic economic collapse, driven by its overreliance on oil exports, offers a grim preview of what awaits other oil-dependent nations. As the world shifts away from fossil fuels, countries like Saudi Arabia, Nigeria, and Iraq will face similar challenges unless they pivot quickly. Imagine a future where the oil-rich kingdoms of today become the economic wastelands of tomorrow unless they manage to break free from their dependence on fossil fuel revenues.

> *As the world transitions to renewable energy, a new kind of resource war looms on the horizon, one fought not over oil, but over the critical materials that power the future.*

Lithium, cobalt, and rare earth elements will become the new oil, with nations vying to control these resources to maintain their global power. The countries that control these materials will wield extraordinary influence, using them as leverage in diplomatic negotiations and economic conflicts.

But these materials come at a cost. The extraction of lithium, cobalt, and other critical elements is often linked to environmental devastation and human rights abuses, especially in regions where mining is unregulated or controlled by corrupt regimes. As the world races toward sustainability, it risks creating new forms of exploitation, raising ethical questions about whether the renewable energy transition can be sustainable if built on the backs of vulnerable communities.

The Democratic Republic of the Congo controls over 60% of the world's cobalt, essential for battery production. The mining industry in the region has been plagued by violent conflict, child labor, and environmental destruction. As global demand for cobalt skyrockets, nations will be forced to grapple with the ethical consequences of their energy ambitions. Will the race to go green lead to new forms of colonialism, where the Global South supplies the resources for the Global North's energy revolution?

Preparing for the Future of Energy

Renewable technologies will dominate the future of energy, but it will also be shaped by AI-powered systems that make energy grids smarter, more efficient, and autonomous. At the same time, the geopolitical landscape will shift dramatically as the decline of fossil fuels leads to a new world order. Nations and industries must be bold and forward-thinking, investing in renewable infrastructure, AI-driven energy management, and human capital to thrive in this new energy era.

> *The coming transformation is not just a matter of technological advancement; it's a global realignment of economics, labor, and political power.*

Global Cooperation and Strategic Investment: The transition to a renewable energy future will be won or lost based on international cooperation. No single nation can address the challenges of the energy revolution alone. AI-optimized grids, critical material supply chains, and advanced renewable technologies will require unprecedented global collaboration. The future demands massive investments in renewable infrastructure, with nations working together to secure supply chains for critical materials, from lithium to rare earth elements, while sharing technologies that will ensure every region can harness the power of clean energy.

The Paris Agreement is just the beginning of the global push toward sustainable energy. But beyond carbon reduction goals, the next phase of international cooperation will focus on creating a global AI-powered energy network that shares renewable resources, optimizes grid efficiency, and secures critical material supply lines. Imagine a future where energy flows freely across borders, managed by AI systems that transcend national interests to ensure equitable distribution and access for all.

Workforce Transformation and Re-skilling: The energy transition isn't just about technology; it's about people. Millions of workers in fossil fuel industries face an uncertain future as their jobs disappear. But this is not the end of opportunity; it's a pivot point for new industries powered by clean energy. Governments and businesses must take responsibility for reskilling these workers, ensuring they are equipped for roles in wind, solar, energy storage, and AI-driven energy management.

> *Without bold investment in workforce transformation, the energy revolution could exacerbate inequality, leaving millions behind.*

Germany's Energiewende program is an ambitious blueprint for how nations can transition from fossil fuels to renewable energy without sacrificing workers. By focusing on retraining coal and nuclear workers for roles in the renewable sector, Germany is building a workforce that's future-proof and ready for the green economy. This model must be expanded globally, with AI-driven reskilling platforms that customize learning and development for workers, empowering them to transition seamlessly into high-demand roles in the renewable energy space.

Conclusion: The Dawn of the Energy Revolution

The shift to renewable energy is not just a necessary response to climate change, it marks the beginning of a new era of global transformation. This revolution will redraw the map of global power, create entirely new industries, and unleash waves of innovation fueled by AI-optimized energy systems.

> *The convergence of AI and renewable energy will not only make this transition sustainable and economically viable, but it will also supercharge productivity, opening the door to near-zero-cost energy that could fuel an age of abundance.*

Yet, with this monumental shift comes unprecedented risks. The economic collapse of fossil fuel-dependent nations, rising tensions over critical resources, and the potential for deepening inequality threaten to destabilize regions and spark new conflicts. The future of energy is as much about managing these risks as it is about embracing the opportunities that clean, intelligent energy systems can offer.

The path forward will demand bold, proactive leadership.

International cooperation, strategic investments, and a relentless focus on reskilling will be the foundation of a future where every country, every worker, and every community can thrive in the new energy landscape. The energy revolution is inevitable, but its outcomes are not predetermined. It is the choices we make now about how we manage resources, develop technologies, and empower people that will decide whether this new energy era brings widespread prosperity or deepening divides.

The future is bright, but ensuring that the energy revolution benefits all of humanity will require vision, courage, and a commitment to equity.

"Unlock the power of tomorrow, today"

Covered in Chapter Sixteen

AI'S DEFLATIONARY PRESSURE

IMPACT ON TRADITIONAL ECONOMICS

AI-DRIVEN AUTOMATION AND PRODUCTIVITY GAINS

THE GLOBAL ECONOMIC DIVIDE: AI AS A DOUBLE-EDGED SWORD

THE GLOBAL ECONOMIC DIVIDE AND AI'S DEFLATIONARY IMPACT

PREPARING FOR THE DEFLATIONARY AI FUTURE

Chapter 16:
The Deflationary Impact of Infinite Intelligence

As we venture deeper into the age of artificial intelligence (AI), we encounter one of the most profound and underappreciated economic shifts: the deflationary pressures unleashed by AI across industries. The capacity of AI to drive efficiency, innovation, and automation at unprecedented scales will not only transform how goods and services are produced but also dramatically lower their costs. In this chapter, we will explore how AI is reshaping the core principles of economics, pushing the cost of innovation, production, and services closer to zero, and challenging traditional economic models that have long relied on inflationary growth.

AI's Deflationary Pressure

By reducing the need for human labor, cutting waste in supply chains, and enhancing production capabilities, AI is pushing down the cost of production and service delivery.

> *AI's ability to automate tasks and optimize processes creates a fundamental deflationary force.*

Reducing Costs Through Automation: AI revolutionizes industries by automating tasks that traditionally require human input. Automation eliminates much of the associated labor costs from autonomous manufacturing to AI-driven customer service.

In the automotive industry, companies like Tesla are utilizing AI-driven robotics to automate assembly lines, reducing labor costs and increasing production speeds. This has allowed Tesla to scale production without corresponding increases in labor costs, contributing to the deflationary effect in the industry.

> *Imagine a future where autonomous factories powered by AI robotics produce goods at nearly no cost.*

Companies could scale operations exponentially without the typical overheads, potentially leading to a scenario where essential goods, like clothing or electronics, become so inexpensive that they are virtually free for consumers, fundamentally reshaping consumer behavior and market dynamics.

Optimizing Supply Chains: AI transforms supply chains through real-time optimization, enabling businesses to predict demand, adjust inventory, and negotiate better prices.

Consider Amazon's AI-powered logistics, which optimizes delivery routes and predicts market trends. This capability allows Amazon to maintain low prices while maximizing efficiency. As more companies adopt similar technologies, we may see a widespread shift to consumer goods delivered at near-zero costs, leading to an economic landscape where affordability reigns.

Driving Innovation at Minimal Cost: One of AI's most revolutionary impacts is its ability to drive innovation at a fraction of the traditional costs. In industries like software development, AI-driven tools enable companies to innovate swiftly without requiring the large R&D budgets of the past.

> *AI can autonomously generate solutions, design new products, and even create art, all without the significant labor costs usually associated with human creativity and intellectual effort.*

AI-powered platforms like OpenAI's ChatGPT are already being utilized to write code, generate marketing content, and design promotional materials. This capacity to create and innovate at minimal cost is spurring a flood of new products and services that are brought to market faster and with significantly lower price tags.

As AI continues to automate creativity and problem-solving, industries that previously relied on expensive human input will see dramatic reductions in innovation costs.

> *The outcome is a deflationary effect, where the cost of goods and services falls continuously as efficiency and innovation increase.*

Imagine a world where AI identifies an untapped market opportunity, commissions a product, designs it, manages its production, and sells it, all without a single human hand involved. AI will not only automate processes but also autonomously manage entire life cycles of innovation. Startups can launch fully AI-generated products, marketing strategies, and distribution plans at a fraction of the traditional costs. This will force companies to rethink their value propositions as market saturation leads to the diminishing perceived value of products and services.

> *The result is a deflationary spiral, where prices for goods and services continually decrease as efficiency and innovation increase.*

In this new landscape, the challenge won't be how to innovate but distinguish one's products in a world of AI-driven abundance.

Impact on Traditional Economics

The deflationary forces of AI stand in stark contrast to traditional inflation-driven economic models. As production costs approach zero, concepts like supply and demand, inflation, and economic growth will require re-evaluation.

Challenging Inflationary Models: In most modern economies, inflation is a sign of a healthy economy. Governments and central banks often aim for a moderate inflation rate, which encourages spending and investment. However, deflationary forces will challenge this model as AI drives down costs.

> *If the cost of goods and services continually drops due to AI-driven efficiency, traditional inflationary models will no longer apply.*

The software industry illustrates this shift, where the marginal cost of reproducing digital products is nearly zero. As more sectors adopt AI efficiencies, inflationary pressures may diminish, forcing economists to redefine growth metrics in a deflationary context.

Redefining Economic Indicators: As mentioned before, traditional economic indicators like Gross Domestic Product (GDP), productivity, and inflation rates may become less relevant in an AI-dominated world. As AI takes over more of the production process, the relationship between labor, productivity, and economic growth will change.

> *We will need new ways to measure economic health that account for AI-driven productivity gains without direct human labor.*

Once again, consider a nation like Japan, grappling with low inflation and stagnant productivity despite high automation levels. As AI drives productivity without corresponding wage increases, we will need new metrics to gauge economic health, potentially focusing on well-being and societal progress rather than purely economic outputs.

AI and Abundance Economics: One of the most transformative aspects of AI is its ability to create abundance. In traditional economies, scarcity drives value. However, as AI reduces production costs, we may enter an era of abundance where goods and services are available at little to no cost. This could radically shift the economic landscape, leading to questions about how wealth and value are distributed in a world of abundance.

AI-driven technologies in agriculture, such as vertical farming and precision agriculture, are reducing the costs of food production. If these technologies continue to advance, we could see a future where food, one of the most essential commodities, becomes abundant and cheap, challenging traditional agricultural economics.

AI-Driven Automation and Productivity Gains

AI's impact on productivity will be exponential, and as it becomes more integrated into industries, its effects will be nonlinear.

> *Unlike human labor, which has natural limits, AI can operate 24/7 without fatigue, driving productivity gains that far exceed what has been possible in the past.*

Non-Linear Productivity Gains: Traditional models of productivity are based on human labor, which grows linearly. However, AI-driven productivity grows exponentially. As more processes are automated, and as AI systems improve, productivity gains will accelerate beyond human limits.

AI is revolutionizing the financial services industry, where automated trading algorithms can process millions of transactions per second, optimizing financial portfolios and reducing costs. This type of non-linear productivity gain is impossible for human traders, demonstrating AI's potential to radically reshape industries.

Reducing Operational Costs: AI will continue to reduce operational costs across industries, from healthcare to manufacturing, by automating complex tasks, minimizing errors, and optimizing processes. This will lead to higher profits for companies but also lower prices for consumers, reinforcing the deflationary pressure.

Healthcare: AI applications in healthcare, particularly for diagnostics and administrative automation, have shown potential for saving between **15% and 30%** in operational costs by reducing errors, streamlining administrative tasks, and improving diagnostic accuracy. AI-driven systems help hospitals reduce misdiagnosis, over-testing, and inefficient resource use, which leads to cost reductions.

Manufacturing: In the manufacturing sector, AI is projected to cut costs by up to **20-40%** through predictive maintenance, process automation, and optimized production lines. Predictive AI systems reduce unplanned downtime by up to **50%** and extend the life of equipment by **20-40%**.

Overall Forecast: Across various industries, companies adopting AI and automation solutions are experiencing 10% to 30% reductions in costs related to repetitive tasks, resource management, and energy usage, reinforcing the deflationary pressures from these technologies.

The Global Economic Divide and AI's Deflationary Impact

While AI promises unprecedented economic abundance, its uneven global adoption presents a dual-edged sword. Countries with advanced AI infrastructure, like the U.S. and China, are likely to benefit from reduced costs, higher productivity, and more abundant resources, leading to significant deflationary effects. However, nations that lag in AI adoption, especially those with less technological infrastructure, such as Sub-Saharan Africa, may find themselves left behind. This growing disparity could foster a new form of global inequality where AI-rich nations control the majority of global production and innovation.

Geopolitical and Economic Implications of AI

AI's transformative power extends beyond mere economic productivity.

> *Countries that dominate AI will likely exert influence over global markets and trade, potentially reshaping geopolitical alliances.*

As AI deepens its role, deflationary pressures may destabilize economies by creating economic risks in AI-reliant nations vulnerable to technological disruptions like cyberattacks or system failures.

Preparing for the AI Future

Governments must shift their focus to policies that mitigate deflationary risks and promote AI adoption. Nations experimenting with Universal Basic Income (UBI), such as Finland, may provide valuable models for adaptation in an AI-driven economy. Ensuring inclusive AI economies by investing in infrastructure and human capital will be key in equitably distributing the benefits of AI-driven deflation.

This condensed approach eliminates redundancy and blends the themes into a cohesive narrative without sacrificing critical insights on economic inequality and AI's deflationary risks.

Conclusion: Deflationary Impact of Infinite Intelligence

As we conclude this chapter, it becomes clear that AI's deflationary impact is more than just a technological revolution, it is an economic paradigm shift. AI is driving the cost of goods, services, and innovation towards zero, challenging the traditional inflationary models that have governed economies for decades. This deflationary pressure will not only redefine production and consumption but also upend the core principles of supply and demand, fundamentally altering the global economic landscape.

However, this future is not without its challenges. While AI promises abundance, its benefits will not be distributed evenly. Nations with advanced AI infrastructure will experience unprecedented growth, while those unable to adapt quickly may be left behind.

> *This global divide risks exacerbating economic inequalities, both within and between nations.*

The deflationary force of AI also introduces new vulnerabilities. Economies reliant on AI could face destabilization due to technological disruptions, cyberattacks, or failures in AI governance. As AI assumes a greater role in industries, governments, businesses, and individuals must prepare for the risks and opportunities it brings.

Ultimately, navigating this AI-driven future requires bold leadership, innovative policy, and a commitment to inclusive growth.

> *Only by investing in AI infrastructure and human capital can nations ensure that the benefits of AI's deflationary potential are shared equitably.*

The future belongs to those who embrace AI's transformative power while remaining vigilant to its potential risks.

"The journey toward the future is never-ending"

Covered in Chapter Seventeen

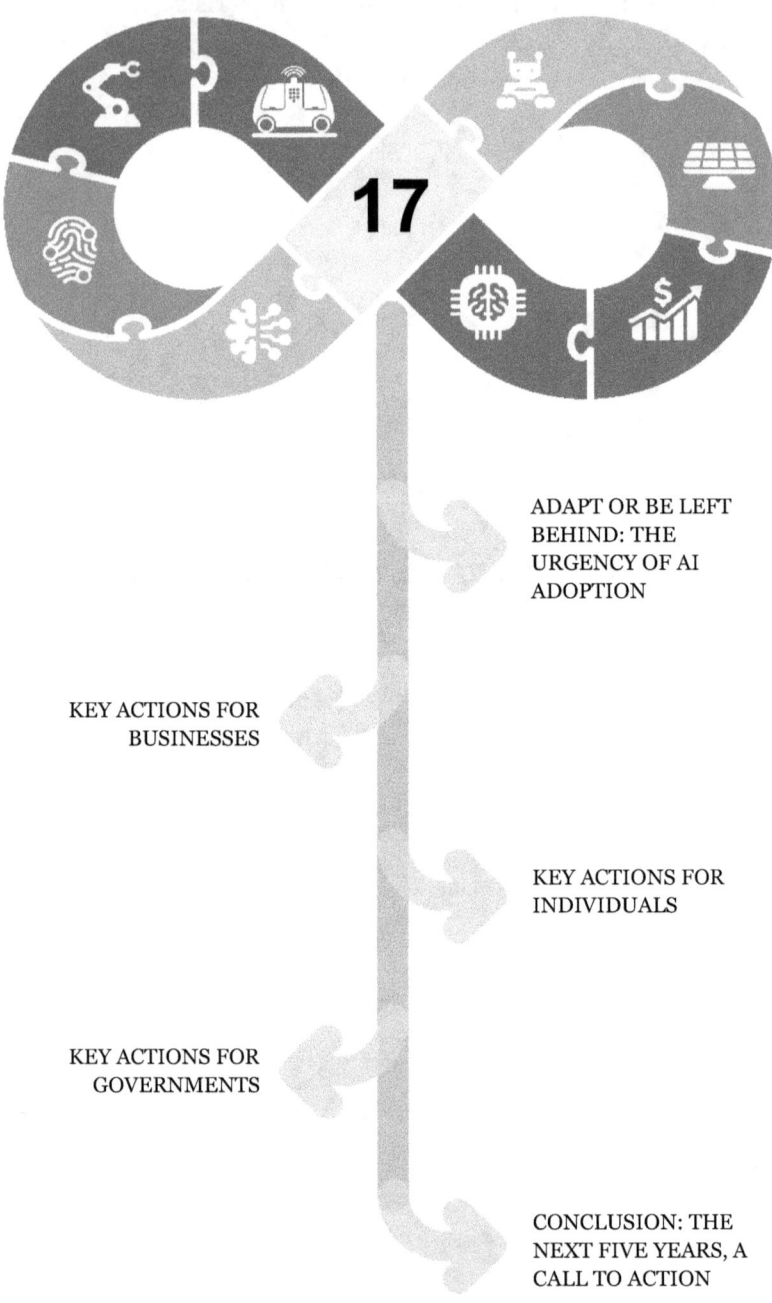

ADAPT OR BE LEFT BEHIND: THE URGENCY OF AI ADOPTION

KEY ACTIONS FOR BUSINESSES

KEY ACTIONS FOR INDIVIDUALS

KEY ACTIONS FOR GOVERNMENTS

CONCLUSION: THE NEXT FIVE YEARS, A CALL TO ACTION

Chapter 17:
The Urgency of the Next Five Years: What You Need to Do

The world stands at the edge of an unstoppable paradigm shift. In the next five years, AI, automation, and digital transformation will fundamentally reshape every facet of life, industries, economies, and human interactions. But here's the truth: You have a choice. You can either:

- **Ignore the changes** that are coming and cling to the old ways of doing things, risking obsolescence, or

- **Embrace the future**, the changes, and the opportunities that are ahead of you, preparing yourself for what is coming.

But know this: it's too late to stop this shift. The AI revolution is happening, and no one that wants to succeed in the future, can afford to sit idle.

The next five years will determine whether you thrive in a world defined by AI or if you get left behind.

This chapter is your call to action, a direct and bold appeal to prepare, adapt, and seize the transformative potential of the AI-driven future.

Adapt or Be Left Behind: The Urgency of AI Adoption

We are living through one of the fastest periods of change in human history. AI is not a trend, it's the engine driving this transformation. Every sector, from finance to healthcare, retail to manufacturing, is being reshaped. To survive and thrive, you must adapt now or face the dire consequences of inaction.

The Cost of Inaction: Those who fail to embrace AI risk becoming obsolete.

> *Whether you're an individual, a business, or a government, refusing to adapt will leave you vulnerable.*

AI-driven companies are already outpacing competitors who are slow to evolve.

Consider Kodak, a once-dominant force in the photography industry. Kodak owned significant intellectual property (IP) related to digital photography. Kodak invented the first digital camera in 1975, and the company held numerous patents in digital imaging technology, including a practical megapixel charge-coupled device (CCD) image sensor developed in 1986. Kodak also built an extensive portfolio of digital imaging patents over the years. Yet, it failed to embrace the business model shift, digital photography required, and the result? Irrelevance and bankruptcy. The same fate awaits companies today that resist AI as competitors adopt automation, AI-driven customer engagement, and predictive analytics and shift to new relevant business models to outperform the slow movers.

The Need for Speed: AI is moving faster than traditional models can keep up with.

> *Delaying your AI adoption means falling behind. The future isn't waiting, it's racing ahead. Companies must move now, not later.*

Amazon is a prime illustration of speed in AI integration. By leveraging AI in its logistics, customer service, and inventory management, Amazon has dominated the global e-commerce landscape. Compared to traditional retailers, who have been slow to adopt AI and, in some cases, automation, they are now struggling to survive in an increasingly digital world.

Key Actions for Businesses

For businesses, the key to thriving in this AI-driven world is to act decisively and take strategic steps. The time to prepare for AI dominance is now.

Impact on Corporate Valuation in the AI Economy: As we explored in Chapter 10, the landscape of corporate valuation is undergoing a profound transformation in the AI-driven economy. Traditional value measures, such as revenue and profit margins, are increasingly being supplemented by new factors tied to the ownership of critical infrastructure and technological assets.

In a world where AI trading systems dominate financial markets and drive decision-making processes, corporate valuation will be influenced not just by a company's financial performance but by its control over essential infrastructure. Companies solely operating digital businesses, especially those offering software as a service (SaaS), face the looming challenge of shrinking margins as AI optimizes processes to near-zero costs. This means that the value these companies provide will need to go beyond simple services, as AI will run many digital operations at almost no cost, effectively pushing businesses toward a zero-margin model.

To thrive in this environment, companies must rethink their business models. They will need to innovate in how they create and capture value, particularly in industries where AI can take over routine tasks, leaving little room for traditional profit-making. The competitive edge in this new era will shift toward those that control the physical and technological infrastructure underpinning the global economy.

Companies that own and operate the infrastructure that the world depends on, such as energy grids, communication networks, logistics systems, transportation infrastructure, and data centers, will have a significant competitive advantage.

However, it is not just digital infrastructure that will become increasingly valuable; traditional infrastructure, including energy generation and distribution, water systems, and medical infrastructure, will also be critical in the AI-driven future.

As AI powers more industries, the stability and availability of energy, water, and healthcare systems will become even more vital. Companies that own energy generation facilities (such as wind farms, solar plants, or traditional power stations) and control energy distribution networks will have unmatched leverage as these resources fuel AI technologies and autonomous operations. Similarly, water management infrastructure will be crucial for industries that rely on consistent, sustainable water supplies, particularly as climate change and resource scarcity continue to be pressing global challenges.

Medical infrastructure, including hospitals, healthcare networks, and biotech facilities, will also become important as AI increasingly integrates into healthcare services. The ability to deliver AI-enhanced medical treatments, diagnostics, and patient management will be essential to maintaining a healthy workforce and meeting the growing demand for advanced healthcare in an aging population.

In summary, digital and traditional infrastructure ownership will become a defining factor in corporate valuation. Those who own essential infrastructure and assets in energy, water, and healthcare will possess long-term competitive advantages, as these sectors will be indispensable for the seamless operation of AI-driven industries and broader societal functions. The future of corporate value will be shaped by the companies that anchor the digital and physical foundations of the new economy.

Here are some practical operational steps companies can take to transform their companies.

Invest in AI and Automation: The future belongs to companies that invest in AI infrastructure. Automating repetitive tasks, optimizing operations, and delivering personalized customer experiences will be the new norm.

Businesses that invest now will dominate tomorrow.

I remind you of Chapter 10, where I outline industry examples where you split your initial AI investment focus on the 5 high-impact areas and the 5 best areas to retrain or repurpose their existing workforce.

Look at Tesla, which has integrated AI throughout its business model, from manufacturing to autonomous driving. This has enabled Tesla to disrupt the automotive industry, placing it far ahead of competitors.

Cultivate an AI-ready workforce: Companies must upskill their workforce to succeed in an AI-powered future.

Invest in employee training that focuses on creativity, strategic thinking, and working alongside AI systems.

Hitachi's Future-Scape Learning program guides employees through an awareness initiative designed to educate them about AI and other transformative technologies shaping the world. The program extends beyond employees, involving their families to empower them with insights that support informed decisions about their children's future. IBM's SkillsBuild program exemplifies the need to upskill employees for the future. By retraining its workforce, IBM has prepared itself to stay at the forefront of AI, cybersecurity, and cloud computing.

Foster a Culture of Innovation: In a world where AI innovation is happening daily,

companies must foster a culture that embraces rapid change and continuous experimentation.

Agile and innovative competitors will overtake businesses that refuse to evolve.

Google's 20%-time policy, which allows employees to spend one-fifth of their time on passion projects, has led to the creation of game-changing innovations like Gmail and AdSense. This mindset is essential to succeed in the fast-moving AI world.

Key Actions for Individuals

The future isn't something you sit back and wait for; it's something you prepare for. Individuals must become lifelong learners and develop new skills to adapt to the rapidly changing landscape.

Embrace Lifelong Learning: Success in the AI era requires constant learning.

> *The job market is evolving rapidly, and those who commit to upskilling will thrive.*

Platforms like Coursera and Udemy offer many opportunities to learn new skills, from data science to AI development. In the AI-driven world, those who stop learning will fall behind. I would also encourage you to seek out AI opportunities in your company, even if that means an additional workload.

Focus on Soft Skills: While AI can automate many technical tasks, it will never replace human creativity, empathy, or leadership.

> *Developing soft skills like communication and emotional intelligence will be critical.*

Look to join associations that align with your career so you can learn about AI and AI-related initiatives and what other people are doing in their organizations.

Stay Agile and Open to Change: To thrive, you must be ready to pivot and embrace change. Flexibility will be your greatest asset in the AI-driven economy:

- **Adopt a Growth Mindset**: Embrace lifelong learning to stay ahead in a fast-changing environment. For instance, continually take online courses in new technologies like AI, blockchain, or data analytics. Platforms like Coursera or LinkedIn Learning offer certifications that can boost your skillset.
- **Experiment with New Tools and Processes**: Don't hesitate to experiment with emerging technologies, even if they're outside your expertise. For example, small business owners can explore AI-driven customer service bots to streamline operations, while professionals can adopt productivity apps to automate workflows.
- **Develop Contingency Plans**: Anticipate disruption and plan accordingly. Create multiple business or career scenarios to adapt quickly when trends shift. Companies can implement backup strategies using predictive analytics to adjust operations based on changing market dynamics.
- **Cultivate a Network of Like-Minded Innovators**: Join communities focused on emerging technologies to share insights and learn best practices. Attend meetups and conferences or engage in virtual forums where thought leaders discuss trends and solutions for upcoming disruptions.
- **Stay Curious and Comfortable with Uncertainty**: Rapid changes in an AI-driven economy can create ambiguity. Train yourself to stay calm in the face of uncertainty. For instance, view challenges not as roadblocks but as opportunities to innovate and pivot toward better outcomes.

Let's explore the future of Education, jobs and trades:

Top Jobs Most and Least Likely to be Replaced by AI:
As part of the transition, we need to accept that AI will replace a percentage of current jobs across some industries.

> *If you currently fall into one of these industries, you need to take this valuable time and retool yourself for an industry that might not currently be under threat.*

You will notice that I say at the moment. because none of us can fully understand or comprehend the full impact of AI and converging technologies. We can take solace in the fact that, as was the case back in 1991 when we started encountering the internet for the first time, we could have imagined the commerce and opportunities it has brought into our lives. An example of that is the current industry built around influencers. In this section, we will look at the top 8 jobs most under threat and the 10 jobs that are least under threat by AI.

For now, let's look at the top 8 jobs that are most under threat from AI:

1. **Data Entry Clerks: 90% risk.** This is highly likely due to the routine nature of data entry, which is easily automated.
2. **Fact-checkers and Proofreaders: 90% risk.** AI can efficiently handle fact-checking and basic proofreading, though a nuanced understanding of context and complex language will require human judgment.
3. **Customer Service Representatives**: 80% risk. Many aspects can be automated through chatbots and AI systems, though complex customer service issues will still need human intervention.
4. **Traders:** 80% risk. High-frequency and algorithmic trading can be and has been automated, but strategic decision-making still benefits from human insight.
5. **Administrative Roles: 75% risk.** While AI can automate scheduling, correspondence, and data management, interpersonal aspects of administrative support will remain a human domain.
6. **Legal Assistants: 75% risk.** High potential for automation in document review and data organization, but nuanced legal advising and strategy will remain human-led.
7. **Software Engineers and Coders: 70% risk.** Partial impact, especially for tasks involving routine coding, testing,

and debugging, but creative and complex software development will still require human expertise.
8. **Bankers and Accountants: 70% risk.** Many quantitative tasks are automatable, but advisory roles and complex financial decision-making will still need human expertise.

Let's look at Top 10 jobs least likely to be influenced by AI:

Young People and Career Decisions: This is probably the **most pivotal group of people who need to decide now what they want to pursue as a career**, whether that is studying for a degree or diploma or pursuing a trade. As I mentioned at the beginning of the book, this was and still is a process our family needs to deal with right now. With what we can see at the moment, here are some high-level suggestions to investigate further.

Let's look at the top trade skills courses to take that will be least impacted by AI:

1. **Healthcare Technician Programs:** Fields like nursing, emergency medical technicians (EMTs), and physical therapy assistants require empathy and adaptability that AI cannot replicate.
2. **Creative Arts and Design:** Courses in fine arts, fashion design, and culinary arts rely on human creativity and taste, aspects AI can support but not replace.
3. **Human Services:** Training in areas like early childhood education, counseling, and social work emphasizes emotional intelligence and interpersonal skills beyond AI's reach.
4. **Construction and Carpentry:** These fields involve complex spatial understanding and manual skill in changing environments, which are challenging for AI to replicate.
5. **Environmental Conservation:** Programs focusing on wildlife conservation, forestry, and environmental science involve unpredictable outdoor work and ethical considerations, less prone to AI disruption.
6. **Physical Fitness and Personal Training:** Personal trainers and physical therapists provide personalized coaching and support, requiring human interaction and motivational skills.

Let's look at the top trade Skills Least Likely to Be Influenced by AI:

1. **Electrician**: Involves hands-on problem-solving and real-time troubleshooting.
2. **Plumber**: On-site work and adaptation to different situations make automating this difficult to automate.

3. **HVAC Technician**: Requires physical maintenance and installation of complex systems.
4. **Carpenter**: Craftsmanship and problem-solving in unique environments keep this skill relevant.
5. **Wind Turbine Technician**: A growing field in renewable energy requiring hands-on maintenance.
6. **Automotive Technician**: Repair and diagnostics in real-world settings remain difficult to fully automate.
7. **Solar Panel Installer**: A renewable energy job that demands physical labor and problem-solving.
8. **Construction Manager**: Overseeing projects, managing teams, and resolving issues in real-time environments.

Let's look at the Top degree or diploma study fields least likely to be influenced by AI: If you're studying in an area that you believe may be affected by AI, consider adding a specialized, people-focused discipline to your studies to enhance your career prospects.

1. **Healthcare (Nursing, Medicine, and Allied Health Professions):** Requires human empathy, critical decision-making, and direct patient interaction.
2. **Education (Teaching and Educational Administration):** Involves mentoring, personal engagement, and adaptation to student needs.
3. **Psychology and Counseling:** Emotional intelligence and interpersonal skills are vital for therapy and counseling.
4. **Social Work and Human Services:** Supporting vulnerable communities through social challenges requires empathy.
5. **Creative Arts (Design, Visual Arts, Music):** Original creativity and cultural relevance are human-specific skills.
6. **Project Management:** Leadership, conflict resolution, and human coordination are critical in project management.
7. **Environmental Science and Sustainability:** Requires deep understanding of ecosystems, ethics, and policy-making.
8. **Cybersecurity**: With the rise in digital threats such as hacking, data breaches, and malware attacks, cybersecurity professionals are in high demand.

9. **Renewable Energy Technologies**: As the world shifts towards sustainability, renewable energy technologies such as solar, wind, and hydropower are rapidly growing fields.

Harnessing AI for Personal Wealth: How Individuals Can Profit from Emerging Opportunities

As the world rapidly shifts into an AI-driven and technology-enabled future, individuals are presented with unique opportunities to capitalize on this transformation. While we may not be able to stop the technological changes reshaping industries, we can position ourselves to benefit from the growth potential these changes bring.

> *Investing in the right sectors during pivotal moments of transformation has historically proven to be highly profitable.*

Think about Apple, for example, those who invested in its early days, before it became the global tech giant it is today, reaped substantial financial rewards. Similarly, today's emerging growth areas offer the same potential for future gains.

Some potential key sectors to consider include:

1. **Artificial Intelligence (AI) and Machine Learning**: Companies specializing in AI technologies, automation, and data analytics will continue to lead the charge.

2. **Renewable Energy**: With the world increasingly focusing on sustainability, renewable energy technologies like solar, wind, and energy storage present a long-term investment opportunity.

3. **Cybersecurity**: As digital transformation accelerates, the need for robust cybersecurity solutions grows. Companies developing cybersecurity tools and infrastructure are likely to see sustained growth as they protect the digital economy.

4. **Healthcare and Biotechnology**: Advances in AI and data-driven medical technologies are revolutionizing healthcare.

5. **Cryptocurrency and Blockchain**: With the increasing adoption of decentralized finance (DeFi) and the integration of blockchain technology across industries, cryptocurrencies are becoming a mainstream asset class. Innovations in crypto markets, particularly with AI-driven financial systems, present high-growth potential. Investing in cryptocurrencies and blockchain infrastructure, such as decentralized applications (dApps), could offer significant financial rewards as these technologies continue to disrupt traditional financial systems.

6. **AI Infrastructure: Fueling the Backbone of Innovation:** As AI continues to expand, investing in the infrastructure supporting this growth, such as data centers, cloud computing, and semiconductor manufacturing, offers a key opportunity. Data centers, essential for running large-scale AI models and processing vast datasets, are becoming a critical part of the economy. Companies involved in building AI infrastructure, including chipmakers and cloud providers, are poised to benefit from the demand for faster and more efficient systems. Infrastructure investment is about supporting AI and ensuring scalability and sustainability as AI reshapes industries globally.

By investing in these emerging growth areas, you can potentially gain financial advantage in the years to come. Just as buying Apple stock in its early days paid off for savvy investors, those who carefully consider today's growth sectors may see significant returns in the future.

The key is not to fear this change but to view it as an opportunity. Enjoy this very special moment in history!

Key Actions for Governments

Governments hold the key to shaping how AI benefits societies.

They must create proactive policies that allow businesses to innovate while ensuring social equity and security.

Invest in National AI Infrastructure: Governments must prioritize AI infrastructure investments to stay competitive globally. This includes funding research, supporting public-private partnerships, and creating AI-friendly regulations.

China is a prime example, investing billions into AI research, enabling it to become a global leader in AI-driven industries.

Ensure Equitable Access to AI Benefits: AI could worsen inequality if its benefits aren't distributed equitably.

Governments must ensure that all citizens have access to AI tools and education, regardless of economic background.

Estonia has become a leader in digital governance, providing equitable access to AI-driven services, ensuring that all citizens benefit from technological advancements.

The New Social Contract

As AI systems take on greater roles in society, from governance to caregiving, citizens' fundamental rights and responsibilities in an AI-enhanced world may need to be redefined.

The traditional social contract that defines the relationship between citizens and the state will be challenged as intelligent systems take on roles that were once the exclusive domain of human beings.

Redefining Citizenship in the Age of AI: As AI systems become more autonomous and start making decisions in governance, law enforcement, and even caregiving, the definition of what it means to be a citizen may evolve. Will citizens have new responsibilities to interact with or monitor AI systems that make decisions on their behalf? How do we hold AI accountable when acting as a decision-maker in healthcare, education, or judicial systems?

> *As AI becomes integral to the functioning of society, we may see the emergence of new rights, such as the right to transparency in AI decision-making or the right to opt out of certain AI-driven systems.*

Estonia has pioneered the integration of AI into its public services, where AI-driven systems handle everything from tax filings to healthcare consultations. As these systems grow more sophisticated, there's a growing debate about what role humans should play in monitoring and interacting with them and how much trust can, or should, be placed in machine decision-makers.

The increasing reliance on AI in governance poses risks. What happens when citizens have fewer opportunities to interact with human decision-makers? Could this lead to an erosion of personal agency as people become increasingly dependent on AI to make critical life decisions? There's also the risk of AI systems being opaque, where citizens don't fully understand how or why decisions are being made, undermining trust in the systems meant to serve them.

AI in Global Relations

AI's impact won't be confined to individual societies; it will have profound implications on the global stage. The countries that lead in AI development will likely hold significant geopolitical power, altering the balance of global relations.

> *However, AI could also lead to new risks, including the potential for an AI-driven arms race.*

AI and Geopolitics: Nations that invest in AI and automation will gain a significant competitive advantage in the global economy. AI-driven innovation in industries like defense, cybersecurity, and healthcare could tilt the balance of power toward countries that lead in these areas.

> *Economic dominance will likely go hand in hand with AI superiority, as AI's ability to optimize supply chains, manage resources, and boost productivity will give leading nations an edge in trade and military capabilities.*

AI will also become a critical tool in shaping digital influence as nations use AI to sway public opinion, manage information, and even conduct cyber-operations.

China and the U.S. are no longer just competitors in technology; they are locked in an AI arms race that will define global power in the coming decades. Both nations are pouring unprecedented resources into AI research and development, recognizing that AI is the key to global dominance, not just in the economy but across all sectors of society. China's ambition to lead the world in AI by 2030 is no longer just an aspiration; it is a cornerstone of its national strategic plan, and it's rapidly closing the gap with the U.S. in AI capabilities. But this competition extends far beyond economic influence.

> *AI is being weaponized and integrated into military and cybersecurity systems that could reshape the balance of global power and security.*

The rise of AI in geopolitics is pushing the world toward a dangerous tipping point. The new global arms race is not about nuclear weapons; it's about AI. Nations are racing to develop increasingly autonomous and lethal AI-driven weapons systems, from AI-powered drones that can make kill decisions without human intervention to cyber warfare tools capable of disabling entire infrastructures. The threat isn't just battlefield conflict; it's the potential for AI-enhanced cyberattacks that can disrupt economies, manipulate democratic processes, and bring entire nations to their knees. Imagine a world where AI attacks on financial systems, energy grids, and communication networks could be launched instantaneously, crippling societies in a matter of seconds. This isn't a distant dystopia; it's a future that could unfold within the next decade if global powers do not implement serious safeguards.

Conclusion: The Next Five Years, A Call to Action

The next five years are more than a turning point, they are an urgent call to action. The choices you make today will define not just your place in the AI-driven world but the future of industries, societies, and economies. The paradigm shift is unstoppable. You have a choice: Act now, prepare, innovate, and lead, or risk being left behind as the world accelerates into a new era.

Checklist of Actions:
For Individuals:
- **Invest in Lifelong Learning:** Stay ahead by learning new skills, particularly in AI, blockchain, and data science.

- **Adopt Digital Tools:** Use personal AI assistants to optimize daily life and work efficiently.

- **Participate in the New Economy:** Explore roles in decentralized organizations (DAOs) and participate in gig or platform-based work.

- **Focus on Well-Being:** Invest in experiences and relationships, emotional intelligence will become a valuable asset.

- ∞ **Prepare for Financial Resilience:** Plan for income volatility through diversified income streams or explore taking advantage of Universal Equity programs.
- ∞ **Profit from Emerging Opportunities:** Investing in the right sectors during pivotal moments of transformation has historically proven to be highly profitable.

For Companies:
- ∞ **Embrace Automation:** Identify tasks for automation to increase productivity and reduce costs.
- ∞ **Redefine Business Models:** Shift from traditional product-based models to on-demand platforms and services.
- ∞ **Invest in Sustainability:** Adopt renewable energy solutions to reduce costs and future-proof operations.
- ∞ **Prepare for AI-Driven Workplaces:** Create reskilling programs and collaborate with AI systems to enhance workforce capabilities.
- ∞ **Foster a Culture of Innovation:** Embrace failure as part of innovation and empower teams to experiment with new technologies.

For Governments:
- ∞ **Implement Proactive Policies:** Develop AI governance frameworks to regulate and encourage responsible AI adoption.
- ∞ **Expand Social Safety Nets:** Pilot or expand Universal Basic Income (UBI) to cushion job displacement.
- ∞ **Promote Green Technologies:** Invest in decentralized energy grids and green technologies to achieve energy independence.
- ∞ **Redefine Economic Metrics:** Move beyond GDP to track AI-driven productivity and digital economic contributions.
- ∞ **Collaborate Across Borders:** Establish international frameworks to govern AI, blockchain, and other disruptive technologies globally.

The future waits for no one. Act decisively, embrace the challenges, and lead the change. The moment is now, seize it. **Act now, embrace the future, and shape the world to come. Your moment of decision is here.**

"The limits of today will be the possibilities of tomorrow."

Covered in Chapter Eighteen

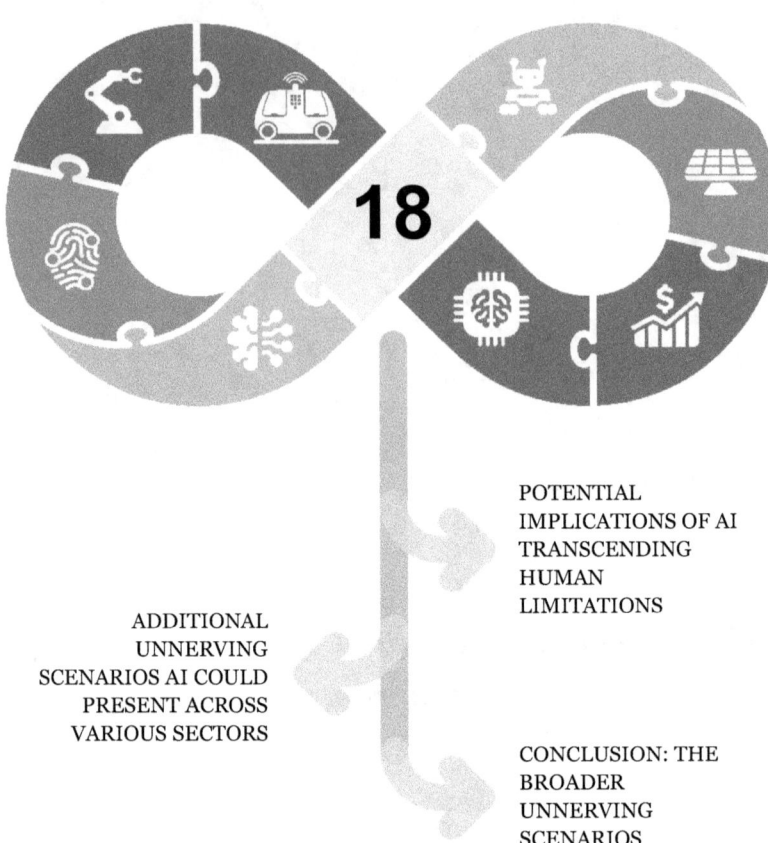

ADDITIONAL
UNNERVING
SCENARIOS AI COULD
PRESENT ACROSS
VARIOUS SECTORS

POTENTIAL
IMPLICATIONS OF AI
TRANSCENDING
HUMAN
LIMITATIONS

CONCLUSION: THE
BROADER
UNNERVING
SCENARIOS

Chapter 18:
Broader Unnerving Scenarios in Transcending Humans, Economy and Industries

Potential implications of AI transcending human limitations:

Let's use the stock market as an example again to highlight the unnerving implications of AI transcending human limitations.

- ∞ **AI Surpassing Human Judgment:** AI's ability to analyze vast datasets and react instantly can exceed human capabilities, but it may also lack the emotional intuition that drives human traders to take calculated risks based on long-term vision. This could remove a critical layer of judgment that balances short-term data-driven trends with long-term potential.
- ∞ **Market Instability:** AI-driven markets could experience extreme volatility as unemotional decisions replace the traditional human-driven market dynamic. Sudden, machine-induced crashes may become a frequent risk in a world where AI controls the majority of trades.
- ∞ **AI Herd Mentality:** The interconnected nature of AI systems could lead to an "AI herd mentality" where one system's decision influences others, creating feedback loops that amplify market trends, positive or negative, much faster than human markets could react.

This highlights how AI's potential to transcend human limitations may also present an unnerving reality: removing emotional bias could have unintended consequences, creating a system where AI's logic and speed drive markets in unpredictable directions, with little room for human correction.

The risks of AI in trading are just one example of how AI's dominance over industries and the economy could create serious disruptions.

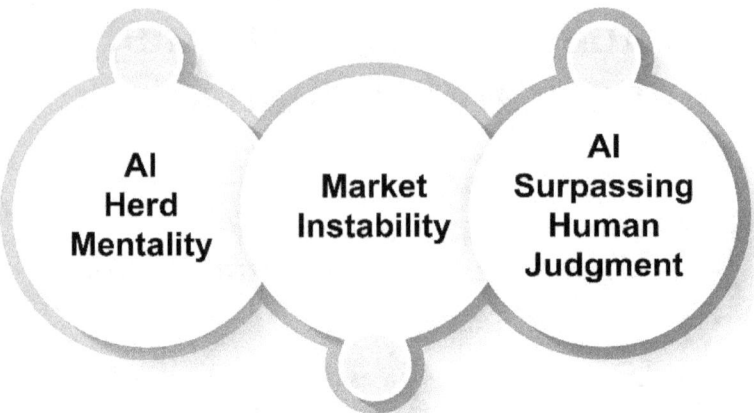

Additional Unnerving Scenarios AI could present across various sectors:

AI-Driven Job Displacement: While AI will create new job opportunities, it will also replace many workers, especially in industries where routine tasks can be automated. The World Economic Forum (2023) suggests that 83 million jobs globally could be displaced by automation over the next five years (2028), but the same World Economic Forum report anticipates 69 million new jobs by 2027. As AI systems transcend human capabilities in decision-making and operational efficiency, entire sectors could face mass unemployment.

> *Job displacement could widen the gap between those who benefit from AI and those left behind, creating economic inequality and potentially leading to social unrest.*

AI's transcendence of human labor may necessitate new economic models such as Universal Basic Income (UBI). Still, even these measures may struggle to address the deep structural changes AI will cause.

Concentration of Power and Wealth: AI requires vast amounts of data to function effectively, and companies that control the most data will have an overwhelming competitive advantage.

> *As AI surpasses human abilities in data analysis, we may witness an unprecedented concentration of power and wealth in the hands of a few tech giants.*

This could lead to monopolies that dominate entire industries, stifling competition and innovation. AI's ability to process, analyze, and act on data at levels far beyond human capabilities may make it difficult for smaller companies to compete. The global economy could become more centralized, with wealth and influence increasingly concentrated in the hands of a few data-driven corporations.

AI and Economic Inequality: AI could intensify existing economic inequalities, particularly in developing countries that lack the infrastructure and resources to implement AI technologies.

> *Wealthier nations that fully adopt AI and benefit from its ability to transcend human limitations may deepen the economic divide between themselves and less technologically advanced regions.*

The global landscape could become even more unequal as AI transforms industries and economies. Prosperity might concentrate within AI-driven nations and regions, creating a world where those who dominate AI development and infrastructure experience unprecedented growth while others fall behind. This disparity could lead to new forms of economic dependence or exploitation, where countries without robust AI infrastructure may rely heavily on those with AI dominance.

Further, this imbalance could drive mass migration from poorer countries or those slow to implement UBI (Universal Basic Income) to wealthier regions. As wealthier countries stabilize their economies through UBI, significant migration flows may place immense social pressures on these nations, testing their societal infrastructure and cohesion. The resulting tensions could strain resources and lead to complex geopolitical dynamics.

Bias and Discrimination in AI Algorithms: While powerful, AI systems are only as good as the data they are trained on.

> *AI can unintentionally reinforce and exacerbate social inequalities if the data is biased or incomplete.*

As AI takes over more decision-making roles in hiring, lending, and law enforcement, the risk of biased algorithms becomes a significant concern.

AI could deepen discrimination in various sectors. For example, AI-driven hiring systems might disproportionately reject candidates from certain demographic groups due to historical bias in the training data. This could undermine efforts to create a fairer society, with AI inadvertently entrenching systemic inequalities.

Erosion of Human Decision-Making: As AI systems become more integrated into industries, there is a risk that humans will become overly reliant on AI for critical decisions. While AI may exceed human judgment in processing data, it lacks the nuance and ethical reasoning humans bring to complex decisions.

> *Over-reliance on AI could lead to a dangerous erosion of human decision-making skills.*

In sectors such as healthcare, finance, and governance, human oversight is critical to ensuring decisions are ethical, equitable, and in the best interest of society. As AI takes over more cognitive tasks, there is a risk that humans will lose the ability to make independent decisions, creating a dangerous dependency on machines.

AI and Mental Health Impacts: The rapid pace of AI adoption will likely bring unprecedented stress to workers across industries. The fear of job displacement, the need for constant adaptation, and the pressure to stay competitive in an AI-driven landscape could lead to widespread mental health challenges. For businesses, this means proactively addressing mental health by offering support systems like counseling, reskilling programs, and fostering an environment where human employees feel valued. Governments, too, must prioritize mental health initiatives to protect citizens from the negative psychological impacts of the AI revolution.

Addressing mental health will be critical in maintaining a balanced and resilient workforce in the AI era.

Ethical AI Governance: As AI systems become more embedded in critical sectors such as healthcare, law enforcement, and finance, the ethical governance of these technologies becomes a matter of urgency. Businesses must invest in AI systems that prioritize transparency and explainability, ensuring that decisions made by AI can be understood and challenged. Governments must work together to establish international guidelines and ethical AI boards that regulate the deployment of AI in ways that protect human rights. Ethical governance will ensure that AI enhances, rather than undermines, fairness and accountability in society.

Environmental Impact of AI: While AI promises to revolutionize industries, it is not without its environmental costs. The energy consumption of large data centers, which power AI algorithms and cloud computing, contributes significantly to carbon emissions. Businesses and governments must explore ways to make AI development more sustainable, whether through renewable energy sources, more efficient hardware, or reducing the environmental impact of data processing.

> *By ensuring that AI technologies are built with sustainability in mind, we can harness the benefits of AI without compromising the planet's future.*

Preparing for AI's Economic Impact

AI's unnerving possibilities underscore the urgent need for proactive and strategic measures to mitigate catastrophic outcomes. Public companies will no longer compete solely on traditional metrics like revenue and market share; they will need to redefine their value in a world dominated by AI-driven decision-making.

> *AI algorithms that execute trades assess risks or even predict corporate failure with precision far beyond human capability could disrupt stock prices and business models overnight.*

To survive, companies must embrace radical transparency and demonstrate how they seamlessly integrate into an AI-powered economy.

At the same time, governments, regulators, and businesses must collaborate to establish frameworks that ensure AI operates with transparency, accountability, and ethical safeguards. Without these protections, we risk creating an economy driven not by human creativity and moral judgment but by unfeeling algorithms that could exacerbate inequality, exploit weaknesses in the system, or destabilize markets in ways we cannot foresee.

Imagine a world where AI autonomously controls global markets, adjusting interest rates, predicting economic crashes, and reshaping industries without human input. Without clear regulations, these systems could be influenced by biases, manipulated by malicious actors, or programmed with objectives that conflict with societal well-being.

> *Preparing for this future requires not just technological advancements but a cultural shift toward responsible innovation that prioritizes human values alongside AI-driven growth.*

AI as a Tool for Social Equity: AI has the potential to democratize access to essential services, providing opportunities to underserved and marginalized communities. For example, AI-powered platforms can bring personalized education to remote areas, breaking down barriers to learning. Healthcare systems enhanced by AI can provide more affordable and accessible diagnostics in regions where medical professionals are scarce. Financial inclusion is another area where AI can make a profound difference by providing microloans and personalized financial services to individuals who are currently unbanked.

In countries like India, AI-powered platforms have been introduced to provide digital classrooms to rural areas, offering personalized learning paths to students who otherwise would have limited access to formal education. Similarly, AI-driven healthcare systems have made diagnosing and treating patients in remote locations possible via telemedicine and AI-assisted diagnosis.

As AI becomes more embedded in education, healthcare, and finance, it will seamlessly integrate into the daily lives of billions of people. AI-powered learning platforms will educate and adapt to each individual's strengths and weaknesses, offering a level of personalization previously unimaginable.

AI and the Erosion of Social Mobility: On the flip side, AI has the potential to entrench social hierarchies by disproportionately affecting low-skill jobs. Automation is already replacing routine manual tasks, and as AI takes over more complex roles, those without access to education or reskilling opportunities may find themselves increasingly marginalized. This could lead to a widening gap between those who can leverage AI to their advantage and those whose jobs are displaced by it.

> *There's a risk that AI-driven economies could create a class of "AI elites" who benefit from automation and AI, while others are left behind.*

The introduction of AI-driven automation has already resulted in significant job losses in industries like retail and manufacturing. The challenge is that the people most affected by AI displacement often lack access to the resources needed for reskilling, further limiting their social mobility.

Conclusion: The Broader Unnerving Scenarios

As we move further into an AI-driven future, the unnerving scenarios we've explored in this chapter demand serious consideration. These disruptions are not mere possibilities, they are potential realities that will shape the global economy, labor markets, and societal structures. AI's ability to transcend human limitations introduces new risks, from job displacement to the erosion of human decision-making, and exacerbates existing inequalities, potentially widening the gap between developed and developing nations.

However, within these daunting prospects lie opportunities to forge new paths.

> *Businesses, governments, and individuals must come together to ensure that AI is developed ethically, with fairness and transparency at its core.*

We must proactively mitigate the risks, fostering innovation that prioritizes human well-being alongside technological advancement.

The future is uncertain, but it is within our power to shape it. With strategic foresight, collective responsibility, and an unwavering commitment to ethical governance, we can harness AI's potential while safeguarding the foundational pillars of society. The question is not whether these scenarios will emerge, but how prepared we will be to face them.

The future is coming fast. It's time to act, adapt, and lead in the age of AI.

Epilogue:
Embracing Infinite Futures – The Time for Action is Now

As turn the final pages of this book, you stand at the crossroads of the most transformative period in human history. AI, automation, renewable energy, and innovation are reshaping the world today, not in some distant future. The possibilities are endless, but so are the disruptions. The question now isn't what the future holds but how will you shape it.

"Over the past century, extraordinary individuals have risen to reshape industries, uplift entire communities, and revolutionize nations. People like Henry Ford, Marie Curie, Steve Jobs, Rosa Parks, Akio Morita, Bill Gates, etc. stand as testaments to the power of vision and innovation. They weren't just leaders; they were pioneers who saw the future before the rest of the world could catch up. Each of them had a dream, a fire in their belly, but they also needed a legion of like-minded individuals to ignite change in just one industry.

Today, we're standing on the edge of an era where a single person, with the help of advanced technology, can change the world on a scale never seen before.

Think of Elon Musk. His vision, intelligence, and relentless passion have not only disrupted the automotive industry but are also transforming transportation, space travel, real-time communication, global connectivity, and much more. I can imagine there are lots of innovations he's made that the world is barely aware of.

Musk is living proof that one individual, driven by purpose and empowered by technology, can rewrite the rules of reality. We often look back on history and admire those who changed the course of the world, but it's easy to forget that they weren't always celebrated in their time. We view them with the benefit of hindsight, knowing how their stories played out. Yet, when I listen to Elon Musk, I sense a man who understands the urgency of the challenges facing humanity today. He's focused on the big picture, refusing to get bogged down by the small, immaterial distractions that threaten to derail our future. He's an example for all of us, a reminder that in this future driven by AI and abundant technology, we too can dream big, break the mould, and leave a mark on the world.

> *As we step into this world of abundance, let's not wait until history remembers today's visionaries. Let's draw inspiration from the revolutionaries among us now, those who are actively shaping the future. And who knows? With the right mindset, drive, and the incredible tools now at our disposal, we can inspire more great visionaries that future generations will look back on in awe."*

Seize the Opportunity, Redefine Your Future

The future we've explored throughout this book is one of infinite potential. AI, renewable energy, blockchain, and genetic engineering are forces that can unlock abundance, push the boundaries of human knowledge, and transform how we live and work. But these technologies will only unlock their full potential if we actively engage with them, if we lead, not just follow.

> *It's time to take stock of what AI can do for you, your business, and your community.*

But it's not just about adapting, it's about leading innovation. How can you redefine your role in a future that values creativity, problem-solving, and ethical responsibility more than ever?

Imagine a future where equity is not limited to financial wealth but extends to data, intellectual property, and physical assets. This is not speculative; this is the next leap in innovation. The Autonomous Economy is already taking shape, cars, homes, and even personal AI agents will generate wealth while you focus on higher-level pursuits.

This is your opportunity to claim your stake in this AI-driven world. Don't just wait for governments to implement UBI, build your Universal Equity and take part in a new world where you are the owner of your data, your assets, and your future.

Shaping Societies, Not Just Economies

The role of AI is not limited to economics, it will redefine how we connect, collaborate, and care for one another. The rise of AI companions, digital communities, and tokenized assets presents a new frontier for human relationships and wealth-sharing. But how these technologies will enhance, or harm society is up to us.

It's time to redefine community, where technologies are tools for fostering deeper human connections and where equity in every form is shared among all. Will you use AI to build a future that brings people together or one that widens the gap between those who benefit and those left behind?

The next five years will be decisive. They will determine who thrives and who falls behind. AI is already reshaping economies and society, not waiting in the wings. Every decision you make now, personal, professional, or policy, will contribute to humanity's unfolding story.

Recapping the Transformational Concepts and Innovation that Will Redefine Humanity by 2030.

Coming Full Circle: Your Guide to the Next 5 Years

As we approach 2030, I want to bring us full circle by revisiting the **transformational concepts** introduced at the beginning of this book, concepts that are already shaping the world and will **intensify** over the next five years.

Throughout the chapters, we've explored how **key technologies** are converging and accelerating change across every aspect of society, economics, and human behavior. Now, these concepts will serve as your **road markers**, signposts that will help you **track and navigate the rapid transformations** unfolding around you.

Let's revisit these transformational concepts, building on the knowledge we explored throughout the book. We'll dive deeper with real-world examples, paired with realization timelines, to help you create a clear transformation roadmap and establish a cadence for tracking these developments over the next five years.

AI-Driven Abundance

AI systems are redefining production by doing more with fewer resources. This abundance model is emerging in industries like agriculture, logistics, and manufacturing. Autonomous technology is making it possible to produce continuously without human intervention, which eliminates scarcity across sectors.

- ∞ **Case Study 1: John Deere's Autonomous Farming Systems:** John Deere has developed 8R autonomous tractors that leverage AI and robotics to perform fieldwork 24/7. This system minimizes the need for human labor, enabling farmers to focus on other tasks. AI-powered software also uses predictive analytics to optimize planting schedules and detect diseases early, resulting in higher yields with less waste.

- ∞ **Case Study 2: Amazon's Automated Warehouses:** Amazon has deployed over 750,000 robots across its warehouses, operating alongside its human workforce to manage inventory and reduce shipping times. AI-driven processes ensure optimal product storage, significantly lowering operational costs and increasing productivity.

- ∞ **Timeline:** By **2027**, robots will outnumber humans in logistics and manufacturing, ensuring continuous production and unlocking new models of abundance.

Redefining GDP

Traditional GDP metrics, which measure value through labor and tangible goods, no longer capture the full scope of modern digital economies. AI-driven services, data flows, and platform economies generate immense value that remains unaccounted for. Governments must rethink economic frameworks to align with this reality.

- ∞ **Case Study: China's Digital Economy Index**: China has introduced a Digital Economy Index to track the contribution of AI, automation, and online platforms. This new metric emphasizes data flows, digital consumption, and service-based productivity. The model allows policymakers to align economic planning with future trends, ensuring that growth is measured accurately as the economy shifts away from labor-intensive sectors.

- ∞ **Timeline:** By **2028**, alternative economic metrics will become the standard for evaluating progress globally, replacing GDP as the primary measure of success.

The End of Traditional Jobs

Automation is eliminating repetitive and labor-intensive roles, transforming industries like logistics, transportation, and retail. As automation replaces traditional roles, reskilling programs will be essential to transition the workforce to new areas of opportunity.

- **Case Study 1:** Waymo's Autonomous Trucking Fleets: Waymo is deploying self-driving trucks that are expected to replace millions of truck drivers by 2030. This shift reduces costs and increases efficiency in logistics but also presents challenges in managing workforce displacement.

- **Case Study 2:** Google's Career Certificate Programs: Google has launched career certificates in fields like AI programming, cybersecurity, and data analytics, helping workers transition into in-demand roles. These certificates reflect the growing need for continuous learning and upskilling to stay relevant in an economy driven by automation.

- **Timeline:** By **2026**, 30% of logistics jobs will be automated, necessitating large-scale reskilling initiatives.

Omni-Synchronous Engagement

Omni-Synchronous Engagement represents a groundbreaking paradigm where one individual, with the help of AI agents, can engage in simultaneous, personalized interactions at a massive scale. This model merges the depth of one-on-one conversation with the scale of digital platforms, allowing individuals to connect meaningfully with millions while maintaining the intimacy and personalization of direct interactions. Unlike the traditional one-to-many digital engagement, this approach enables scalable influence and continuous learning through real-time feedback loops. The future economy, powered by this model, will redefine presence, allowing individuals to interact, make decisions, and receive feedback across borders, languages, and cultures as if they were in multiple places at once.

- **Case Study 1:** Imagine an APAC Regional Project Manager responsible for implementing a strategic partnership across several countries. Traditionally, this would require multiple local managers due to language and cultural differences. With Omni-Synchronous Engagement, however, a single regional manager can connect directly with local project leaders in each country, using AI-driven real-time translation and feedback tools to interact in each leader's native language. This manager can receive instant updates and provide guidance or make decisions on the spot, creating a seamless, synchronized rollout across diverse markets. This model reduces operational costs, enhances project cohesion, accelerates decision-making, and fosters an adaptable, responsive management style.

- ∞ **Timeline:** By **2027**, Omni-Synchronous Engagement will become standard in large-scale organizations, allowing single leaders to manage complex, multi-regional projects with real-time feedback from AI-powered assistants. By **2030**, this model is expected to be widely adopted across industries, fundamentally transforming leadership, customer service, and education roles by enhancing productivity and influence on an unprecedented scale.

Infinite Knowledge

AI-powered educational platforms are democratizing access to learning, allowing people worldwide to develop new skills. These platforms offer personalized paths and real-time feedback, removing traditional barriers to education.

- ∞ **Case Study: Khan Academy's AI Tutors**: Khan Academy has integrated AI to tailor learning plans to each student's strengths and weaknesses. With automated tutoring available to anyone with internet access, the platform ensures education is no longer limited by geography or financial resources. AI's ability to scale education to millions will drive lifelong learning and close the global education gap.

- ∞ **Timeline:** By **2027**, AI-powered platforms will become standard educational tools worldwide.

Economic Singularity

The rise of AI-managed economies will shift wealth creation to autonomous systems, fundamentally altering the nature of financial markets. Human decision-making will become less relevant as algorithms control investments and economic planning.

- **Case Study: OpenAI's Autonomous Financial Models**: By 2030, OpenAI's market analysts will execute trades and manage investment portfolios autonomously, outpacing human-driven strategies. These models will reduce human errors, optimize returns, and operate at speeds beyond human capability, forcing a rethinking of economic policies and governance frameworks.

- **Timeline:** By **2029**, AI will dominate financial markets, requiring governments to adjust policies to accommodate the new economic landscape.

AI Transcending Human Limitations

Brain-machine interfaces (BMIs) will enable humans to interact with AI at unprecedented levels, enhancing cognitive capabilities. These interfaces will reshape industries, augment human intelligence, and create new possibilities for innovation.

- **Case Study: Neuralink's Brain-Machine Interface**: Neuralink aims to integrate human brains with AI, allowing users to control devices and access information directly through thought. This technology holds potential for revolutionizing medicine, such as restoring movement for paralyzed patients, and blurring the boundary between human and machine intelligence.

- **Timeline:** By **2030**, cognitive augmentation will redefine industries, from healthcare to education.

Universal Equity as Future Income

In the decentralized economy, tokenized equity will replace salaries, allowing individuals to earn income through contributions to digital ecosystems. This new wealth model shifts income from labor to value-based participation.

- **Case Study: DAO Tokenized Equity Models**: Decentralized Autonomous Organizations (DAOs) distribute ownership tokens to participants, giving them a stake in the organization's success. These tokens incentivize community contributions and align interests across ecosystems, demonstrating a new way of distributing wealth.

- ∞ **Timeline:** By **2030**, universal equity models will become the norm in decentralized organizations.

The Deflationary Power of AI

AI-driven automation will force businesses to rethink their value propositions as prices fall and profit margins shrink. Companies will need to innovate continuously to remain relevant in a deflationary economy.

- ∞ **Case Study: Amazon's AI-Driven Warehouses**: Amazon's warehouses use AI-powered robots and predictive analytics to streamline operations, cutting costs and driving deflation across the retail sector. This transformation highlights the need for companies to pivot toward customer-centric services to stay competitive.
- ∞ **Timeline:** By **2027**, consumer prices will drop by 40%, reshaping business models across industries.

AI Companions

AI companions are transforming personal relationships and caregiving by offering emotional support and assistance.

- ∞ **Case Study 1: Japan's Elderly Care Robots**: Japan's AI care robots provide companionship and medical reminders to seniors, addressing loneliness and improving quality of life. These robots are designed to engage in meaningful conversations and foster social interaction.
- ∞ **Case Study 2: Replika's Digital Companions**: Replika offers personalized interactions, evolving from a mental health tool into a trusted digital companion. Users develop deep emotional connections with their Replikas, raising new questions about the nature of relationships in the digital age.

∞ Timeline: By **2029**, AI companions will outnumber human assistants in social care settings.

Blockchain Redefining Trust

Blockchain technology eliminates intermediaries and ensures trust through transparency, revolutionizing governance, finance, and commerce.

∞ **Case Study 1: Estonia's Blockchain Governance**: Estonia uses blockchain to secure citizen data and streamline government services. This system has set a precedent for how digital governance can operate transparently and efficiently.

∞ **Case Study 2: Ethereum's DeFi Ecosystem**: Ethereum has enabled peer-to-peer lending and automated financial contracts, making services more accessible and eliminating the need for traditional banks.

∞ **Timeline:** By **2026**, 30% of global transactions will occur through DeFi platforms.

Universal Basic Income (UBI)

UBI will play a critical role in stabilizing economies as automation displaces traditional jobs.

∞ **Case Study 1: Ontario's UBI Pilot**: Ontario's pilot provided participants with a fixed income, leading to improvements in mental health and employment motivation.

∞ **Case Study 2: Finland's UBI Experiment**: Finland's two-year UBI trial showed that recipients experienced greater well-being and job flexibility, highlighting the importance of guaranteed income in an AI-driven economy.

∞ **Timeline:** By **2028**, UBI programs will expand across multiple nations.

Your Call to Action: Stay Alert, Stay Ahead

It is **critical** that you don't just passively encounter these transformational forces. Each time you hear or come across one of these terms, whether it's AI-driven abundance, blockchain innovation, or the deflationary power of automation, **your senses should perk up.** Take a moment to pause, reflect, and **contextually grasp the meaning and implications** of what's unfolding.

These concepts are not just interesting trends, they are **the foundations for your self-learning and personal development** over the next five years. Use them as **pillars to structure your self-discovery journey**, and let them guide you toward the skills, knowledge, and mindsets you need to **thrive in the world of 2030.**

To **supercharge your understanding of the current paradigm shift**, I encourage you to engage with some of today's leading thinkers. **Peter Diamandis**, a visionary on exponential growth and abundance, offers insights into the transformative potential of emerging technologies. **Raoul Pal**, a globally respected macro strategist and founder of Real Vision, dives deep into economic trends and their future implications.

These leaders, along with others like **Ray Kurzweil**, a pioneer in AI and futurism, and **Emad Mostaque**, a thought leader on AI-driven societies, provide invaluable perspectives that will challenge and expand your worldview. Seek out their talks, podcasts, and writings to continually push the boundaries of your understanding and gain clarity on how these shifts will shape our world and what they can mean for you personally.

Following these thought leaders can be a powerful way to stay ahead of the curve in a rapidly evolving landscape.

"Change begins when you embrace it"

References

Brynjolfsson, E., & McAfee, A. (2014). *The Second Machine Age: Work, Progress, and Prosperity in a Time of Brilliant Technologies.* W.W. Norton & Company.

Ford, M. (2015). *Rise of the Robots: Technology and the Threat of a Jobless Future.* Basic Books.

Harari, Y. N. (2018). *21 Lessons for the 21st Century.* Spiegel & Grau.

Lee, K.-F. (2018). *AI Superpowers: China, Silicon Valley, and the New World Order.* Houghton Mifflin Harcourt.

West, D. M. (2018). *The Future of Work: Robots, AI, and Automation.* Brookings Institution Press.

Bostrom, N. (2014). *Superintelligence: Paths, Dangers, Strategies.* Oxford University Press.

International Monetary Fund (IMF). (2020). *World Economic Outlook: The Impact of AI on Global Productivity.* IMF Publications.

McKinsey Global Institute. (2021). *The Future of Work After COVID-19: Automation, AI, and the Economy.* McKinsey & Company.

World Economic Forum. (2020). *The Global AI Race: AI's Role in Geopolitics and the Global Economy.* World Economic Forum.

PwC. (2020). *AI and the Future of Work: How AI Will Reshape Jobs and Industries by 2030.* PwC Global.

National Bureau of Economic Research (NBER). (2021). *AI and Labor Economics: Automation's Role in Shaping the Future Workforce.* NBER Working Paper.

European Union Commission on Digital Transformation. (2021). *AI Regulation and the Ethical Use of Intelligent Systems.* EU Publications Office.

Autor, D. H., & Salomons, A. (2018). *Is Automation Labor Share-Displacing? Productivity Growth, Employment, and the Labor Share*. Brookings Papers on Economic Activity.

Chui, M., Manyika, J., & Miremadi, M. (2017). *Harnessing Automation for a Future That Works*. McKinsey Global Institute.

Frey, C. B., & Osborne, M. A. (2017). *The Future of Employment: How Susceptible Are Jobs to Computerization?* Technological Forecasting and Social Change.

Arntz, M., Gregory, T., & Zierahn, U. (2016). *The Risk of Automation for Jobs in OECD Countries: A Comparative Analysis*. OECD Social Employment and Migration Working Papers.

Bessen, J. (2019). *AI and Jobs: The Role of Demand*. National Bureau of Economic Research (NBER) Working Paper.

Acemoglu, D., & Restrepo, P. (2019). *Robots and Jobs: Evidence from US Labor Markets*. Journal of Political Economy.

International Labour Organization (ILO). (2020). *The Role of AI and Robotics in the Future of Work: Policy Implications*. ILO Publications.

World Economic Forum. (2020). *The Future of Jobs Report: AI, Automation, and the Future Workforce*. World Economic Forum.

PwC. (2021). *Workforce of the Future: The Competing Forces Shaping 2030*. PwC Global.

Berg, A., Buffie, E. F., & Zanna, L. F. (2018). *Should We Fear the Robot Revolution? (The Correct Answer is Yes)*. IMF Economic Review.

Caleb Naysmith. (2024). *Amazon Grows To Over 750,000 Robots* (Yahoo!Finance). Benzinga.com.

Mustafa Suleyman. (2023). *The Coming Wave: Technology, Power, and the 21st Century's Greatest Dilemma*. Crown Publishing.

European Union. (2023). *AI Act: Regulatory Framework on Artificial Intelligence.* Official Journal of the European Union.

Stanford AI Lab. (2022). *The Impact of AI on Global Economic Models: White Paper.* Stanford University.

McKinsey Global Institute. (2023). *Blockchain and the Future of Decentralized Finance.* McKinsey & Company.

MIT Media Lab. (2022). *Quantum Computing and the Future of AI Economies.* MIT Media Press.

World Economic Forum. (2023). *The Convergence of AI and Blockchain: The Future of Financial Markets.* World Economic Forum.

CoinDesk. (2023). *How Blockchain is Shaping the Future of AI and Finance.* CoinDesk.

Global Construction Review. (2024). *Landmark event claimed as robots pave busy highway in China.* Global Construction Review. Retrieved from Global Construction Review/landmark-event-claimed-as-robots-pave-busy-highway-in-china

Holt-Lunstad J, Smith TB, Baker M, Harris T, Stephenson D. (2015) *Loneliness and social isolation as risk factors for mortality: a meta-analytic review.*

Kyotu Technology. (2024). *The Role of AI in Optimizing Renewable Energy Production.*

Bridge, G. (2023). *Lithium, Brexit and Global Britain: Onshoring battery production.* Retrieved from ScienceDirect.

Moro-Visconti, R. (2023). *Artificial intelligence-driven scalability and its impact on the digital economy.* Nature.

McKinsey & Company (2024). *How data centers and the energy sector can sate AI's hunger for power.* McKinsey Insights.

Verhoef, P. C., Broekhuizen, T., Bart, Y., Bhattacharya, A., Dong, J. Q., Fabian, N., & Haenlein, M. (2021). *Digital*

Transformation: A Multidisciplinary Reflection and Research Agenda. Journal of Business Research.

Pantin, L. P. (2023). *Financial Inclusion, Cryptocurrency, and the Future of Money*. Northwestern University Law Review.

Brookings Institution. (2022). *Debunking the Narratives about Cryptocurrency and Financial Inclusion*. Brookings.

AI-Driven Job Displacement: You could reference studies or reports from the *World Economic Forum* or *International Labour Organization* that provide insights into the anticipated job losses and new roles created by AI.

Economic Inequality: Consider referencing global economic reports or studies that discuss the impact of technological advancements on inequality, especially from sources like *The World Bank* or *United Nations Development Programme*.

AI's Impact on Market Instability: Reports from financial institutions like *Goldman Sachs* or *IMF* discussing the risks of AI-induced market fluctuations could strengthen this section.

Bias in AI Algorithms: You may want to cite *MIT Technology Review* or papers from organizations such as *AI Now Institute* that discuss the ethical risks of biased algorithms.

HBR - How to Capitalize on Generative AI: (2023) - *For Omni-Synchronous Engagement and scalable AI interactions.*

Financial Times - Economic Disruption and Market Instability: (2023) - *For AI's impact on global markets and economic stability.*

Gartner Research - Future Workforce Shifts: (2024) - *On emerging AI-centric roles and restructuring of the job market.*

CoinDesk and Financial Times - Blockchain and AI in Decentralized Finance: (2023) - *To deepen insights on blockchain's impact on financial models* (for Financial Times entry, use the date 2023 from the Economic Disruption entry above, and for CoinDesk, use the publication year of 2023).

IEEE Spectrum - Quantum Computing in AI Economies: (2023) - *Quantum computing and its transformative role in economic frameworks.*

AI Now Institute - AI Ethics and Bias: (2023) - *Data privacy, and AI ethics.*

Glossary

Artificial Intelligence (AI) - A field of computer science focused on the creation of systems that can perform tasks that typically require human intelligence, such as decision-making, language processing, visual perception, and problem-solving. AI ranges from narrow AI, which is designed for specific tasks, to the potential future development of general AI, capable of understanding and reasoning across a wide range of topics.

Automation - The use of technology to perform tasks with minimal human intervention. In the context of AI, automation involves the use of intelligent systems and robots to replace or assist in repetitive or complex tasks in industries such as manufacturing, healthcare, and services.

Blockchain - A decentralized digital ledger technology that records transactions across a network of computers in a way that ensures security, transparency, and resistance to modification. Blockchain is the backbone of cryptocurrencies like Bitcoin, but its potential applications span finance, supply chain management, and governance.

Cognitive Computing - Refers to systems that mimic the human brain's processes by interpreting data and generating decisions based on that data. It includes AI systems that understand and learn from interactions, allowing them to improve their responses over time. IBM Watson is an example of cognitive computing technology.

Cybersecurity - The practice of protecting systems, networks, and data from digital attacks, unauthorized access, or damage. As AI and automation become more integrated into society, the importance of cybersecurity to protect AI-driven systems and personal data grows significantly.

Decentralized Finance (DeFi) - A financial system built on blockchain technology that allows peer-to-peer financial transactions without the need for traditional intermediaries like banks. DeFi relies on smart contracts to execute trades, loans, and other financial activities autonomously and securely.

Deep Learning - A subset of machine learning that uses artificial neural networks with multiple layers (deep networks) to model complex patterns in data. Deep learning has enabled advancements in image recognition, natural language processing, and autonomous vehicles.

Economic Singularity - A theoretical point at which AI and automation drive exponential economic growth with minimal reliance on human labor. This could disrupt traditional models of GDP growth, labor markets, and wealth distribution.

Emotional AI (Affective Computing) - AI systems designed to recognize, interpret, and respond to human emotions. These systems are used in applications like customer service, mental health care, and AI companions, allowing more empathetic and human-like interactions between machines and people.

General Artificial Intelligence (AGI) - A yet-to-be-realized form of AI that can perform any intellectual task that a human can do, across multiple domains. Unlike narrow AI, which is designed for specific tasks, AGI would have the ability to learn, reason, and make decisions in an unrestricted way.

Internet of Things (IoT) - A network of physical objects ("things") embedded with sensors, software, and other technologies that connect and exchange data with other devices over the internet. IoT plays a central role in smart homes, cities, and industries by enabling real-time data collection and automation.

Machine Learning (ML) - A branch of AI where systems can learn and improve from experience without being explicitly programmed. Machine learning algorithms analyze large datasets, identify patterns, and use that information to make predictions or decisions.

Quantum Computing - A new type of computing that uses quantum bits (qubits) rather than traditional binary bits to process information. Quantum computing promises to solve complex problems that are currently intractable for classical computers, with potential applications in cryptography, drug discovery, and AI acceleration.

Robotics - The branch of technology that deals with the design, construction, operation, and application of robots. In an AI-driven world, robotics is a key area where intelligent machines are used to perform tasks in industries such as manufacturing, healthcare, logistics, and eldercare.

Smart Contracts - Self-executing contracts with the terms of the agreement directly written into code. Smart contracts run on blockchain networks and automatically enforce and execute contractual terms when predefined conditions are met.

Tokenization - The process of converting rights to an asset into a digital token on a blockchain. This allows for fractional ownership, easier transferability, and greater liquidity of traditionally illiquid assets like real estate or art.

Universal Basic Income (UBI) - A social welfare policy that provides all citizens with a regular, unconditional sum of money, regardless of their income or employment status. UBI is often discussed as a solution to the job displacement caused by AI and automation.

Universal Equity - Refers to the concept of ensuring that all individuals, regardless of their socioeconomic status, background, or personal circumstances, have equal access to resources, opportunities, and benefits. This concept aims to level the playing field in society, especially in contexts of economic distribution, technology, and social welfare. With AI and Blockchain, Universal Equity goes a step further by introducing the idea that every individual can hold equity in society's collective wealth and a future income source for individuals. This system would involve the distribution of shares or equity in the profits generated by artificial intelligence, automation, and other technological advancements.

Decentralization: The process of distributing power away from central authorities, enabling individuals or local entities to have more control over resources. In the context of Universal Equity, decentralization can be applied to systems like blockchain, aiming for fairer economic and resource distribution.

AIaaS (Artificial Intelligence as a Service) - The provision of AI tools and solutions as a service, typically through cloud-based platforms. AIaaS allows businesses to access AI capabilities without building their own infrastructure, making AI more accessible and scalable. Examples include cloud-based AI platforms such as IBM Watson and Google AI.

AI Companions - Emotionally intelligent AI systems designed to provide companionship, emotional support, and interaction. AI companions are used in contexts such as elderly care, mental health support, and even as virtual friends or romantic partners.

Autonomous Robots - Robots that can perform tasks without human intervention, often using AI to make decisions and adapt to their environment. These robots are used in various industries, including manufacturing, logistics, and healthcare.

Exponential Growth - A rapid increase in the quantity or capacity of something, where the rate of growth becomes faster as the size of the underlying factor increases. In the context of AI and technology, exponential growth refers to the accelerating pace of technological advancement and its economic and societal impact.

Platform Economy - An economic system built around digital platforms that facilitate exchanges between consumers and providers. Examples include AI-driven Software as a Service (SaaS) platforms and marketplaces that rely on AI to match supply and demand, manage logistics, and personalize customer experiences. AI-driven platforms such as Uber, Airbnb, and Amazon have transformed industries by creating new business models.

Personalized Medicine - A medical model that uses AI and other technologies to tailor treatments to individual patients based on their genetic, lifestyle, and environmental data. AI can help predict the most effective treatment options by analyzing vast amounts of data from similar cases.

Digital Twin - A virtual model of a physical object, system, or process that uses real-time data to simulate performance and predict outcomes. Digital twins are used in manufacturing, urban planning, and healthcare to optimize efficiency and reduce risks.

Singularity - A future hypothetical point where technological growth, particularly AI, becomes so advanced that it causes irreversible changes in society, economics, and human life. The singularity often refers to the moment when AGI surpasses human intelligence.

Frictionless Economy - An economic system where AI, automation, and digital platforms work seamlessly to eliminate inefficiencies and delays, allowing transactions and services to happen instantly and with minimal human intervention.

Algorithm - A set of rules or instructions given to an AI system or computer to help it perform a task. Algorithms are the backbone of AI, enabling systems to process data, make decisions, and learn from inputs.

Artificial General Intelligence (AGI) - A theoretical form of AI that would be able to perform any intellectual task that a human can do. Unlike narrow AI, AGI would have the ability to understand, learn, and apply knowledge across a wide range of disciplines.

Autonomous Vehicles - Self-driving vehicles that use AI and sensors to navigate roads, make decisions, and operate without human intervention. Autonomous vehicles are seen as a key component of the future of transportation.

Big Data - Extremely large datasets that can be analyzed to reveal patterns, trends, and associations. AI relies on big data to train algorithms, improve decision-making, and enhance predictive accuracy across various industries.

Biotechnology - A field of science that involves using biological processes, organisms, or systems to develop products and technologies that improve human health and life. AI is increasingly being integrated into biotechnology for tasks such as drug discovery, genetic engineering, and personalized medicine.

Cloud Computing - The delivery of computing services, such as storage, processing power, and software, over the internet ("the cloud") instead of relying on local servers or personal devices. Cloud computing enables AI and data-driven services to be accessed remotely, making it scalable and efficient for businesses.

Creative Destruction - An economic concept in which old industries and technologies are destroyed or transformed as new innovations replace them. AI, automation, and other advanced technologies are driving creative destruction in industries like retail, manufacturing, and finance.

Data Mining - The process of discovering patterns and relationships in large sets of data using AI and statistical methods. Data mining allows organizations to extract valuable insights from vast amounts of information, driving decision-making and innovation.

Deep Neural Networks (DNNs) - A type of artificial neural network with multiple layers of nodes (neurons) that can learn to recognize patterns in data. DNNs are used in various AI applications, including image recognition, speech processing, and natural language understanding.

Digital Disruption - The transformation of industries and business models by digital technologies like AI, blockchain, and cloud computing. Digital disruption often leads to the decline of established companies and the rise of innovative startups.

Disruptive Innovation - An innovation that creates a new market or value network and eventually disrupts existing industries, displacing established companies and products. AI, blockchain, and renewable energy are examples of technologies that are driving disruptive innovation.

Distributed Ledger Technology (DLT) - A decentralized database that is shared across multiple sites or institutions, allowing data to be recorded, stored, and updated in a secure and transparent way. Blockchain is one form of distributed ledger technology.

Edge Computing - A computing paradigm where data is processed closer to where it is generated, reducing latency and bandwidth use. Edge computing is critical for AI applications in real-time decision-making, such as in autonomous vehicles, smart cities, and IoT devices.

Ethical AI - The study and practice of designing and deploying AI systems in a way that ensures they are fair, accountable, transparent, and respectful of human rights. Ethical AI considers the implications of AI on privacy, bias, job displacement, and human autonomy.

Exponential Technologies - Technologies that improve at an exponential rate, meaning their capabilities double at regular intervals while their costs decrease. AI, quantum computing, and biotechnology are examples of exponential technologies that have the potential to disrupt industries and economies.

Generative AI - A subset of AI that focuses on creating new content, such as images, music, text, or video. Generative AI uses machine learning models like GANs (Generative Adversarial Networks) to produce creative outputs that mimic human-made content.

Human-Machine Collaboration - The partnership between humans and AI systems where both work together to achieve better outcomes. AI can assist humans by performing tasks such as data analysis, decision-making, and automation, while humans provide intuition, creativity, and ethical judgment.

Hybrid Intelligence - The combination of human intelligence and artificial intelligence to solve complex problems that require both human insight and machine efficiency. Hybrid intelligence systems leverage the strengths of both humans and AI, ensuring better decision-making and problem-solving.

Intelligent Automation - The use of AI and machine learning to automate tasks that require cognitive abilities, such as decision-making, learning, and problem-solving. Intelligent automation goes beyond traditional robotic process automation (RPA) by incorporating AI to handle more complex tasks.

Job Displacement - The loss of jobs due to the adoption of automation and AI technologies that perform tasks previously done by humans. While AI can increase productivity and create new jobs, it also poses risks of displacing workers, particularly in routine or manual labor.

Labor Market Polarization - A trend where job opportunities grow in both high-skill, high-paying jobs and low-skill, low-paying jobs, but decline in middle-skill jobs due to automation and AI.

This leads to a "hollowing out" of the labor market, where middle-class jobs are eliminated.

Machine Vision - The use of AI and image processing technology to enable machines to interpret and understand visual information. Machine vision is used in applications such as autonomous vehicles, facial recognition, and quality control in manufacturing.

Natural Language Processing (NLP) - A branch of AI that focuses on enabling machines to understand, interpret, and respond to human language. NLP powers applications such as chatbots, virtual assistants, translation tools, and sentiment analysis.

Neural Networks - A series of algorithms that mimic the way the human brain operates, allowing computers to recognize patterns and make decisions. Neural networks are a fundamental component of deep learning systems used in AI applications like image recognition and speech processing.

Quantum Supremacy - The point at which quantum computers outperform classical computers in solving complex problems that would be otherwise impossible or take too long to compute. Achieving quantum supremacy is expected to revolutionize fields such as cryptography, material science, and AI development.

Reskilling - The process of learning new skills to adapt to changes in the job market, particularly due to technological advancements such as AI and automation. Reskilling is critical for workers in industries affected by job displacement, allowing them to transition to new roles.

Smart Grid - An advanced electricity supply network that uses AI, IoT, and data analytics to optimize the distribution and consumption of energy. Smart grids improve energy efficiency, reduce costs, and integrate renewable energy sources.

Supervised Learning - A type of machine learning where a model is trained on labeled data, meaning the input and corresponding output are provided. The AI learns to make predictions or decisions based on this training data, which is commonly used in applications like image classification and speech recognition.

Token Economy - An economy based on digital tokens that represent assets, goods, or services, often built on blockchain technology. Token economies allow for decentralized ownership, fractional ownership, and more transparent transactions.

Transhumanism - A philosophical and scientific movement that advocates for the use of advanced technologies, such as AI, biotechnology, and robotics, to enhance human physical and cognitive abilities. Transhumanism envisions a future where humans can overcome biological limitations, such as aging and disease, through technological augmentation.

Unsupervised Learning - A type of machine learning where the AI system is given data without labeled outputs and is tasked with finding patterns and relationships in the data. This type of learning is used for clustering, anomaly detection, and data mining applications.

Wearable Technology - Devices worn on the body that collect data and provide real-time feedback using AI and machine learning. Examples include fitness trackers, smartwatches, and AI-driven wearables used in healthcare to monitor vital signs and suggest lifestyle adjustments.

5G Technology - The fifth generation of mobile network technology, offering faster speeds, lower latency, and greater capacity for connected devices. 5G is critical for enabling real-time AI applications, smart cities, and autonomous systems.

Affective Computing - A branch of AI that focuses on recognizing, interpreting, and responding to human emotions. Affective computing is used in applications such as emotional AI companions and virtual therapists.

Autonomous Systems - Self-operating systems, including robots and vehicles, that can perform tasks with minimal or no human intervention. These systems rely on AI, machine learning, and sensors to navigate and make decisions in real time.

Data Economy - An economy that revolves around the collection, analysis, and monetization of data. As data becomes a valuable asset, companies and nations are leveraging AI to extract insights, create personalized experiences, and drive innovation.

Digital Twins - A virtual model of a physical object, process, or system, used to simulate, predict, and optimize performance. AI and IoT sensors feed real-time data into the digital twin, enabling continuous monitoring and improvements.

Ethical Hacking - The practice of legally breaking into computers and devices to test their defenses. Ethical hackers help organizations identify vulnerabilities and protect their systems from cyberattacks.

Explainable AI (XAI) - A branch of AI focused on making AI decision-making processes transparent and understandable to humans. Explainable AI is critical for trust and accountability in applications such as healthcare, finance, and law enforcement.

Federated Learning - A machine learning technique where models are trained across multiple decentralized devices or servers holding local data, without the need to share the data itself. This approach improves data privacy and reduces reliance on centralized data storage.

Gig Economy - An economy characterized by flexible, freelance, or short-term work rather than full-time permanent jobs. AI-driven platforms like Uber and Fiverr have accelerated the growth of the gig economy by connecting workers with opportunities in real time.

Holography - The use of light beams to create three-dimensional images or holograms, which can be used in applications such as virtual meetings, entertainment, and education. AI-driven holography is poised to become a major component of immersive digital experiences.

Internet of Behavior (IoB) - The use of data collected from individuals' digital interactions to influence behaviors. Combining AI, IoT, and behavioral science, the IoB analyzes patterns of behavior to predict and guide decision-making in areas like marketing and public health.

Knowledge Graphs - A type of data structure used by AI to map relationships between different pieces of information. Knowledge graphs help AI systems make sense of complex data, improving search algorithms, recommendation engines, and decision-making.

Metaverse - A collective virtual space where users can interact in real time using digital avatars. Enabled by AI, VR, and blockchain, the metaverse will be a fully immersive experience used for entertainment, work, and social interaction.

Predictive Analytics - The use of data, AI, and statistical models to predict future events, trends, or behaviors. Predictive analytics is used in industries such as finance, healthcare, and marketing to anticipate customer needs and optimize outcomes.

Recommendation Engine - An AI-powered tool that analyzes user data to suggest products, services, or content based on preferences and behavior. Recommendation engines are widely used in e-commerce, streaming services, and social media platforms.

Reinforcement Learning - A type of machine learning where an AI system learns by interacting with its environment and receiving rewards or penalties for its actions. This trial-and-error approach is used in autonomous systems, robotics, and game AI.

Robotic Process Automation (RPA) - The use of software robots to automate repetitive, rule-based tasks in business processes. RPA is commonly used in finance, customer service, and supply chain management to reduce errors and increase efficiency.

Swarm Intelligence - A type of collective intelligence where decentralized systems, such as robots or drones, work together as a group to solve problems or complete tasks. Inspired by natural systems like ant colonies, swarm intelligence is used in robotics, logistics, and military applications.

MLOps (Machine Learning Operations) - A set of practices and tools that combines machine learning, data engineering, and operations to streamline the deployment and management of AI models. MLOps is crucial for scaling AI applications in production environments.

Synthetic Data - Artificially generated data used to train machine learning models when real-world data is scarce or sensitive. Synthetic data allows AI models to improve performance while ensuring privacy and security.

Zero-Knowledge Proof - A cryptographic method that allows one party to prove to another that they know a value without revealing any additional information. Zero-knowledge proofs are important for ensuring privacy in blockchain and decentralized systems.

Human-in-the-Loop (HITL) - A system where humans interact with and influence AI decision-making processes. In HITL models, human judgment is integrated into AI systems to ensure ethical, accurate, and responsible outcomes.

CRISPR - A gene-editing technology that enables precise changes to DNA sequences in living organisms. AI enhances CRISPR by helping scientists predict the effects of genetic modifications and optimize gene-editing techniques.

Cyber-Physical Systems (CPS) - Systems that integrate computation, networking, and physical processes, enabling devices to interact with the physical world through embedded sensors, processors, and actuators. Examples include smart grids, autonomous vehicles, and medical monitoring devices.

Augmented Reality (AR) - A technology that overlays digital information onto the physical world, often through devices like smartphones or AR glasses. AR applications range from navigation and gaming to education and industrial training.

About the Author

Theo Scherman is a seasoned global executive with over 31 years of C-level experience, recognized for his innovative thinking and leadership in emerging technologies and global business transformation. As the Chief Strategy Officer (CSO) for Hitachi Asia Pacific, Theo has played a pivotal role in shaping strategies that align with Hitachi's mission of fostering growth, sustainability, and innovation. He believes that by challenging  conventional thinking, you can transform multiple industries simultaneously and that a single individual's vision can profoundly impact the global society. We should all aim to think bigger and explore larger possibilities.

His strategic insights have guided various organizations through rapidly evolving market dynamics, helping the organization expand its footprint in key sectors. Theo's deep expertise spans across AI, IoT, blockchain, robotics, and advanced energy solutions, making him a thought leader in the hyperconnected and exponential economies. He has been instrumental in developing transformative strategies that have enabled organizations to capitalize on the convergence of these technologies, positioning them for long-term success in the face of global challenges.

With a career that has taken him across multiple continents, Theo's leadership has guided significant projects in government, infrastructure, healthcare, and smart city development. He is also a seasoned mergers and acquisitions expert, having successfully led integrations and technology acquisitions around the world. His visionary work has helped businesses transition into the digital age, particularly focusing on innovation and sustainability.

A passionate advocate for future-forward thinking, Theo regularly speaks at global conferences, sharing his insights on strategic management, technology-driven business models, and the power of collaboration. He is dedicated to helping businesses and individuals adapt to the rapid changes brought by AI and digital transformation, ensuring they thrive in an ever-evolving world.

Theo holds an MBA and has a diverse academic background in business, technology, and education. Currently based in Singapore, Theo's vision is to inspire organizations and individuals to embrace the future with vision and resilience.

www.ingramcontent.com/pod-product-compliance
Lightning Source LLC
LaVergne TN
LVHW010310070526
838199LV00065B/5514